FAKE!

Books by Clifford Irving

NOVELS

On a Darkling Plain
The Losers
The Valley
The 38th Floor

NON-FICTION

Fake!

FAKE!

The Story of Elmyr de Hory,
the Greatest Art Forger of Our Time

by
CLIFFORD IRVING

HEINEMANN : LONDON

William Heinemann Ltd

LONDON   MELBOURNE   TORONTO
JOHANNESBURG   AUCKLAND

SBN 434 36801 6

Printed in Great Britain by
Fletcher & Son Ltd, Norwich and bound by
Richard Clay (The Chaucer Press) Ltd, Bungay Suffolk

for
Edith,
with
love

AUTHOR'S NOTE

I do not think it hyperbole to call this an incredible tale, even though it is a true one. But since the history of Elmyr de Hory and his business associates, Fernand Legros and Réal Lessard, has never been fully told before and until recently was completely unknown outside the inner sanctums of the art establishment, the astute reader is bound to ask one very pointed question. "If the secret was so well kept for twenty-one years, then how did the author find out?" Before I begin, I feel the obligation to provide an answer.

The Mediterranean island of Ibiza, which figures so prominently in the following narrative, has been my home base for the last fifteen years. Legros and Lessard, who often visited Ibiza, were acquaintances of mine, and Elmyr de Hory was a close friend. One day in the spring of 1967, under great stress and in need of help, Elmyr made an amazing confession to me and later amplified this confession by narrating in detail his life's story. A writer usually hunts for his stories in the world about him or in the jungle of his personal needs; only rarely is one thrust upon him. But that is what happened.

I have noticed in this most curious world that anything is possible, and that what seems highly improbable is merely beyond the current reach of one's imagination. Still, a native skepticism combined with a respect for the laws of libel—as well as a realization that my principal informant was testifying against himself and therefore might not be entirely reliable—led me to go forth from my island home to Paris, Geneva, London and New York, in order to verify and perhaps correct what I had been told. Certain people were extremely helpful to me in these research trips: particularly Klaus Perls of the Perls Galleries in New York, Fred Schoneman of the Schoneman Galleries, Herbert Kende of Selected Artists Galleries, Ruth Gelmis of *Look* magazine (whose long and independent research was invaluable), Alvin S. Lane, Dewey Ebbin, Joseph Stone of the District Attorney's Office in New York County, Peregrine Pollen of the Parke-Bernet Galleries, Frank Perls of Los Angeles, Hervé Odermatt of Galerie

Hervé and Philippe Reichenbach of Galerie Reichenbach in Paris, and Agnes Mongan of the Fogg Art Museum in Cambridge, Massachusetts. Their cooperation gratified and in some instances astonished me. I also thank Leo Rosten, in his capacity as Editorial Adviser to *Look,* and my publisher and friend, Frank Taylor, for their continuous enthusiasm.

Last, but hardly least under the circumstances, I thank Elmyr de Hory/von Houry/Herzog/Cassou/Hoffman/Raynal/Dory-Boutin.

Clifford Irving

Ibiza
February 1969

If fools
did not go
to market,
cracked pots
and
false wares
would not
be sold.

JEAN LE MALCHANCEUX
(in the twelfth century)

FAKE!

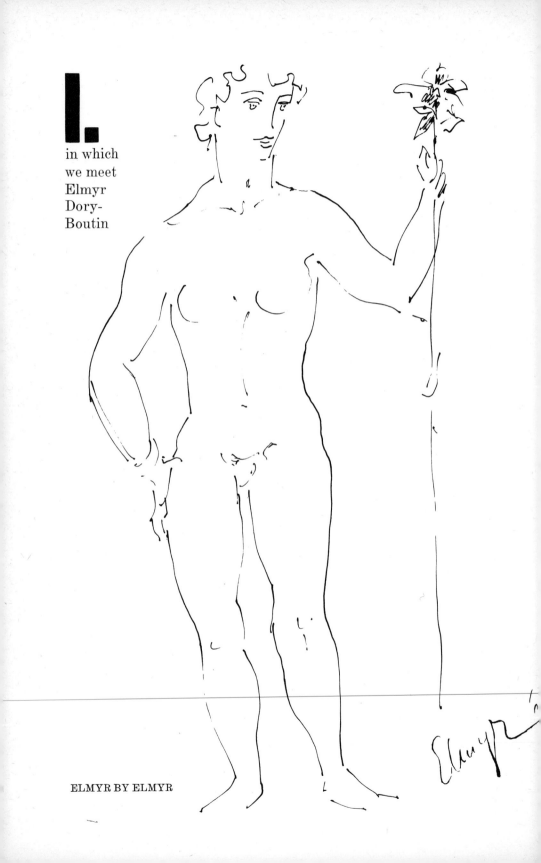

I.

in which
we meet
Elmyr
Dory-
Boutin

ELMYR BY ELMYR

In the summer of 1961, with as little fuss and fanfare as possible, a dapper, middle-aged, expatriate Hungarian bachelor gentleman calling himself Elmyr Dory-Boutin rented a comfortable suburban house on the Spanish Mediterranean island of Ibiza. His hair was dyed an apparently ageless jet black, he sported a monocle on a gold chain, all his sweaters were of cashmere, and during his seven-year residence on the island he came to wear a wristwatch from Cartier and drive a red Corvette Sting Ray convertible. He spoke five languages—all fluently, none perfectly. In English, for example, he was on less than friendly terms with the past imperfect: he "did go" rather than went to the Duquesa's cocktail party; he "did live" once in America rather than lived. A rumor soon spread among the members of Ibiza's rather sophisticated foreign colony that he was a black sheep of the Hungarian royal family in exile—perhaps a lesser prince, in the least a baron of the blood. Offering a sly smile, Elmyr—the stress falls on the second syllable, to rhyme with *dear*—neither admitted nor denied it. With his twinkling large brown eyes, cultivated suntan, mischievous laughter and protruding ears, he had more the air of a slightly wicked forest elf: he wouldn't eat you up, but he might very well cast a spell on you. He was a charming epicurean gentleman of leisure, who did, as far as anyone could make out, absolutely nothing in the way of productive labor. He was, he let it be known, "an art collector."

For three years he lived quietly in the modest rented house and then, high on a cliff behind the fifteenth-century walls of the old town of Ibiza, had built for himself a modern white-walled villa, complete with kidney-shaped swimming pool, sun terraces, multicolored flower gardens and a magnificent panoramic sweep of dark blue sea three hundred feet below. Called La Falaise, the house looked like a Hollywood set designer's wistful version of a Mediterranean hideaway. You mounted a flight of stone steps and entered through what seemed the back door of an unimpressive façade; inside, however, a large cool hallway led to two separate sleeping apartments. One of them was Elmyr's, and the other was called, because of its monocolor decor, "The Red Apartment." Upstairs a vast living room stretched the length of the house, adjoined by a dining alcove and modern American-style kitchen. This was revolutionary, considering that most people on Ibiza still cooked on charcoal.

There were also servants' quarters—and on the lower level of the house yet another room, whose windows were shielded from view of prying eyes on both the road and the terraces leading to the swimming pool. This last room was reached by an outside staircase from an area behind the kitchen. Aside from the architect (who had been told it was to be an extra guest room) and the builders and the maid (who was forbidden to clean it), only three people knew of its existence.

In the winter Elmyr traveled abroad. In the summer he sat around Ibiza's sidewalk cafés and Arlene Kaufman's bar La Tierra with his painter friends from the artists' colony, or had them up to La Falaise for poolside barbecues and Hungarian goulash by candlelight, to share with him *la vie de bohème trois étoiles*. If he wanted to call himself an art collector that was perfectly all right with them, too; he bought their paintings, which wasn't necessarily proof of his taste but certainly signified his good intentions. Did he really know anything about art? Well, someone had heard a tale—origin unremembered—that in his youth, in Budapest or perhaps Paris, Elmyr had been a fashionable portrait painter. It was a good story but no one quite believed it. Another claimed that very early one morning he'd seen Elmyr, in white shorts, sandals and dark glasses, wandering along the port, doing watercolor sketches of the fishermen mending their nets. Everyone laughed. The rich, they speculated, are probably lonely and certainly bored. On one occasion a Russian emigré painter, Pierre Dmitrienko, who had won major prizes at the Venice and Tokyo Biennales, happened to glance at a pen-and-ink drawing, an unsigned nude, that lay carelessly on Elmyr's desk.

"You did that?" Dmitrienko asked. When Elmyr nodded, Dmitrienko looked closer, "But," he said, mildly astonished—"that's a—that's not a bad drawing at all. Aren't you joking? Didn't someone else—"

"Yes, of course," Elmyr said hurriedly. "Someone else. I'm just joking."

Ibiza, part of the Balearic group and sometimes called the Saint-Germain-des-Prés of the Mediterranean, is a lovely island, warm and swinging in summer, bearable in winter, cheap in any season. It is also a tight little island where everybody minds everybody else's business and not much indiscretion goes unnoticed. The Ibiza expatriate community is a kind of microcosmic and visually psychedelic United Nations: on any given morning, sitting in the sunshine of the *paseo* outside the Café Alhambra, you can find a handful of Dutch hippies, a few American novelists and leftover beatniks, a covey of mini-skirted birds who look as if they had only that morning flapped their pretty wings and fled mama's nest in London or Stockholm, at least a dozen painters from anywhere in the world, a couple of mustachioed retired English civil servants and maybe even a slumming German millionaire or two. Some of these people work, but the leading occupation of the daylight hours —nothing even comes a close second—is Gossip. And its principal subject as well as its most inventive author, from the day he set foot on the island, was Elmyr Dory-Boutin.

Most people assumed that Elmyr had inherited his fortune, however large or small it might be, for if there was one unanimous opinion about Ibiza's suave, well-groomed Hungarian resident (the barber climbed the hill to his house every Sunday morning) it was that he had never done a day's work in his life, never could and never would. Another common rumor, virtually accepted as fact, held that the money came from a family collection of French Fauve, Impressionist and Post-Impressionist art—Dufys Vlamincks, Renoirs—smuggled out of Hungary after the war. Two young Paris art dealers, Fernand Legros and Réal Lessard, both of whom paid occasional brief visits to Elmyr on Ibiza, were supposed to be in charge of sales. Legros was a man in his early thirties, a nervous, smooth, Latin-looking, fast-talking, sharp-eyed, slightly effeminate Egyptian-born naturalized American. He liked to tell people that in his youth he had been a ballet dancer, that he was married and that he had a fourteen-year-old adopted son. It was true that he was married.

Réal Lessard was ten years younger, a good-looking, curly-haired French-Canadian, later to be described euphemistically by the world press as Fernand Legros' "traveling companion and personal secretary." He was a pleasant young man with a quick smile that showed beautiful white teeth, a cheerful disposition and innocent, fawnlike, soft brown eyes. Most of Elmyr's friends liked Réal and wondered how he could get along so well with Fernand, whose manner was brusque and often offensive and who looked, as one observer put it, "like the kind of sleazy gigolo who creeps up on you at 4 A.M. in Montmartre to sell you dirty pictures." It was assumed by almost everyone who knew them on Ibiza that they were homosexuals, although this was a subject that both Fernand and Réal declined to discuss. They lived, so it was rumored, in a palatial apartment on the Avenue Henri-Martin in Paris, and they were supposed to travel all over—Brazil, Japan, New York, Texas, South Africa—buying and selling their expensive wares. Elmyr, out of the goodness of his Hungarian heart, had evidently given them their start in the art business. In 1964 the island was startled to see him suddenly riding around in a dark red Mustang converti-ble, which, he shyly explained to the less fortunate, was a gift from his friends Fernand and Réal—obviously in gratitude for his patronage and the no doubt excellent commissions on the sales of his Dufys, Vlamincks and Renoirs.

But Elmyr offered no real clue as to his past. Close friends often asked him who he *really* was (they meant: what was his title? why had he left Hungary?), and his silence or smiles or evasive an-swers clinched it; he was certainly somebody other than soigné, coquettish, simple Elmyr. "If I was ever depressed enough to tell you my secret," he said one day to Edith Sommer, the young Ger-man painter and an intimate friend, "you'd be as shocked as if I told you I was Martin Bormann." He saw her expression. "I'm not a murderer," he added hastily. "That's not my scene at all. But you would be just as shocked as if I was."

His scene, as he put it, was best depicted by his favorite stories, which always began with himself strolling down Main Street in Kansas City or sipping an apéritif at some fashionable café on the Champs Élysées or Rome's Via Veneto; and then, quite unexpec-tedly, who would confront him but his "old friend" Judith Ander-son, or his "old friend" Tennessee Williams, or ditto Princess

Aga Khan, Salvador Dali, Prince Yussoupov, Baron Scézeny, Zsa Zsa, or Agatha Ratibor—"her mother was Hungarian, too; she was a princess, you know; there was a German state, my dear, called the Duchy of Ratibor"—at any rate, one of these glittering figures whom he had not seen for years would turn a corner and, with a combination of delight and disbelief, shriek, gasp or bubble his name: "El–*myr*?" The question mark was always implicit, as though he had risen like a phoenix from his own ashes. In telling the story of such encounters, Elmyr always seemed to share some of the long-lost friend's joy, as if in a vanished world where there had always been time for idle hours and gentle remembrance, nothing could be more beautiful than one spring day on the Via Veneto, quite unexpectedly, to bump into "El–*myr*?"

Whether or not the tales were true, no one of course had the slightest idea; although they had a clear ring of authenticity, there was something about Elmyr's almost desperate need to be a name-dropper that made one wonder. But his pleasure in himself was often infectious, and those who liked him, like Edith Sommer, called him a "generous, sentimental, warm-hearted man" (he was constantly lending small sums of money to young people, painters, friends or even casual acquaintances, most of which sums he never saw again), "a gentleman of the old school," witty, charming and debonair, as well as "the best cook on the whole island." Those who disliked him (or weren't invited to his chicken *papricas* dinners) labeled him a snob and a parasite; or, like one English-woman, dismissed him as "that tiresome little man. Always talking about Central European royalty whom one had never heard of, and whom one in any case doubted *he* had ever met."

Yet Ibiza in those days was a peaceful sort of place, with or without dissent about Elmyr. Then, in the opening months of 1967, the first hints of scandal, like the rattling of teacups before an earthquake, began to appear in the European and American press. The story was a confusing one, lacking details and confirmation, but it seemed to involve the forgery and sale of some extremely valuable paintings. Of its three main characters, the two villains were those agile and shadowy young men, Fernand Legros and Réal Lessard, Elmyr's friends and the supposed salesmen of his family art treasures. The third, playing the rôle of *ingénue* and victim, was a Texas oil millionaire named Algur Hurtle Meadows, to whom bad Fernand and bad Réal were reported to have sold forty-four fake paintings by French masters—an all-star list featuring Dufy, Degas, Vlaminck, Modigliani, Picasso and Derain. Legros was evidently the mastermind of the duo, and with Lessard had been calling on Meadows in his Dallas home on and off for several years, carting the paintings round in the trunk of a rented car like a Fuller Brush Man. The fakes always came with impressive documentation—certificates from the family of the painter, a record of sale at some auction house like the Parke-Bernet Galleries, and often a statement of authenticity by one of several Paris experts, formally recognized by the French government as *experts auprès du tribunal*, which meant, in effect, that their word was law.

Meadows was boss of the General American Oil Company and had acquired a reputation in business as a shrewd bargainer and master trader. To him, Legros and Lessard were "just peddlers."

"They'd come down here," he said to a reporter, "with a Modigliani for $100,000, which I knew was the selling price anywhere. The next day they asked $75,000 and I told them to take it away. When it came time for them to leave Dallas I would always think of some excuse to be busy. They'd court me like a virgin. No, I was busy that night. The next night? No, we were having some friends over. During the day, then? Well, I never knew exactly. Two or three weeks would go by. They kept telling me they had to leave town. Well, I said, I haven't asked you to stay. If you want to sell it to me, I'll give you $45,000. They took it."

The value of the disputed works, if genuine, was put somewhere in the area of $2 million, although Meadows was rumored to have paid considerably less. Whatever the price, however, it seemed to be quite a coup. But there was no talk yet in the press of prosecution. If he wanted justice in France, Meadows would have to enter a complaint against a person unknown, and when the French newspapers picked this up they began referring to Legros as Monsieur X. Some reports had it that he employed a "factory" of artists somewhere in the South of France, but there was evidently no attempt at further investigation. Strangely, or so it seemed to most people who heard the tale or read of the accusations, Fernand Legros and Réal Lessard were still at liberty. Moreover, they were apparently still in business.

When Elmyr was asked about all this he either shrugged nonchalantly or essayed a bored chuckle, as if to say ''Boys will be boys, and Texas oil millionaires will be Texas oil millionaires.'' His laughter, however, had a certain thin and worried quality, and everyone on Ibiza was instantly convinced that the nervous Hungarian was somehow involved in the con game. The question was how. Had he financed Fernand and Réal in their skulduggery? Was he being blackmailed? Had he foolishly signed some papers which linked him to the swindlers? Had some of the alleged fake paintings come from his family collection? *Was* there a family collection?

Apparently unperturbed by such suspicions and conjecture, Elmyr flew off to Madrid in March of 1967 with several other members of Ibiza's jet set to attend a theater opening and a round of parties given by friends. Almost immediately following his departure from the island, the headlines of French newspapers proclaimed fresh scandal. A batch of paintings—two Dufys, two Vlamincks and a Derain—put up for auction at the suburban town of Pontoise, near Paris, had been denounced by the French police as fakes and their ownership attributed to Fernand Legros. Did this mean, someone wondered aloud to Elmyr, that the collection of supposed fakes sold to Meadows in Texas had been merely the tip of an iceberg? Elmyr shrugged again. ''You know, my dear,'' he said, ''in my experience the newspapers have a terrible tendency to exaggerate these things.''

A week later, perhaps in response to the events at Pontoise and an article about them in the French newspaper *Le Figaro,* a Socialist member of the Japanese Diet brought up the question of the authenticity of three paintings, a Dufy, a Derain and a Modigliani, purchased in 1963 and 1964 for the Japanese National Museum of Western Art in Tokyo. Government funds had financed the purchase; the seller, once again, had been the ubiquitous Fernand Legros.

The official price quoted by the Tokyo press for the Dufy and the Derain was the equivalent of $70,252, although unofficial estimates were considerably higher. Whatever the cost, the name Fernand Legros was now synonymous with the sale of fraudulent art. Curiously enough, no one had yet shown any great concern, at least in print, over the identity of the man or men (there was still occasional casual mention of a "factory" in the South of France, or perhaps even the Balearic Islands of Spain) who had turned out all the fake paintings, which now numbered over fifty.

In the middle of April 1967, Fernand Legros, in the company of two young bodyguards, arrived by overnight boat from Barcelona to the island of Ibiza. In his new red Buick he drove up the hill to La Falaise. He broke in, changed the locks and coolly announced to the community at large that "this house is mine, not Elmyr's. He has no right here, and I intend to live in it."

Elmyr returned from Madrid a week later: black hair a trifle gray above the elfin ears, monocle missing, white-faced, furious and protesting. Yet the police made no move either to evict or to punish Fernand. Elmyr ran round town, rallying the support of his friends at the Alhambra and in La Tierra, hiring and firing lawyers who refused to promise him instant justice. In a few days the case came before the local judge, who studied all the pertinent documents and then gave his decision. The house clearly belonged —had, in fact, *always* belonged—to Señor Fernand Legros, although a private agreement gave Señor Elmyr Dory-Boutin the right to live in it during his lifetime. Therefore the two gentlemen would have to share their living quarters.

For three weeks then, maintaining an uneasy truce, Elmyr and Fernand lived together in La Falaise. But in the meantime a new, peculiar rumor began to gain momentum in Ibiza's buzzing sidewalk cafés. Someone had had the temerity to suggest that he— "El-*myr*?"—had done all or part of the alleged fake paintings sold in Dallas, Pontoise and Tokyo. Someone else remembered, a few years back, having heard that someone else had spoken to someone else, who'd said *they'd* seen an oil painting of Elmyr's that looked like "a poor copy of a bad Matisse."

The implications of this story were finally scotched by Erwin Broner, the German-American architect who had designed and built La Falaise. He had visited Elmyr many times in the previously rented villa and from time to time had surprised Elmyr at work on an oil or watercolor. One morning at the Café Alhambra, a month after the unhappy return from Madrid, Broner, richly amused, said: "Listen Elmyr, they're telling that you're the genius who made those fake paintings Legros sold in Texas. You know, everyone can talk about it and everyone can believe it, but we—I and my wife Gisela—we know it's not true. We've *seen* your paintings. You could never have done it. You don't have that kind of talent." He warmly squeezed Elmyr's shoulder. "And the funny thing is, some people told me the other day that underneath La Falaise there's a secret studio where you did your 'masterpieces.' So I laughed at these ignoramuses and said, 'Well, I built the house and there's nothing but rocks! And he's every morning until one o'clock sipping Cinzano at the Alhambra, in the afternoon he's taking his siesta, in the evening he goes out— so when do you suppose he did those forty paintings?'

"No, my friend," he reassured Elmyr. "Let them all vilify you. I know you are innocent."

Elmyr smiled wanly and said, "Thank you very much. Very kind of you, Erwin." He excused himself from the table.

That evening, for the last time in his life, he confronted Fernand Legros in the living room of La Falaise. Fernand sat with his feet propped on Elmyr's coffee table, calmly smoking a Dutch cigar. The two men, the older Hungarian and the young naturalized American, were alone.

"I can't go on like this," Elmyr said pitifully.

"Then just go," Fernand suggested, smiling.

"Where? Why are you torturing me? This is my home. I have nowhere to go. You could live in the South of Spain if you liked. If you stay here they'll come for you, they'll find us together—I'll go to jail, Réal will go to jail, you'll *certainly* go to jail."

"In which case," said Fernand, puffing on his cigar, "it will be my greatest last pleasure to take you and your criminal-minded friend with me."

Elmyr sighed like a man grieving. "I can't stand it any longer," he said.

"Then go," Fernand repeated, with no change of expression.

There was no more to say. A beaten man, Elmyr left the room.

On June 11, 1967, a few days after the conversation at the Café Alhambra in which he was pronounced incapable and innocent, he vanished from the island of Ibiza. Once again he was on the run— as he had been on the run, it seemed to him, nearly all his life.

2.

in which we
trace Elmyr's
youth and
wartime
escapades,
and watch
his career
unfold
in Paris.

MATISSE BY ELMYR

he beginning of Elmyr's fantastic saga took place on an April afternoon in 1946, in Paris. But to know the man who lived then in a cramped artist's studio on the rue Jacob, painting portraits of his rich and socially illustrious friends, one must go back in time to the Budapest of the 1920s, when Elmyr Dory-Boutin—born Elmyr de Hory—was a boy, and from there to a concentration camp for political prisoners high in the Carpathian Mountains. Let us take the brief and instructive journey: Portrait of the Artist as a Young Aristocrat.

Elmyr's family were landowners, with large estates and vineyards near Lake Balaton in central Hungary. His mother came from a family of Jewish bankers who had always served the kings of the Austro-Hungarian Empire; his father, in the decades between the wars, was appointed Hungarian ambassador to Turkey and then to two South American republics. His son rarely traveled with him, for when he was sixteen Elmyr's parents were divorced. Before that traumatic event he had lived the secure, spoiled life of the only child of wealthy parents. After it, everything seemed to change. His mother married again, a man younger than herself, and Elmyr had even less place in her affections than before.

He had been brought up in what was called the *Kinderzimmer*, a wholly separate part of the house, by a wet nurse and a progression of French, German and English governesses. The wet nurse lived with the family until Elmyr was fourteen, and when something went wrong in his life she was the one who comforted and sheltered him; he was closer to her than to either of his parents. As a child he was afraid to be alone in the dark, and the nurse would sit by his bedside until he had fallen asleep.

His earliest memory was of a time when he was perhaps five years old. He awoke one night; the room was dark, he was alone and frightened, and he crawled from bed and made his way quietly through the house to the *grand salon*.

"I walked down the huge curving staircase and into the *salon*. There was my mother, wearing a dark red silk suit and a big feather hat, and some people standing around her . . . she was a very beautiful woman, and she always had a score of young men around her. Suddenly somebody pointed to me standing in the door. I came running to her, probably crying—she picked me up and when I wanted to kiss her she said, very angrily, 'You kiss my powder away.' That's my oldest souvenir of memory.''

It was the kind of luxurious Central European life that was to go quite out of fashion with the advent of two world wars. "We ate always with real silver," Elmyr recalled, "and always off Meissen china. In the season we traveled to Biarritz, Ostende, Karlsbad and Paris. We all had horses, carriages and servants. My mother went to the greatest Paris fashion houses for her clothes and furs —I remember a portrait of her where her arm is covered from wrist to elbow with diamond bracelets. In our home all the portraits stood in a gallery, depicting at least three generations of the family." Elmyr himself was painted as a small boy, standing next to his mother, wearing white shorts, black pumps, white stockings and a white frilly collar, leaning against Mama's Louis Quinze chair. "The portrait," he once said wistfully, "disappeared during the Second World War.... But how I would love to see it again...."

At sixteen, with the divorce, Elmyr was catapulted out of this sheltered life. Naturally upset, and then extremely restless, he announced his desire to travel abroad; his mother refused her permission. He had another and more secret problem, too, which perhaps she had just begun to understand. With his loyalties fragmented and his security shattered as a result of the divorce, Elmyr lacked a father to both guide him and provide a figure of authority at a critical age. He was a good-looking and well-spoken young man. Homosexuals—of whom there were a fair number in the aristocratic *salons* of Budapest—sensed his confusion and his need, and were strongly attracted to him; and he found himself, at first with fear and doubt, but later with alacrity, reciprocating their affection. He was fond of girls, and he had one or two romantic flirtations before he was twenty-one, but they were no more than flirtations, and he was inevitably drawn toward the company of older men whom he admired and wished to please. Once he had taken the step, he saw no turning back. It was to color and shape his entire life.

By sixteen he had also begun to show some artistic talent, and since it seemed a proper pastime for a young gentleman he was sent by his mother to art school in Budapest. Considering his secret life, however, living at home was difficult, and at the age of eighteen, after repeated arguments and scenes, he finally persuaded his parents to allow him to leave Budapest to study in Munich.

It was a great adventure for a Hungarian boy to be in Munich on his own, but the air of his new freedom proved intoxicating. Life in one sense suddenly became easy for him; as an attractive and rich young man he was considered in certain circles an extremely desirable companion, constantly courted, constantly flattered. He was vulnerable, and homosexuality became his way of life. As Elmyr tried to explain it many years later, ''I was at the mercy of a strange European society whose morals had been damaged through the First World War, and which was then in complete flux. What was true of the society was also true of me.''

In another sense, life was hard. Living alone at a *pension,* Elmyr was out on the town or with friends almost every night; but he went every day to his art school, the Akademie Heimann, whose approach to the arts of drawing and painting was strict and classical. If he was a nocturnal *bon vivant,* he was still a diligent and excited student from nine to five. On the drawing of a single hand, or on one nude, he had sometimes to work two weeks, six hours a day, until Moritz Heimann himself was satisfied with the result.

''I had a rigid training,'' Elmyr explained, casting back on his youth for an explanation of what happened twenty years later, ''and I was greatly taken by the Impressionists, who were the big artistic influence at that time. I remember looking at my first Picassos, which I didn't quite understand. I did see one classical period Picasso at the Galerie Tannheuser, a portrait of a woman, so superbly drawn with a fine brush that I was flabbergasted. I dreamed about the painting for months. But Picasso was already in an abstract cubist stage, and I didn't understand it. The first Chagall I saw was also a complete mystery to me—no contact at all. Because somehow my surroundings and upbringing excluded that. There was another school in Munich, the Akademie Hoffman, more advanced and more abstract. Unhappily, it seems to me now,

I didn't go to that school. Maybe after all these years I see it was a mistake."

After Munich Elmyr decided he wanted to continue his studies in Paris and, somewhat reluctantly, his family agreed to finance this second stage of his education. In Paris he studied at the Académie la Grande Chaumière under Fernand Léger, and in 1926—he was twenty—one of his paintings was submitted to and accepted by the annual exhibition of the Salon d'Automne. It was a great day for the young artist; perhaps, in the light of what happened afterward, his greatest. The painting was a landscape, a view of Cagnes-sur-Mer, and it hung in the same room with a painting by Maurice de Vlaminck.

Elmyr stayed in Paris off and on until 1932, living, like so many artists, in Montparnasse, which was at the zenith of its heroic age. Vlaminck had worked there in the previous decade; so had André Derain, Kees van Dongen, Albert Marquet and, until 1928, Henri Matisse. Picasso had been a frequent visitor. "Like most young painters in the *quartier*," Elmyr later liked to claim, "I knew them all. Of course I was just a boy then, and they probably didn't know me as much more than a face in the crowd of young people that was always hanging around. But I was sitting with them night after night at the Café du Dôme, or the Rotonde, for years. I was friendly at first with Léger, because he was my teacher, and his wife, and also later with Vlaminck, whom I admired because he had such great style as a man. Gertrude Stein was there, and Hemingway and Alice Toklas and Peggy Guggenheim, and Fujita and Man Ray. I was friends with Paul Valéry, the poet, and with Leon Zadkin. That was the great time in Montparnasse—the twenties—when suddenly everything that was vitally new burst upon the scene and dazzled the world. I was a witness, I was part of it. I was introduced to James Joyce—the Shakespeare Company met in Sylvia Beach's little bookshop in the rue de l'Odéon, where Joyce read from his work. I hadn't the faintest idea what he was talking about, but I listened with great curiosity."

Unlike most young painters in the *quartier,* however, Elmyr received from his family as much money as he needed to keep up the life of a young expatriate aristocrat. If he was short of cash and wanted suddenly to take a trip to St. Tropez with a new friend, he simply went, and en route telegraphed to Budapest for funds. This happened often. "Too often," Elmyr later lamented. "I was never held to a specific allowance, which caused me a lot of trouble, because I had and have absolutely no sense of the reality of money. Later, with Fernand Legros and Réal Lessard, I paid for this."

Before 1940 then, Elmyr was a kind of playboy artist living in two distinct worlds: that of the painter and that of fast-moving, moneyed international society. To be a homosexual, or "gay," was hardly a disqualification for either, if one had wit, good looks, youth, and talent to boot. Elmyr participated in one more group exhibition, this time at London's Redfern Gallery, and he painted the portraits of such rich friends as Prince Yussoupov, Mrs. Potter Palmer of Chicago, and the Duke of Kent; but he was not, by any stretch of the imagination—including his own—a dedicated artist. He was a gifted, elegant drifter. If a good friend liked a certain drawing he would simply say "Take it." He had no real ambition and put little value on his work, which, like his life, he considered a form of amusement and not much more. "If Gertrude Stein was right," he commented many years later, "and there was indeed a 'lost generation,' I was certainly a charter member of it. I was very bright and bubbly on the surface, but underneath I felt as desolate and barren as Mr. Eliot's 'Waste Land.' I was a most unhappy young man. I felt doomed. You see, I wasn't a very strong character. I didn't see that I had any alternative."

With the advent of the war, the alternative arrived with the jackboots, taking a form Elmyr had failed to anticipate. He returned to Hungary just after the *Anschluss*. Less than a year later he was taken as a political prisoner to a camp in Transylvania. He had no politics and belonged to no party, but he had been a little too intimate with an English newspaperman in Budapest and had lived most of his life in France, which in the eyes of the Horthy regime was enough to make him suspect. As Elmyr put it, "I was obviously too colorful a person for the safety of the state."

Fortunately, when the camp commandant discovered that Elmyr was a painter, he commissioned a portrait. Elmyr, in fact, had let it be known that he was ready and willing to oblige.

"It was a bitter winter," he explained, "and the camp was on top of the Carpathian Mountains, in Dracula's land. Six feet of snow lay on the ground, and the temperature was below zero. The Commandant had a wood stove in his room. So I painted him very slowly, in the greatest detail, wearing every single one of his medals. With the preliminary sketches it took me at least three months to finish. That was the first time my artistic talents helped me to survive, but not the last."

He was released, only to be arrested again a year later, and this time he was packed off to a camp in Germany. During an interrogation the Gestapo beat him and broke one of his legs, and he was removed to a hospital outside of Berlin. One day, to his amazement, he noticed that the front gate was open. Taking a deep breath, he walked through the hospital grounds, on his crutches, out into the street. He never looked back. He had friends in Berlin from before the war; they agreed to help him, and three months later he had made his way back to Budapest. When the war ended and the Russians had occupied the city, he was still there.

His parents were dead. The family's fortune—the Meissen, the horses and the Swiss bank accounts—had been confiscated by the Germans, and now the family vineyards at Lake Balaton were about to be communized by the Red Army. With Swedish diplomatic papers and a handful of small diamonds sewn into the lining of his coat, Elmyr turned his back on Hungary forever and headed for France. The Swedish papers proved useless and the diamonds took the place of his passport when it came to crossing borders and checkpoints in the occupied zones. In September 1945 he reached Paris. Léger, his old teacher, was there to welcome him as a friend; Leon Zadkin was there, Philippe de Rothschild was there. It was like the old days, and it was marvelous to be back, with one terrifying difference. Elmyr had no money.

But he had a talent, and he could paint. He took a cheap room in the rue Jacob, and there, for the next six months, he led the undisguised double life of a struggling artist and expatriate Hungarian aristocrat. It was a time, just after the war, when all over France a small unhorsed army of impoverished barons and counts was walking the streets and knocking on doors with suitcases full of dia-

De Hory:
Paris (Summer).
An early work of
Elmyr's, painted in 1946
in Paris at his studio
in the rue Jacob.

mond tiaras, gold snuff boxes and rolled-up Watteaus and Fragonards. Less fortunate in that sense than most, Elmyr de Hory had escaped from the holocaust of Central Europe with nothing except his artistic abilities and his expensive tastes. He was poor, he was a painter, and he was no longer young; for lack of hope in postwar Europe the combination was hard to beat. To old friends like Tommy Esterhazy, the Countess of Palfy and Philippe de Rothschild he sold his paintings for prices averaging about $100, and later for that amount he did portraits of the Baron de Thierry's two sons. But the Paris art galleries, when he offered the landscapes and nudes, shrugged their collective shoulders and politely declined to buy.

Elmyr was a poor man on the April afternoon in 1946 when Lady Malcolm Campbell, a friend who lived at the plush Hôtel George V, paid a visit to his studio in the rue Jacob, happened to glance at a drawing on the wall, and said: "Elmyr ... that's a Picasso, isn't it?"

It wasn't a Picasso. It was a de Hory, a little line of a young girl's head, unsigned and unframed. Elmyr smiled—the slightly wicked elf's smile—at his good friend Lady Campbell.

"How do you know it's a Picasso?" he asked.

"I know something about Picasso," she said, with a certain nonchalant air of authority. "And I remember you told me that you knew him fairly well before the war. He didn't sign a lot of those drawings from his Greek period. It's a very good one. Tell me, would you like to sell it?"

"Well, why not?" Elmyr said—softly sighing—after a while. "How much you give me for it?"

So it was that by accident a career had been launched which would last more than twenty years, span five continents and find a major place in the history of art. But at the time Elmyr had no visions of the future and no idea what was in store for him; he was just bewildered and delighted. The agreed price was £40 sterling; with that much cash he could live for two months. The drawing had taken him all of ten minutes on a rainy March afternoon.

In a few days Lady Campbell left for London, and Elmyr forgot the incident as quickly as possible. He had needed the money badly, but still he felt a little guilty at having hoodwinked a friend—even a rich friend.

Then three months later the elegant lady in question returned from England. The Thierrys gave a cocktail party, where she swept a nervous Elmyr into a corner.

"I must confess, darling, I feel a bit odd about that Picasso drawing you sold me. I was rather short of cash in London, so I took it to an art dealer I know. He gave me £150 for it. Dear sweet Elmyr, don't look so shocked. Won't you lunch with me tomorrow at the Ritz?"

Dear sweet Elmyr was indeed shocked. Were such things possible? I must find out, he decided. He had no money again, and he saw no special reason why he should resist the temptation. To ease his conscience, he recalled that Fernand Léger, his teacher, had confided to his friends in Montparnasse that in his younger days he had faked Corots. In later years Elmyr would also claim that Vlaminck, the great Fauve painter, had not hesitated to paint some Cézannes when he was out of funds. "It was common knowledge among his friends in Paris," Elmyr said. No art historian or dealer has ever corroborated this, and there seems little doubt that it was an effort on Elmyr's part to find worthy precedents for actions that rarely failed to make him uneasy. The point, of course, is that Elmyr *believed* that it was so. Whatever the truth about Vlaminck, it seemed to Elmyr the time-honored prerogative of the artist facing starvation—provided he had the genius to implement his secret scheme.

Declining the offer of lunch at the Ritz, he went instead to his studio, consulted some old catalogs and then spent an hour making pen-and-ink drawings in the so-called classical style, *circa* 1925, à la Picasso. The work went swiftly and Elmyr found it surprisingly easy, which made him wonder: could it possibly be any good? He did about six female heads, then selected what he considered the two best. An American girl dropped in for a drink just before dinner. "Would you mind taking off your clothes," Elmyr asked politely, "and sitting in that wicker chair?" She didn't mind—she knew him, and there was nothing to fear—and he did a nude drawing of her, a profile in line.

"Thank you, my dear."

It was a success, he decided, on the first try. In the morning he studied the drawings with a fresh eye. They were good, there was no doubt of that—but under the scrutiny of an expert, would they really pass as Picassos? For a moment Elmyr decided to call the whole thing off; it seemed too absurd, and he had visions of himself being marched toward the Sûreté in the grip of cold-eyed *gendarmes*. Then, he thought, what is the alternative? At least in jail they won't let me starve.

Shortly before noon he entered an art gallery in the rue de Seine on the Left Bank, where the dealer was a complete stranger to him. He carried three drawings under his arm in a cheap cardboard portfolio; his hands were sweating. As casually as he could, he introduced himself and explained that he had known Picasso in Paris before the war, that the drawings had been a gift. He was regretfully selling them, he explained, because the war had left him destitute. The dealer nodded—it was a common enough experience. He examined the drawings for about five minutes, while Elmyr walked round the gallery, admiring a Dufy here and a Matisse there, and from time to time wiping his palms on the sides of his freshly pressed trousers. At last the dealer said: "*Mais oui, c'est bon*—how much do you want?" The only argument was one of price. Ten minutes later Elmyr walked out in the gentle sunshine of the rue de Seine with cash stuffed in his pocket—the equivalent of $400.

"It was probably more money than I'd had in my hands at one time in seven years," he recalled long afterward. "It was so easy I couldn't believe it. And I didn't even feel guilty, because I hadn't done it out of viciousness, to harm anyone, or even with the idea of making a fortune. It was a matter of survival. When you went through the ordeal of the war, then even if you had stronger morals than I had, you found you could do things that were absolutely unthinkable in the past. The criterion of morality in 1946," he added, "was quite different than in 1920, in the beautiful world we lived in when we were children."

To prove his point that he hadn't done it "to make a fortune," the moment he had money in his pocket he went back to painting his own landscapes and figure studies. But nothing sold. And the money dwindled, then vanished. He had never in his life been held to a budget; money was something that appeared by magic when you sent a telegram to Budapest; it was handed to you by gracious bank tellers in Kitzbühel, Monte Carlo, Deauville, Biarritz and Rome. It was meant to buy Château Yquem wine, lunch at the Ritz, clothes at Knize, nights of love and laughter and expensive gifts for friends. For Elmyr it still had no reality. By August the profit from the three Picassos was gone.

By August, also, he had admitted the fakery to a close friend, a twenty-two-year-old Frenchman named Jacques Chamberlin. Chamberlin had no money, either, but he had youth, brashness, good looks and a pedigree in the art world. He also had an idea. His father, a Bordeaux industrialist who had died in the war, had been a well-known collector of Impressionist paintings. The collection had been carted off by an S.S. *Obergruppenführer* and vanished in the bombing of Berlin. One evening, over a drink at the Café Flore, Chamberlin blithely suggested that he and Elmyr go into partnership.

"You make the drawings, and I'll sell them. I'll say they're all that's left of my father's collection. We'll travel through Europe together, we'll make money, and we'll have a marvelous time."

The prospect sounded amusing as well as potentially profitable, and again there seemed no reason to resist the temptation. And again Elmyr, after a while, sighed and said: "Well, why not?"

This time, however, he took a little more care in the preparation of the work. He went to a Picasso exhibit and he studied volumes of Picasso reproductions. He had noticed that the dealer on the rue de Seine had held the paper up to the light, searching for an identifying watermark. In a cheap art supply shop on the Left Bank, Elmyr bought a block of old prewar paper, already beginning to yellow slightly around the edges. Then, in his studio, in one week, he made a dozen Picassos.

Until the summer of 1946 he had only his outdated Swedish diplomatic papers and a temporary *carte d'identité*. Chamberlin, however, had a friend in one of the government bureaus who procured for Elmyr a French passport, and with it Elmyr and Chamberlin and Chamberlin's English girlfriend set out *à trois* on a grand tour of Europe. They covered Brussels, Amsterdam, London, Geneva, Lausanne and Zurich, ending their first swing on the Côte d'Azur in October. Then they returned to London. Elmyr in later years remembered the journey with nostalgia; after the rigors of the war and the misery of his year in Paris it was indeed, as Chamberlin had promised, ''a marvelous time.'' Money was plentiful, comfort was available, and there was a certain euphoria resulting from their being always on the move—and since Chamberlin did all the selling, Elmyr had no need to wipe the sweat from his palms before entering an art gallery. They couldn't quite afford Claridge's and the Carleton Hotel in Cannes, but they dined in the best restaurants, ordered the best wines and traveled first class in Wagon-Lits. Elmyr worked leisurely a few hours every morning in his hotel room. Each time a sale was made the trio went out on the town to celebrate. Chamberlin loved good wine. Whatever scruples Elmyr may have had were drowned effectively in Haut-Brion '34 and Mouton-Rothschild '29.

The sales record was perfect. For one thing, Picasso drawings were still cheap; and not once, in a dozen of the best art galleries in Europe, did Chamberlin fail to sell whatever he had in his portfolio. In Brussels he sold two figure studies privately to the director of the Beaux-Arts museum. The profits, as agreed, were split down the middle. It was in London, however, the second time around, that Elmyr began to suspect he was getting somewhat less than his share. Until then he had taken Chamberlin's word at face value, but one day, browsing through Mayfair, he walked into the Redfern Gallery and saw—he claimed—one of his Picassos hanging on the wall in the front room. The price was so high that, even allowing for any reasonable mark-up on the part of the gallery (which no longer has records for that period, so that the point cannot be clarified), it was still a revelation that signaled the end of the business relationship with young, enterprising Jacques Chamberlin. Accusations followed, then arguments, and finally an end of trust. The days of the partnership were clearly numbered, and in February 1947 Elmyr said adieu and flew to Copenhagen, alone.

He had his new French passport, about $1000 in cash and some prewar friends scattered throughout Scandinavia. By the time he reached Stockholm, the cash had almost disappeared. If Chamberlin had been so successful, Elmyr thought, why not me? What was there to fear? If there was trouble he could always claim that he was innocent, that he had inherited the drawings from his family who had bought them from dealers before the war in perfectly good faith. He walked into a Stockholm gallery and asked if they would be interested in some classical-period Picasso drawings; he was, as in Paris, a refugee Hungarian aristocrat out of funds— nothing less than the truth. Three men, including a curator from the Stockholm Art Museum, marched up to Elmyr's room in the Grand Hotel. A businesslike trio, they examined and discussed the five pen-and-ink drawings for over an hour. Which gallery had sold them? "Ah, that I don't know," Elmyr confessed. "My father came back from Paris to Budapest around 1937, and he had them with him. I tell you frankly, that's all I know."

While Elmyr sweated and dried his palms on his trousers, the Swedish dealers retired to the bar downstairs for a private council. Then they made their offer: for all five, the Swedish equivalent of a solid $6000. It was almost double what Elmyr had hoped for.

Three days later he received the check. It was the first time he had made a sale by himself for such a sum of money—even the three days' wait had been a kind of purgatory for him, and he had been so nervous that he threw up twice in his hotel bathroom. He had become convinced that the galleries would eventually write to Picasso or Picasso's dealer in Paris for some sort of authentication, and if Elmyr was around when the answer arrived he would spend three years in a Swedish prison. He cashed the check and went straight from the bank to a travel agency. On reflection, however enlightened the Swedish penal code, it seemed a good time to leave Stockholm.

With so much cash in hand, all things were possible. He was weary of a war-ravaged Europe and a little worried, too, that if he returned to France it would be a simple matter for the authorities to find him. Looking at the bas-relief airline map in the travel agency, it seemed that the farthest one could travel from Europe and still remain in what Elmyr considered the civilized world was Rio de Janeiro. He had never been to South America. Well, why not? Prudently—and prophetically—he bought a one-way ticket.

3.

in which Elmyr
journeys to
Brazil, thence to
high society life
in New York and
points West, and
has a portfolio
flung at him in
Beverly Hills.

BONNARD BY ELMYR

Rio de Janeiro was a steppingstone, a breath taken, a momentary halt in what would prove to be for Elmyr de Hory the grand and fateful design of his life. He had just celebrated his fortieth birthday. He was a mature man who had lived his entire adult life dependent either on his family or his wits. What he owned, in emotional or pecuniary capital, he spent. He never considered the future. In this sense he was still completely childlike: he had a child's trust that no one meant to do him harm and that the future would be cosy and warm. Companions to that trust were a child's charm and a child's guile.

"It was deep winter when I left Stockholm," he reminisced many years later, cheerfully and blithely, as was his habit, "and I wore long woolen underwear and a fur coat. I flew KLM. The first stop was Copenhagen, where during the one hour waiting I was nearly raped in the restroom by a Danish officer in uniform. I declined the invitation. Then a night's stopover in Lisbon, then Dakar, then Natal—then finally Rio. It was full blazing summer and I was still in my long woolen underwear. I thought I'd faint from the heat. I nearly exploded. I knew no one in Rio. I went to the Copacabana Hotel, the best in town, and the main hangout later on of Fernand Legros and Réal Lessard—naturally at my recommendation. And then I rented a very beautiful little house from a Frenchman, up on Gloria Hill. I started to paint my own paintings, as I'd promised myself, and I very quickly made friends."

Arriving with the first postwar wave of rich European travelers, Elmyr was received with open arms into Brazilian society. He painted the portraits of Brazilian financiers: Oswaldo Aranha, second president of the U.N. General Assembly, and General Humberto Castel Branco, later to be President of Brazil. The fee was high. He didn't have to do Picassos. In those days, of course, he never thought of it as a way of life, a career. It was something he had forced himself to do in the interests of survival.

Had he committed a crime? That never occurred to him. "I was terribly naïve," he explained. "When I had money I didn't even want to think about what I'd done. Of course, at the back of my mind, probably, I did realize that if I ever got into financial trouble

I could always fall back on it. It was like a private insurance policy."

He was to cash it sooner than he planned. Rio de Janeiro, after a while, bored him. In August, 1947, with previous introductions from Léger and Consuelo St. Exupéry in Paris, as well as from all his new Brazilian friends, Elmyr flew to New York to pay what he thought would be a brief visit to the United States. He had never been there and he was filled with curiosity. His visa was good for three months. As it turned out, he overstayed that limit somewhat —by more than eleven years.

Three weeks in New York was enough to meet, as Elmyr put it, "everybody who was anybody." Agatha Ratibor helped with introductions. He started out in a suite at the Essex House and when he moved to a duplex apartment on East 78th Street the guest list at his housewarming party included Zsa Zsa and Magda Gabor, Anita Loos, Averell Harriman, Lana Turner, Anita Averell, Dan Topping and René d'Harnoncourt, then a director of the Museum of Modern Art. Elmyr had known Zsa Zsa in Budapest, and in New York she commissioned him to do a three-quarter-length portrait, nude, with a guitar leaning against her thigh at a strategic angle. "She complained," Elmyr remarked to a friend, "that one of the tits were too much in the center. I was paid for it, but very poorly."

Miss Gabor's recollection is somewhat different. "Yes," she said recently, "I remember him well. But he never painted my portrait. In 1949 he came to visit me at the Plaza and sold me two Dufys—he said they were Dufys—for $5000. They were fakes. . . . Now I can get my money back."*

Through Zsa Zsa he met Anita Loos and painted her portrait,

---

* At the risk of starting the Hungarian equivalent of a vendetta, it seems worthwhile to quote Elmyr's *riposte* to this story, as related in *Look* (Dec. 10, 1968). "Two Dufys?" he said. "On the face of it, that's absurd. Can you imagine Zsa Zsa buying even *one* Dufy?"

Miss Gabor also added, to explain Elmyr's claim that he had painted her portrait: "All Hungarians are liars." The list of paintings in the catalog for Elmyr's show at the Lilienfeld Galleries in January 1948 (see page 33) includes, in any case, a *Portrait of Zsa Zsa.*

De Hory:
Epilogue.
An oil painting by
Elmyr, done in 1947
in Río de Janeiro.

too. "A very big portrait," he said. "She was very upset about the result, however, and wrote me that it was 'too naturalistic to show to the public,' whatever that means. And she never paid me for it and she never gave back the painting. I said, 'Give it back or pay, you're not a poor woman.' But she never did. I asked Averell Harriman to intercede for me, and he told me, 'Elmyr, I think you're completely in the right, but I'm such an old friend of Anita's that it's not worth breaking up the relationship over such a matter.' You see, that's what they call diplomacy. In Central Europe we understand it only too well."

(Miss Loos says succinctly: "Yes, he painted my portrait. He asked me if he could, and I said yes. Then he gave it to me as a gift. It was so awful I gave it to my maid, and she ripped it up and threw it out.")

He painted Magda Gabor, too, but it was understandable, with the suites and the cocktail parties and the new Knize suits for which he paid close to $300 each, that the money left over from Stockholm and Rio soon dwindled. He had ballyhooed himself as a fashionable artist, and the Lilienfeld Galleries on 57th Street invited him then to give his first one-man show. It came at an opportune moment. It was a fine gallery; Vlaminck and Feininger had showed there, too, and there were Chagalls and Dufys hanging on the walls. This, thought Elmyr, was his great chance. It was also make-or-break for him in the New York art world. If he sold well, his future was virtually assured.

Two rooms of the gallery were filled with portraits, brightly colored landscapes and figural compositions. The January opening night was a social success—but a financial disaster.

"All of the *haut monde* of New York was there," Elmyr recalled. "The *vernissage* was on the night of an awful snowstorm. People couldn't get taxis, they had to walk through a blizzard, and still they came. You couldn't move, it was so packed. You couldn't even see the paintings. My friends said it was the most glittering event of the social season.

"However, I sold only one portrait. I didn't make enough money to cover the expense of the catalog. It was a bad year—I think it was the first postwar recession and the stock market wasn't good

LILIENFELD GALLERIES

21 EAST 57TH STREET   *   **NEW YORK CITY**

ARTISTS REPRESENTED IN

OUR COLLECTION

VLAMINK	*SERGER*
DERAIN	*RUBIN*
UTRILLO	*MANDIN*
CHAGALL	*CHIRICO*
DUFY	*BRAQUE*
CHABAUD	*FEININGER*
MONET	*SERISAWA*
COURBET	*DREWES*
ulRIEUD	*A. DREFS*
LAURENCIN	*BASSFORD*
WAROQUIER	*HORY*

AND OLD MASTERS

OF IMPORTANCE

The list of painters
on view at the
Lilienfeld Galleries
in 1948 when Elmyr
was exhibited there
under the pseudonym of Hory.
Included were Vlaminck,
Derain, Chagall and Dufy.

either. Salvador Dali had an exhibition at the same time in another gallery on 57th Street and *he* didn't sell anything. Once that winter, in bitter cold January, I was invited to a party at the home of Jorge de Cuevas and, just as I arrived, Dali and his wife stepped out of a taxi. He was carrying a huge package. I asked him what it was and he said, 'Paintings.' To show to the guests, naturally, to try and sell something. And he, mind you, was not de Hory, but Dali."

The critics called Elmyr's work "charming, capable, attractive, romantic in its approach," and added that "de Hory leans to an expressionist palette in some of his best works." *Art News* said: "His lively realism, reckless paint and lush colors strike the well-known chord of the School of Paris as do his subjects—French ports, harlequins and facile portraits." Yet only one painting was sold.

The financial failure of the exhibition plunged Elmyr into a black depression. It meant one of two things. He could accept the lot of the struggling artist—tighten his belt, live on baked beans and Tip Top bread, give up his duplex and move to a cold-water loft on the lower East Side; he could become one of the legion of painters who frequented warm Greenwich Village coffeehouses in the wintertime and never missed a gallery opening where free *hors d'oeuvres* and wine were offered to the ever-hungry mob. He could return to Paris, assuming he could raise the fare, but that simply meant swapping baked beans for *croissants* and the East Side loft for a grubby Montparnasse garret. He was too old, he decided, for such romance—too old and too spoiled. He liked cocktails at the Plaza. The sound of rats gnawing in the eaves of artists' garrets set his teeth on edge.

The alternative, of course, was to cash his wonderful insurance policy. He had already put it to the test shortly after his arrival in New York. A foreboding had seized him, and he had decided to find out—in the event of future emergency—if it was still as valid in the United States as it had been in Paris and Stockholm. Sitting down at the living-room coffee table in his Essex House suite, he did a single Picasso drawing and a very large Picasso gouache. For the drawing he had no more vintage French paper, and he didn't dare risk an American watermark; instead, he went downtown to the used-book shops on Fourth Avenue and bought some old, oversized French picture albums of the 1920s—*Gothic Cathedrals* and *Views of Paris*. Carefully scissoring out the blank pages at the end of the books, he set to work. "The gouache," Elmyr related many years later, "was about 24 inches by 40 inches. Once Picasso had made a sculpture called *L'homme à l'Agneau*—'The Man with the Lamb,' a big bronze. I was quite fond of it and my gouache, you might say, was a study for the finished sculpture. At least that's how I presented it. I didn't even have the money to frame it properly."

He took the gouache one Saturday morning to the Perls Galleries on 58th Street and left it over the weekend with the gallery owner, Klaus Perls. "He wanted to examine it more closely," Elmyr says, "and show it to some other experts." On Tuesday Elmyr returned, bringing the Picasso drawing as well. "Perls was very happy to see me, and delighted that I had something else to sell him, too. After the usual haggling he offered me $750 for the gouache and $250 for the drawing, and I reluctantly accepted the offer."

Klaus Perls, later to become president of the American Art Dealers Association—and who, nineteen years later, an older and wiser man, was to walk into the Meadows living room in Dallas and say, without hesitation, "Fake!"—thus became, as Elmyr one day recalled with a certain childlike innocent pleasure, "my first American victim."

In January the show at the Lilienfeld Galleries was about to close. Most of the critics had been kind to Elmyr's work, but some had declined to review the exhibition on the grounds that his work was eclectic, unoriginal, curiously out-of-date, his style either too reminiscent or frankly borrowed from the early twentieth-century French masters. It seemed a hint too broad to resist—the hand of Fate gently pushing him forward toward his destiny. There were bills to pay, the gallery itself was dunning him for costs, and Elmyr already owed more money than he had in his dwindling bank account. Once more he faced, as he put it, "the grim everyday life."

The show closed. "It was cold in New York," Elmyr says, "and I yearned for the sunshine." With a small sigh of regret, he packed his bags.

"All I needed was some old paper, Chinese ink and a feather pen. I decided to go to California—I had a great curiosity to see America. I thought already that it was a wonderful country."

Once he had made the decision to resume his briefly interrupted career as a forger of French art, Elmyr went at it with all the dedication and skill he could muster. He was not without a sense of guilt, however, and certainly not without fear of the consequences.

He solved the former problem in a time-honored manner. I'm only doing it for a little while, he told himself, and because I have no choice. It's either that or starve. The moment he had accumulated a little capital, he would quit and go back to painting his own work. One day his talent would be recognized, and he would be famous. As for his fear of the consequences—what could he do except take all possible precautions and then hope for the best? He decided, with typical wishful thinking, that if he were found out by any of the galleries the worst penalty he faced would be deportation. He had already overstayed his three-month visa, which meant he was now in the United States illegally. He had long ago developed the pessimistic mentality of a displaced person and professional refugee; he was sure that with no visible means of support and no money in the bank, if he applied for a renewal it would be denied him. And he wanted to stay. Europe in retrospect seemed like a wasteland; America was the land of opportunity, the new world. Fortunately it was possible to move from state to state in America and check into hotels without producing one's passport or identity card.

He had already realized that he had one great plus going for him. He was a European gentleman, and the species was in short supply in the new world. They were listened to, they were treated with respect and often with slight awe. With his perfectly cut clothes, his excellent manners and cultivated middle-European accent, his arched eyebrows and elegant monocle dangling on its gold chain, he was the archetype of gentility that had seen more opulent days but was still a symbol of distinction and tradition in an otherwise vulgar world. He took full advantage of it.

Normally, art gallery owners buy important works of art from one another, from established private art dealers whose business it is to travel from city to city and ferret them out wherever they may be in hiding, or bid for them in reputable auction houses like the Parke-Bernet Galleries in New York, Sotheby's and Christie's in London, and the government-operated Hôtel Drouot in Paris. But occasionally they will buy privately from small or large collectors who, wishing to avoid the publicity of public auction, offer them something directly or through an intermediary. If he has any suspicion as to the authenticity of the work, the gallery owner may try to check with a museum or send a photograph of the painting and a sketch of its supposed history to either a relative of the artist or a presumed authority on his life's work. But the process, obviously, can be a lengthy one, and there are temptations to shortcut it—especially if the price is cheap and the seller's credentials are in order.

Elmyr's approach to art dealers in Los Angeles and elsewhere was a simple one: the drawings he reluctantly offered for sale were part of a small collection, all he had managed to save from his family estate in Hungary in the last days of the war before the Russian occupation. With time, as he traveled up and down the West Coast from Hollywood to San Francisco, Portland, Seattle and San Diego, he became the Baron de Hory. He used different titles as they suited his mood. Zsa Zsa had told him: "In America, people like that sort of thing. A baron becomes a count, a count becomes a duke. You have to puff yourself up a little. That's what the Americans expect. They love it." Later, wondering if the authorities might be on the lookout for homeless and visaless Elmyr de Hory, he adopted several pseudonyms, or *noms de vendeur*: he sold as L. E. Raynal, Elmyr Hoffman, Louis Cassou, Elmyr von Houry, and Baron Herzog. Cassou and von Houry were purely fictional. There had been a famous French art historian called Maurice Raynal, and it seemed to Elmyr that the name in its new context might awaken echoes of authority. The Hoffmans and Herzogs were simply old Hungarian families with known art collec-

Picasso:
Still Life with Jug.
Painted by
Elmyr in 1951.
This painting was
accompanied by a
forged certificate from the artist,
stating that he had done
the canvas in Paris
in 1946. (See p. 41.)

tions. Elmyr passed himself off as a cousin who had lived in Paris. He never implied, however, that he had too large a personal inventory, for the great collections were fairly well known and often catalogued in esoteric volumes which might be found on dealers' shelves or in public libraries.

Arriving in Los Angeles for the first time in 1948, Elmyr checked into the Ambassador Hotel and went to work. He was getting a little bored with turning out Picassos, and he decided to try his hand now at Matisse and Renoir as well. It was strictly an experiment, but the experience with Klaus Perls in New York had given him a fresh confidence—not only in his ability, but in the gullibility of first-rate art dealers. He went to a nearby bookstore and bought all the volumes that reproduced Matisse and Renoir drawings. He studied them carefully for a day or two, made some preliminary sketches for several hours on scrap paper until his hand had developed a fluency for the particular line that he wanted to reproduce, and then, with pen and better paper, set to work. He worked not feverishly, but smoothly and quickly, as he always did. If a drawing was going to turn out "right," it had to be "right" from the beginning; it couldn't be corrected later on. His speed of accomplishment was the result of the felicitous marriage of careful study and extraordinary skill, and three days later, with a full portfolio, he walked into one of the more fashionable galleries in Beverly Hills.

"I went with the new Matisse and Renoir drawings. I was most curious to see how they would be received. I was sure of my ability to do Picasso, but I'd really had no experience before then at Matisse and Renoir. I might have been a little nervous, but obviously it didn't matter. I sold three Matisse pen-and-ink nudes on the spot—absolutely unquestioned. After that, the owner of this particular gallery always bought everything I offered him. He passed them along to the film colony at a 500 per cent profit."

Elmyr's other favorite dealer in Los Angeles was Earl Stendahl, whose private gallery was near Hollywood Boulevard not far from Grauman's Chinese Theatre. Stendahl must have scented a small gold mine in this congenial Hungarian with an apparently inexhaustible supply of Matisse and Picasso drawings whose true value he obviously didn't understand. A Stendahl customer, one of the great collectors of Southern California, eventually left his entire collection to the museum in Philadelphia, where he had been born: it included three works by Elmyr.

Things were going so well then that after a few months Elmyr decided to branch out. He had a yen to visit Texas—an astute and far-seeing choice, considering that it was 1949 and little publicity had been in circulation about millionaire oilmen and their urge for instant culture. Elmyr explained it later with disarming sincerity: "I'd gone to some Western movies, and I wanted to see the cowboys."

On the eve of his trip he dropped by the Stendahl Gallery to dispose of his last Matisse, and the dealer nonchalantly asked him if he had, by any chance, "something cubistic by Picasso." It was a period that of late had begun to interest Mrs. Stendahl, who had "a little collection of her own." Elmyr frowned and tried to remember. Ah yes, wait, he had *one*—not a terribly important one, he explained, but a very small and pretty gouache.

Could he bring it round in the morning, Stendahl wanted to know, before he flew to Texas?

"Well," Elmyr said thoughtfully, "I'll try to pass by, but I'll be very busy in the morning packing and getting my things ready. I don't promise."

He went back to his hotel room and in the space of about three hours, after several false starts, made a little cubist drawing, perhaps three by four inches—pen, Chinese ink, a little red and black tempera. He dried it for an hour by holding it as close as he dared to the hot electric bulb of the bedside table lamp. In the morning, neatly mounted but unframed, it was brought to Stendahl who, shrugging and wrinkling his nose, said, "Ah, yes, you're right, it's not much. It's really of no special importance. Will you take $500? Hmmm . . . well . . . let me show it to my wife."

Elmyr took off that evening, bound for Houston; but in Dallas, where it was necessary to change planes, there was some confusion with his luggage. By the time he had located it the plane was gone and, as he recalled philosophically—and with his own original sense of English grammar—"I was stucked in Dallas." He was _cette peinture est de moi_

PARIS 24 mai 46

Picasso

"This painting is by me
Paris 24 May 46 Picasso."
Elmyr forged this
certificate when he painted
the still life shown on page 38.
Klaus Perls later said
that the letters
in the forged signature
are too far apart and that
the "P" is badly formed.

rather annoyed, particularly when he learned that the bars in the city closed at eleven o'clock. He took a room in the Adolphus Hotel and had begun to skim through the local newspaper when he spotted a front-page story about Jacques Fath, the Paris fashion designer, who was about to give his first show of *haute couture* in Texas at the Neiman-Marcus department store. Elmyr had known Fath fairly well in Paris. Although it was 1 A.M. he called the desk and was told, as he suspected, that Fath was also staying in the Adolphus, which was the best hotel in town. Elmyr rang through, and ten minutes later Fath arrived in his room, wearing a gorgeous flowered-silk dressing gown. After they had talked for a while, Elmyr mentioned that he would be leaving the next day for Houston.

"Ah, don't," begged Fath. "Give Dallas a chance; it's a most amusing town. And tomorrow there is a big cocktail party at the Marcuses. They own Neiman-Marcus, which I assure you, *mon cher*, is the most elegant and exclusive department store in America."

"But tell me," said Elmyr, after he had finally agreed to stay, "fashion and elegant department stores aside, what are you really doing here in Texas?"

"I, too," Fath confided, "have come to see the cowboys."

In Dallas, the capital of instant culture, Elmyr was an instant success. He stayed four months. Fath introduced him to the Marcuses, the Hunts, the Murchisons and the Halliburtons, who were visiting from Florida ("Meadows wasn't around," Elmyr recalled. "I think he was still out drilling for oil"), and a few weeks later he found himself living in a plush rented house and giving cocktail parties for Dallas millionaires. If you dine with the rich, goes an old Hungarian proverb, you wind up paying the bill. "The trouble in Dallas," Elmyr commented, "was that any portrait that didn't look like a country-fair photograph, they didn't like. I couldn't make any money. I was just a little too modern for them." Still, to make ends meet, he managed to paint a few portraits and sell a few drawings. A widow from Lubbock in West Texas sent her private plane to Dallas to pick him up for lunch, bought several of his Matisses from a Dallas dealer and invited him to Colorado Springs for a summer vacation.

"I was a great attraction," Elmyr recalled. "I liked Texas, and I liked Americans. I was amazed how generous and how easygoing they all were. They opened their houses and their arms to anyone who came along. Really, I liked America more and more."

His tourist visa had already lapsed; and now, to compound the felony, the French passport expired. It occurred to Elmyr that if he left the country he might never be able to get back in: he was homeless, stateless, and of course unemployable. He decided definitely to stay.

He spent the summer in Dallas and then as a guest of the Lubbock widow at the Broadmoor Hotel in Colorado Springs, where he met Huntington Hartford. He was then invited by the A & P heir, and eventual patron of his own New York art museum, to be a houseguest in Hollywood. "I had no idea how rich he was," Elmyr had to admit. "I thought he owned some grocery stores, that's all. In Budapest it meant a man standing behind a counter and cutting salami—it wasn't exactly the man you invited for dinner to your home. And as far as art was concerned, at least at that time, he didn't know an oil from a watercolor. But I liked Hunt. He gave some marvelous Sunday brunch parties around his swimming pool with dozens of beautiful boys and girls."

In the fall Elmyr returned to Los Angeles, and it was then that he was found out for the first time and had his first unpleasant brush with an art dealer. The man was Frank Perls, who had been in business in Beverly Hills since long before the war, and whose brother Klaus had already been victimized by Elmyr two years previously in New York. The Perls brothers' resulting interest in fake art was one day to earn them the respective nicknames of "The Witch Hunter of the West" and "The Witch Hunter of the East." In 1952 Elmyr found out why.

According to Elmyr he had taken some drawings to Perls, who "hardly looked at the work, but must have heard about me before from some other dealer. He said to me one day, amiably, 'I know you're doing forgeries. You better be careful.' He wasn't threatening me at all. He couldn't, because he wasn't sure. He said the climate in Southern California wasn't as healthful as the tourist brochures advertised. It was a gentle hint to leave town.''

It was hardly gentle. What happened, according to Frank Perls, is this:

One day a well-dressed gentleman with a large portfolio under his arm came into the gallery on North Camden Drive in Beverly Hills and asked Perls, sitting at his desk near the door, if he would be interested in some French drawings. Perls, who was in a good mood and likes to joke, smiled and said, ''Are they filthy French drawings?''

''No,'' Elmyr said stiffly, ''these are drawings which I have inherited from my family.''

He then introduced himself as Louis Raynal, and mentioned that he was a relative of Maurice Raynal, the French art critic who had written one of the first books on Picasso. Perls was interested, and when he looked at the drawings he was immediately impressed. Elmyr had been busy. There were three early Renoirs, two classical-period Picassos, a few Matisses from the 1937 period, and a Modigliani portrait of Soutine. Perls studied the Renoirs first and was surprised and elated by their perfection. One of them, he thought, seemed a small masterpiece. He was pleased with the Picassos also. When it came time to inspect the Modigliani, however, Perls' sharp eye suddenly saw something—perhaps a concept in the composition, but basically something indefinable—that reminded him curiously of the Renoirs he had just looked at. He went back to the Renoirs, then back to the Picassos. Then he studied the Matisses. He shuffled through them quickly, one after another—and then he understood, almost as a revelation, that all the drawings had been made by the same hand.

At this point Perls' good mood abruptly vanished. He abandoned the portfolio, politely asked Elmyr to sit down with him at the desk, and then asked for his address. A little nervously, Elmyr adjusted his monocle and explained that he lived in Kansas City; he was only visiting friends in Hollywood. He also volunteered the information that he had authentications for all of the drawings from the Galerie Robert Desnos and Manju Gorowskaja in Paris, for which he had paid $25 apiece.

"That's very interesting," Perls said.

He went back to the portfolio, slid the stack of drawings neatly inside and carefully knotted the strings on three sides to keep them in place. Then he threw the portfolio across the room at Elmyr sitting at the desk. Elmyr ducked—then, white-faced and shaking, he picked it up. The monocle on its gold chain had popped out of his eye.

"Get out," Perls said.

Elmyr did, hurriedly. Perls followed him out the door onto Camden Drive.

"You have two seconds to get off the block and twenty-four hours to get out of town. I have your address—if you're not gone by then, I'll call the police. Every single one of those drawings is a fake."

By this time, the drawings safely tucked under his arm, Elmyr had recovered some of his composure. He tapped the portfolio and tried to smile.

"But they're good ones," he said, "aren't they?"

"They certainly fooled me for a few minutes," Perls replied to this plaintive comment. "Now you've got one more second to get off the block."

Elmyr started running, and Perls ran after him to the corner of Camden Drive and Brighton Way. There he stopped, and Elmyr continued down Brighton Way, monocle flapping in the breeze.

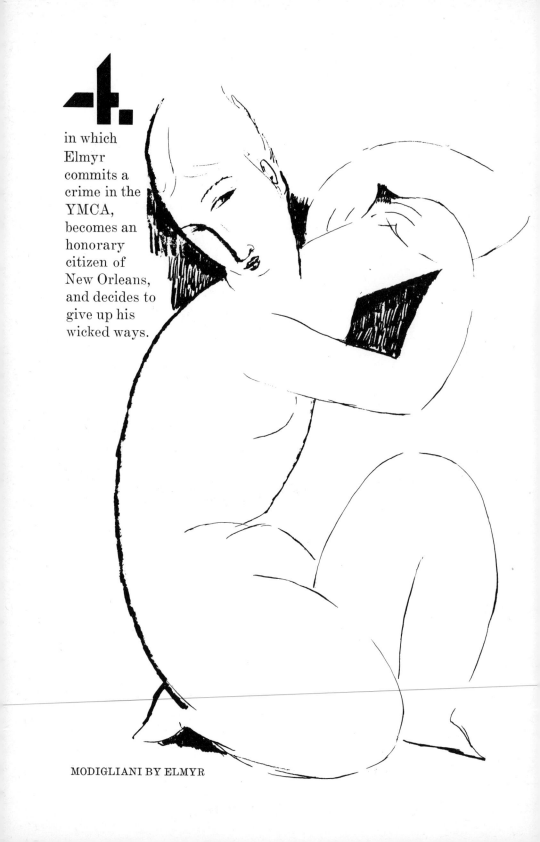

4.

in which
Elmyr
commits a
crime in the
YMCA,
becomes an
honorary
citizen of
New Orleans,
and decides to
give up his
wicked ways.

MODIGLIANI BY ELMYR

This, in one sense, was Elmyr's apprenticeship as an art forger, and he worked hard at it, learning and constantly expanding his capabilities. He had already experimented with a few small oils by Picasso. He sold them in Los Angeles and San Francisco and when he returned to New York for a visit in 1949 he made his first extended series of Modigliani drawings. It was the start of a long and profitable relationship, for from the beginning Elmyr felt what he called "an affinity with Modigliani as a creative personality" that he had never felt for any other artist. He did some Renoirs, too, which were easy to sell and brought better prices than Matisse and Picasso, both of whom were still alive and producing. But the most significant work of that period for Elmyr was a Modigliani portrait in oil.

"I moved from drawings to paintings perhaps because of the challenge involved. An oil, you know, taking into mind the possibilities of texture and color, is theoretically far more complicated— you have the chance to do a major masterpiece. And, of course, there's much more money in it. I remember the year before I was at Fanny Brice's house in Hollywood, and she'd just got a big Modigliani oil, a portrait, and when I asked her she admitted to me without hesitation that she'd paid $12,000 for it. I was absolutely flabbergasted. I told her it was a fantastic price. I said: 'My dear, I sincerely hope it gives you pleasure, but as an investment it simply won't stand up.' A year or so later she died and I met her son in New York, who mentioned to me that he'd just had an offer of $25,000 for it. So I thought, well, well, well. . . .

"It was a terribly exciting thing to do, my first Modigliani oil, an important development in my career. It was the portrait of a young girl, a subject that Modigliani treated many times. I let it dry for two months, which I realized later was hardly long enough, but then—in 1949—I needed the money and I didn't understand too much of the technicalities. I showed the painting to Montgomery Clift. I had an apartment on East 62nd Street and he lived nearby, and he thought it was wonderful. I wouldn't sell it to him, of course, because he was a friend, and in any case, to protect myself, I had only thus far sold to dealers. In Europe a dealer can't sue or take you to jail if he buys a fake from you; he is supposed to be an expert and responsible for his business decisions. So I took the Modigliani to a man named Vladimir Margouliès, the owner of the Niveau Gallery.'' (The Niveau is now under the new management of Mme. Margouliès. Margouliès himself is dead and the records of the gallery, which in any case did not list every transaction, do not go back in time to 1953. Therefore what took place according to Elmyr can neither be confirmed nor disproved.)

''There were the usual arguments about price. He kept it a week to have it expertised and then peeled off $6000. One painting! It gave me a new dimension.''

Elmyr's sales technique had so far depended on three factors: the quality of the work of art itself, its authenticity or ''rightness,'' and his personality as a salesman. The idea there, of course, was that he *wasn't* a salesman, but a gentleman art collector in temporary need of funds. Fernand Legros' standard procedure, fifteen years later, of adding a documented pedigree and an expert's certificate of authenticity never occurred to Elmyr. ''I did never dream I could get one,'' he said. ''I simply wouldn't have dared to ask!'' On occasion, it was true, he did provide an expertise ''signed'' by the painter himself—Matisse, for example, or Picasso—but this he considered completely in the spirit of his basic gamble.

He would walk into a gallery, establish his credentials as first a connoisseur and second a refugee aristocrat, and then vaguely ask if the gallery would be interested in a certain drawing that he ''happened to have in his possession.'' He rarely carried it with him the first visit, as he had done with Frank Perls. If it were a Modigliani, for example, he might say that it had been in his small collection for many years, perhaps since 1933, when it had been given to him by the wife of Moïse Kisling. Kisling was the young painter with whom Modigliani had shared a studio in Montmartre. Because he had lived and known these people intimately in Paris, Elmyr also knew precisely who might have been in a position to acquire a Modigliani, a Picasso, a Braque, a Léger. He knew who might have been the painter's mistress and close friends, or the lover of the painter's wife. He knew the names of the European collectors and dealers, like Flechtheim in Berlin, who were buying and selling cheaply in the twenties and thirties. It was quickly obvious to most of the American art dealers that Elmyr was the genuine article, and this in turn influenced them to assume that what he had for sale was equally genuine.

When he brought the drawing round the next day and the dealer saw that it was not only a Modigliani but a *good* Modigliani, no further documentation was needed. If the dealer so requested, Elmyr left the piece behind for a few days' consideration and consultation. There were undoubtedly many instances where the dealer had cause to wonder if what had been offered him was fake, if only because Elmyr's asking prices were usually cheap. But it seems fair to assume that precisely because they were so cheap, a good many dealers who might otherwise have been suspicious decided to buy while the opportunity presented itself and worry about it afterward—or not worry about it. If Elmyr was out to bilk the art buyer, he surely in some cases had his silent accessories after the fact.

"I never forced a sale," he maintains categorically and with an almost fierce pride. "I'd come back on the appointed day, we'd talk about the weather for a while, and then it was just a question of haggling price. Until then everything had been discussed on a strictly gentlemanly basis. They'd gossip about different collectors and recent exhibitions, talk about the quality of the drawing, who might have posed for it, how poor Modigliani used to sit in cheap cafés and make sketches of prostitutes at the next table, how sad it was he'd died unknown, and so forth. But then it came time to talk price. Then all the cultural veneer falls away, and they become what they really are—merchants in a Turkish bazaar, fighting tooth and claw to buy cheap and sell dear. They reminded me exactly of used car dealers. And they don't even have the professional knowledge of a used car dealer. A used car dealer may try to cheat you—but at least he can tell the difference between a Ford and a Cadillac."

That year in New York he sold through auction at the Kende Galleries on 57th Street, and on other occasions to such bulwarks of the art establishment as the Niveau Gallery and M. Knoedler &

Co. As Klaus Perls recalled, "He would suddenly reappear with the story that he'd just come back from a quick trip to Paris, where he'd 'found' an old drawing or oil from his 'collection.' As recently as the summer of 1967 my wife and I walked into an art dealer's apartment in Paris and on the far wall I saw a Picasso, another of those *Man with a Lamb* gouaches. I said instantly: 'Where did you get the de Hory?' The dealer—I'm afraid I can't mention his name—said, 'How did you know? How do you know that name? As a matter of fact it was *given* by Picasso to a man named de Hory.' And he pointed out where it was inscribed, for all the world to see, *À mon ami Elmyr de Hory. Picasso.*"

By the late forties Elmyr had been living for several years in the United States and had made some new friends in the international set. People found him witty and knowledgeable; he was a chic addition to any Beekman Place cocktail party, and his apparently inexhaustible reservoir of tales about prewar European aristocracy gave him a ready audience in all the New York *salons*. The fact that he was a refugee accounted for his comparative poverty; his flamboyance and casual attitude toward money were all the more appreciated by the budding jet set. Elmyr, of course, lived from day to day—he had little idea where his next thousand dollars was coming from; providence and his curious talent would somehow provide. One of his good friends—to protect his reputation now, Elmyr prefers to call him "Jean-Louis"—was an art collector, a rich young Frenchman who had inherited some $10 million worth of Renoir and Degas pastels which hung in stunning profusion on the walls of his Paris apartment. He was also homosexual, and he and Elmyr traveled together on one occasion by car throughout the Western states "to see the cowboys." Perhaps because Elmyr had to visit some art galleries en route, perhaps because of their mutual admiration of the Impressionists, or perhaps because from time to time he owed Jean-Louis money, Elmyr let slip to him what it was he did in his spare time to pay the rent at the Essex House and buy drinks at the Plaza. Elmyr was by nature indiscreet, and it was only with difficulty that he managed to keep his great secret. Jean-Louis, when he found out what was going on, was astounded. At first he refused to believe it, but Elmyr provided proof on the spot by quickly producing a Matisse drawing in their San Francisco hotel room.

"Naturally," Jean-Louis remarked years later, "I tried to talk him out of it, because it seemed so dangerous. But he pointed out that it was the only way he could live unless he wanted to throw himself at the mercy of his friends. And I think, in a peculiar way, he loved to do it, too. He loved the risk, and of course he enjoyed the sense of accomplishment. He was like a child. You might as well have tried to talk a three-year-old out of throwing mudpies."

Once, when he was staying in a suite at the Waldorf-Astoria, Elmyr, for a reason which seemed obscure to many of his friends, also took a room at Sloane House, a New York YMCA. Jean-Louis visited him there. A good many illegal acts have no doubt been committed within those hallowed precincts, but this was perhaps the most bizarre: in his little room Elmyr was happily at work on a Modigliani oil. Jean-Louis, en route to a cocktail party, arrived to pick Elmyr up and found him in his shirtsleeves, painting.

"Why are you doing that *here*?" he asked, amazed.

"I can't get oil paint all over the carpet at the Waldorf," Elmyr explained. "Here," he said, handing his friend the brush. "Put in some of that blue background color while I get dressed."

Jean-Louis obliged, and thus fulfilled an art collector's dream: to paint, or at least help to paint, a masterpiece.

With time and new intimacies a few other trusted friends were also let in on the secret. It was again a rash move on Elmyr's part, but his judgment was proved correct; not one of his friends, in all the years to come, ever gave him away. For one thing, Elmyr minimized his accomplishments. For another, no one quite took him at his word. One of these friends at the time had the idea to set him up in a West Coast art gallery of his own, but when the subject was broached Elmyr turned down the offer. He later explained it this way:

"I had no papers, no status. I couldn't go into public life. Also, I never wanted possessions. I never had the feeling that it would be good for me to have a lot of money, a big house and the usual responsibilities. That need obviously escaped my makeup completely. When God gave out brains I must have thought he said 'pains,' so I said 'Give me as little as possible.' I never looked ahead. I didn't enjoy insecurity, but I didn't really give a damn about security. In the back of my mind, I suppose, I may have counted that if I got into trouble someone would help me. In my relationship with my close friends I never used them—if I asked them for something they knew there was no other way out for me, I really needed it. They never said no. In that way I'm a lucky person. Most of my life I had friends who were good and kind to me, and somehow I think that's more than most people can say.''

His ''good and kind'' friends, however, often began to weary of Elmyr after a season or two of his high-pressure Magyar charm.

''In our crowd he was definitely what you would call 'a second stringer,' '' one of them reminisced, nearly twenty years later, in the comfort of his Park Avenue apartment. ''He was rather frantic about his sex life, and that became a bit of a bore. The name-dropping, too—he couldn't tell a story without a dozen digressions about this baron or that young prince with whom, naturally, he confided, he'd slept in Paris or Cannes or Kitzbühel. Still, taken in small doses, he was amusing. He painted an oil portrait once, of a young and rather intimate friend of mine. He had given him an elongated neck and eyes without pupils or irises. I looked at it and burst out laughing. 'But my dear Elmyr,' I said, 'you've resurrected the ghost of poor Amadeo Modigliani!' He didn't think that was very funny—you see, he had intended it to be an original. It more or less ended our friendship—he had no sense of humor about what he considered his 'serious' work.''

In early 1951 he set out, a Hungarian Gulliver, on the second leg of his travels about the United States. He visited Florida for the first time and then New Orleans, whose atmosphere, particularly in the *vieux quartier,* made him nostalgic for Europe. He took an apartment in the rue Royale and stayed the whole winter—laying in a stock of Matisse and Modigliani for the spring season—and became friendly with Tennessee Williams and Robert Ruark, who was quartered in an apartment above the Old Absinthe House. The proprietor had a small historical museum and he commissioned Elmyr to do a painting of the Café Lafitte and the blacksmith's shop on Bourbon Street. This led to Elmyr's meeting the mayor of the city, Morrison deLesseps, and deLesseps, impressed by Elmyr's legitimate talents, came forward with a second commission of a somewhat different nature. The old City Hall of New Orleans contained a number of important vintage American paintings: historical scenes of Civil War battles, blood and gore and tattered flags flying, portraits of Generals Lee and Stuart, even a portrait of Abraham Lincoln. There was also a Watteau. Neglected for decades, they were all in poor shape, badly stained and chipped, and the Mayor asked Elmyr to undertake a major restoration job. Elmyr accepted. He worked in the basement of City Hall for three months, was paid a fee of $5000 and became an honorary citizen of New Orleans with a parchment that said so and a gold key to the city.

He was probably the only honorary citizen of New Orleans or any other American city who was also a fugitive, for when he tried there at the consulate to renew his long-expired French passport, he was refused. Strangely enough, he had no idea then that he was eligible to apply for a Nansen passport for stateless persons; and by now he was afraid to make any official application to the U.S. government for fear that somewhere in the past a complaint had been lodged by some art dealer. For that very reason, once he'd made a series of major sales to any particular gallery, as to Stendahl in 1949, he crossed it off his list. He was in the curious position of a man who had committed a crime which could easily be traced to him, and yet had no way of knowing if the crime had ever been discovered. He had no papers now except his California driver's license. Still, he thought, it's better to be a fugitive in America in 1952 than in Europe in 1944. There was *some* progress.

He drifted northward, via Kansas City, where he stayed for several months and sold a Matisse and one Picasso to the William Rockhill Nelson Gallery of Art and Atkins Museum of Fine Art; to St. Louis, where he found the tastes ran more to Renoir *sanguine* drawings; to Chicago, where he tried his hand at watercolors by his old friends, the darlings of the Fauve period, Derain and Vlaminck.

It was a long, arduous trip, he was not overly fond of the Middle

West, and he was tired of drifting. Each time he looked into a hotel mirror he seemed to see a new gray hair. He was tired of hotel mirrors, too—it was no way for a man to live. By the time he reached California again he was weary in both body and soul, footsore and fed up with the subterfuge that had become his way of life.

He realized suddenly one sleepless night that it had been four years since the day he'd said to himself, "I'll just do it till I get together a little capital, and then I'll quit and paint my own work." What had happened to that resolution? He knew well enough, and it depressed him. He still was unable to think of forgery as a career, a life's work. The thought was horrifying—one day, surely, he would be caught, and he understood now that a prison cell and not deportation would be the result. He had sold in the past six years some hundred drawings, a dozen gouaches and watercolors and about four or five small oil paintings. What had he to show for it? Whatever he earned, he spent. All that he owned in the world, besides the rings on his fingers and $1500 in traveler's cheques, could fit into his three calfskin suitcases. The art dealers were starting to become rich men on what they'd bought from him, and he was still an unknown painter. The years were passing by; he was forty-six years old: the prime of life. His real crime, he suddenly decided, was against himself—that he had created no important body of work that was his own, that he had failed to profit on his talent the way he should.

And yet there were facts to face. He needed money and the luxuries it could buy. He was a foreigner, he had no home wherein to rest his head, no family to encourage him. If for a moment he could see himself as a forger and not a painter, then it was clear that he had served his apprenticeship. He had six solid years of experience, he knew the market and he knew his own capabilities: he was a consummate professional. As a painter he would in effect be just at the beginning of a precarious career. As a forger he was already launched; he could survive easily, and survive in comfort.

The debate in his mind took place on more than one sleepless night over a period of several months during his third westward trip. He brooded incessantly. He lost weight; he seemed to live on a diet of coffee and tranquilizers. And then, reaching Los Angeles in the winter of 1952, Elmyr de Hory made what surely deserves to be called a brave and principled decision—however quixotic and sentimental, however unrealistic and ill-fated. Almost with a snap of the fingers he said: "I quit." He would start from scratch. He would give up faking completely and become what he'd always wanted to be and believed he was—a painter.

5.

in which Elmyr
paints pink
poodles in L.A.,
does a
Modigliani self-
portrait, and is
undone by a
Lincoln
Continental.

DERAIN BY ELMYR

He knew exactly how difficult it would be, that for the first years he would make just enough money to survive and not more. He found a room and kitchenette near Pershing Square for eleven dollars a week. Setting up an easel next to the Castro convertible, he bought prepared canvas boards —they were cheaper than good canvas and wooden stretchers—and started to work on small paintings.

He worked for six months until his money was nearly gone. An artist may not be the best critic of his own work, but Elmyr liked what he had done. It was the best he could do, he decided, and that was a satisfying thought. Tucking the paintings under his arm, he boarded a bus and went to a few small but good galleries, where an unknown painter might reasonably expect an audience. He wore one of his $300 Knize suits, Brooks Brothers shoes and a shirt with his initials stitched on the pocket.

"Are *you* the painter?" one of the gallery owners asked him.

"Yes, of course. Why?"

"Look at you. You don't *look* like a painter."

Whatever the reason, the galleries declined to buy or give Elmyr an exhibition. One or two were willing to take a few paintings on consignment, but would offer no guarantees to hang them even in the front room. It was a terrible disappointment to Elmyr, not to mention a financial blow. He had counted on selling *something,* and now he had no money. There was of course one clear avenue toward solvency—but he had promised himself; he had said "I quit."

He hurried home. For one week he got up at seven o'clock in the morning and put together a collection of what he considered the most mundane commercial work—flamboyantly painted seascapes, still lifes with roses, landscapes with palm trees and gorgeous sunsets. A few years before, during one of his stays in New York, he had sold similar things under mildly similar circumstances to some wholesale furniture shops on Third Avenue; he had even at one time done a batch of flower paintings for a Westchester County interior decorator who needed them to liven up some all-beige living rooms. Now he went forth again, still in his Knize suit, to make the rounds of the interior-decorating shops on La Cienaga Boulevard in Beverly Hills. This time the paintings sold—for ten and twenty dollars apiece. Decorators bought them the way they might buy ashtrays and vases, for functional value and a quick sale. They were often rude to him, treating him like a peddler; they always bargained. One man, who liked the landscapes and bought several of them, asked Elmyr: "Can you paint for me a series of pink poodles? I have a woman customer who—"

"That," the artist replied with dignity, "is not in my line. Thank you just the same."

It was a strange time in Elmyr's life, for during that year in Los Angeles he was not really unhappy. He would one day look back on it with a certain wistfulness—as many people look back on those times, usually in youth, when they live on the margins of society, when needs are few and the simple pleasures are the most gratifying. He had no car, no money to eat out in anything better than a Hollywood Boulevard hamburger joint. Most of the time he cooked at home on the two-burner stove in the hot little apartment. At one point, to economize, he was buying day-old bread—and this, one must remember, was after a suite at the Essex House, a duplex apartment on Manhattan's East Side and the best hotels in every city. But he wanted to "go straight," he didn't want to do a single Picasso more.

Los Angeles had a particular appeal to him, too. He was fascinated by the shadowy night life of the downtown area near Pershing Square where he lived—an underground world, full of dangers and forbidden pleasures. "It was exactly like a book I read many years later," Elmyr said, "—*City of Night,* by a boy named John Rechy. For all I know I might have met Rechy there. But that book awakened strange memories in me."

Young men drifted into town from all over the United States; you met them for a night, sometimes a little longer, and then they drifted out again. They came to Pershing Square and the nearby bars like hungry bees in search of dark honey. About that time Elmyr became friendly with a young ex-Marine boxing champion named Jimmy Damion—he had been saddled with a dishonorable discharge for hitting his commanding officer; "But," said Elmyr, "he was a sweet, undemanding and beautiful person"—and they decided to share the rent.

Almost immediately a curious bit of good luck came Elmyr's way. In 1950 he had been in Chicago, where he had sold several drawings to a French art dealer in business there. He had also left behind, on consignment, a large Derain watercolor. Now, three years later, rummaging one day through his papers in Los Angeles, he came upon the receipt for the Derain. He had completely forgotten about it. I wonder, he mused, what ever happened. What could he lose? Taking the chance, he telephoned collect to the dealer in Chicago. The charges were accepted. "Here is Elmyr de Hory," he began, and quickly identified himself.

"Good God," the dealer said. "I thought you must be dead. I've tried to contact you, I looked for you all over the country! That Derain watercolor you left, someone's been begging me for it for over a year, but I couldn't sell it because we never agreed on the price you wanted. If you'll take $400 I can sell it tomorrow."

"I've been ill," Elmyr said quickly. "In the hospital in Los Angeles. I had pneumonia. And amnesia. I'll take the $400 if you can wire it right away."

Two days later he had the money, and a week later he and Jimmy Damion moved to a new and larger apartment on Melrose Avenue, between Griffith Park and Hollywood.

Elmyr kept painting and trudging round to the decorator shops every Friday afternoon, selling his flower compositions and even a few pink poodles. He had to be careful in the smarter sections of the city not to bump into any old friends; he was too proud to meet them under such circumstances, and he had told no one he was in Los Angeles. Then, with his new windfall of money from Chicago, he decided he needed a car. Jimmy's presence pushed him to work a little bit harder to provide. It was to become a familiar pattern in Elmyr's life, and one that would prove his financial undoing. He may have had little personal need for possessions, but as he grew older he found himself in a position similar to that of a middle-aged bachelor who covets the company of attractive young girls. In Elmyr's case, of course, it was the company of attractive young men, and it was usually necessary to offer them something more than charm, worldly experience, and fading looks. He had two compulsive needs: to impress his young friends and to spend money when he had it. The combination was devastating.

One day an interior decorator on La Cienaga, with whom he had become moderately friendly after selling a dozen seascapes, offered him an old 1946 Chevrolet coupé in exchange for three large still lifes. The deal was made. A shift car was a total mystery to Elmyr, but Jimmy, who loved to drive, said to him, "I'll be your chauffeur. I'll get a cap and gray gloves."

After that, with the car, life was far more pleasant. The bus system in Los Angeles was not the best, the distances to travel were great, and previously Elmyr had often to walk from dealer to dealer. If he had been offered ten dollars for a painting when he'd hoped for twenty-five, he was often so weary that he didn't even argue; he took what he could get.

And then one week the possibility he dreaded most became a reality. The dealers on La Cienaga were overstocked, surfeited with de Hory seascapes and flower compositions.

"Pink poodles?" Elmyr offered.

"Sorry," said the decorator.

He sold only one painting, for ten dollars. The rent was overdue, and in the Melrose Avenue section of cheap apartment buildings that catered to new arrivals and transients, you paid on time or you packed.

It was a Friday afternoon, the banks were closed, and Elmyr needed cash. With another brief sigh of regret at dreams unfulfilled and promises about to be broken, he went to his luggage and took out his materials. He worked quickly from an old photograph in an art magazine. An hour later, wearing his best dark suit and a sincere Brooks Brothers tie, L. E. Raynal, resurrected like a Transylvanian vampire from the long sleep of the undead, presented himself at the Dalzell Hatfield Galleries in the Ambassador Hotel with a small Modigliani self-portrait for sale.

"I don't buy drawings," Hatfield explained. "Only paintings and major works. Sorry. But my wife has a little collection of her own, and she's very fond of self-portraits. Let me just give her a ring and describe it to her."

The "wife with a little collection of her own" was a story that sounded vaguely familiar, but Elmyr was too desperate to indulge his skepticism.

Amedeo Modigliani:
Portrait de l'artiste.

Drawn by Elmyr
in Los Angeles in 1953.

"How much?" Hatfield asked, after his wife had had her description.

Elmyr hesitated. He couldn't say too much because he needed the money too badly, he couldn't say too little for fear the dealer would become suspicious.

"Two hundred fifty?"

"I can give you two hundred cash."

A month later the drawing was sold to James Alsdorf of Chicago, who then had and still has one of the largest Modigliani collections in the world. Elmyr discovered this four months later in a newspaper article entitled "Discovery of a Modigliani Self-Portrait." According to Elmyr, the drawing which he had made on the back page of a book printed in the 1920s, a little yellowish around the edges and bought at a downtown junk shop for a dollar, was praised as a masterpiece and reproduced in three columns.

Ablaze with curiosity, Elmyr telephoned a dealer he knew in Chicago in the hope of finding out how much Alsdorf had paid. The dealer guessed "around $4000"—which turned out to be something of an exaggeration. But Elmyr had no way of knowing that, and the thought of Hatfield's profit made him feel slightly sick. He felt like a man who has sold a stock cheap and then watched it rise to astronomical heights.

He had already been forced to branch out in business beyond La Cienaga Boulevard to decorator shops as far south as Laguna Beach, La Jolla and San Diego, and as far east of Los Angeles as Pasadena. Almost immediately after his discovery of the Modigliani in the newspaper, Elmyr met the owner of a small art gallery in Pasadena who took a fancy to his more serious work, the oils he had been unable to sell in Los Angeles the year before. The Pasadena dealer was short of cash but long on transportation. He offered Elmyr, in exchange for several large oil paintings, a silver-gray 1947 Lincoln Continental that had belonged to his son before he went into the Army. It was an expensive and beautiful car in excellent condition, and Jimmy Damion, Elmyr's ex-Marine roommate, went wild over it.

"How can we afford to run such a car?" Elmyr protested.

The old Chevy was already on its last legs and had just had the clutch replaced; on the freeways Jimmy always had to drive in the inside lanes at thirty miles per hour. It broke down on the way back from Pasadena, while Elmyr was trying to make up his mind about the offer of the Lincoln. A nearby garage mechanic told him, "If you spend ten bucks to fix that heap, it's too much." A junk dealer a few blocks away came round and offered him five dollars for it. "Okay," Elmyr said. Then he telephoned the art gallery owner in Pasadena and said, "I thought it over. It's a deal."

Looking at his new car and remembering what had just happened with the Modigliani self-portrait, Elmyr suddenly decided the hell with everything. His elegant Lincoln Continental no longer fitted the image of a poor painter in a cramped apartment on Melrose Avenue. It was due the car, he reckoned, to live a little better.

"My curiosity for the Bohemian life in America is quite satisfied," he announced that evening to Jimmy Damion. "So—let's take our beautiful car and drive East, slowly, stopping at the major centers of culture and art. Elmyr is coming up in the world again."

He had made a momentous decision. He had decided to rise from the ashes, to make the leap from defunct apprentice to working journeyman.

6.

in which a
journeyman
painter retires
to Florida, goes
into competition
with Sears
Roebuck, makes
$160,000, and
comes a cropper
with the FBI.

DUFY BY ELMYR

"Coming up in the world" meant a base of operations, a home, a workshop befitting his new status. The trip East was only mildly successful, so that upon his arrival in New York Elmyr found himself with only a few hundred dollars in cash. But then a few days after he and Jimmy had settled into a room at the Ansonia Hotel on West 73rd Street he had a stroke of luck. After calling various friends he was invited to a cocktail party, where he was introduced to a French art dealer recently arrived from Paris. Somehow the Frenchman had been given the impression that Elmyr was a *courtier,* or private art dealer. He drew Elmyr aside. Did he have, the dealer wanted to know—or did he know anyone who had for sale—any drawings by Henri Matisse?

"I'll ask around," Elmyr promised.

"If you hear of any, let me know. I'm at the Plaza."

In his room at the Ansonia Elmyr sat down at the hall table, adjusted the table lamp and in about two hours made three full-sheet Matisse drawings. The next day he telephoned the Plaza.

"*Three?*" The dealer was delighted. Elmyr scurried round.

"Superb! Beautiful! Naturally, they are on consignment with you—there is a percentage for you which is included in the price?"

"Naturally," said Elmyr.

"How much?"

"Five hundred dollars each, including my percentage."

Without quibbling a second, the French dealer wrote a check. He would be able to sell the drawings for at least double. In 1969 they were worth between seven and ten thousand dollars each; to Elmyr, then, in 1955, the $1500 meant freedom. A week later he and Jimmy Damion left New York.

Elmyr was weary not only of living from one day to the next, but also of running from one city to another, of trudging from gallery to gallery with his wares tucked under his arm like a traveling brush salesman. The elements of his dream suddenly came into focus: warm sun, blue sea, a cosy little place of his own, money, comfort—and yes, even a little security. He had a plan, too, something he had long considered but had not thought to implement until a much later date in his life. But the years had passed quickly. The time was now. And the place, he decided, was the congenial eastern coast of Florida.

Jimmy Damion served him in the capacity of traveling companion, secretary and chauffeur. They drove south at a leisurely pace in the Lincoln Continental and took a pleasant bayside apartment in Miami Beach.

Then Elmyr began writing letters. They went something like this:

Dear Sir: I am in possession of a Matisse drawing, pen and ink, from period 1920–1925, representing a woman seated at a table with a bouquet of flowers, and for personal reasons I would like to dispose of it. If you would be interested, I will gladly send you a photograph. . . .

The first letter went to the City Art Museum of St. Louis. Three days later a telegram arrived: they were interested. The photograph was sent and a price was arranged, pending examination. He rolled the drawing into a tube—"I heard that if you sent anything by U.S. mail, and it turns out there's something wrong with it, the government can make you trouble. So I did ship everything always by Railway Express." A week after receipt of the drawing, the museum arranged the purchase for a private collector in St. Louis and the money was wired to Miami Beach. With a fine impartiality, similar letters went forth in the course of the next two years to art galleries and museums all over the United States.

In the mornings, when the apartment was empty save for himself, Elmyr carefully double-locked the door and went to work. He had previously spent several days in the New York Public Library, skimming through all the available books on Impressionist, Post-Impressionist and Fauve art, and then made the rounds of bookstores on Fifth Avenue to pick up whatever volumes he thought necessary for his reference library. The investment had come to more than $400, but he was now equipped with a shelf of books and portfolios that gave him all the examples he needed. By noon he was finished with work for the day, and he would join Jimmy on the beach for a swim. In the evenings they watched television or went to an occasional movie, and there were weekend trips in the Lincoln to Palm Beach and the Seminole Indian reservation and Key West. It was a pleasant domestic life, which would have bored Elmyr beyond belief had it not been so remunerative. His "private collection" soon expanded to include drawings, gouaches, watercolors and small oil paintings by Matisse, Picasso, Braque, Derain, Bonnard, Degas, Vlaminck, Laurencin, Modigliani and Renoir. He also made some minor changes on facsimile reproductions of Renoir drawings, which he then signed and passed off as originals. His sales record, had it been known to them, certainly would have been studied with envy by Sears, Roebuck or Montgomery Ward— it had never been, and probably never will be, surpassed in the mail-order business. It was nearly 100 per cent, with no returns. Whatever Elmyr deigned to offer, Elmyr sold, and in the entire two years the authenticity of only two drawings was ever questioned prior to sale.

It was hardly a hit-and-run operation. Sometimes the museums would hold the work for three, four, five and six weeks, to mull the price or seek the advice of other experts before they made the decision to buy. Elmyr was cagy about the origins of the paintings—if a gallery owner or museum curator telephoned to ask how M'sieur Raynal or Baron Herzog had come by such-and-such a Braque and Degas, he would be deliberately vague: "They were acquired in France many years ago by my family. . . ." But to the serious and determined buyer, vagueness obviously was no deterrent.

Elmyr sold by mail in that period to modern art museums and galleries in New York, Philadelphia, St. Louis, Chicago, Seattle, Baltimore, Washington, Boston, Cleveland, Detroit, Dallas and San Francisco. He concentrated particularly on Matisse, who had died less than a year earlier, on the assumption that his work would now rise in value. "I thought he was an important painter," Elmyr explained later, "though," he added parenthetically, "highly overrated. He had a large output. But there was a great amount of business wheeling and dealing involved, and I guessed that the dealers would hold a lot of the work off the market and keep the price up artificially."

Sometimes, after a sale to a museum had been consummated, the director would write to Elmyr on behalf of one of the trustees or "friends of the museum," asking if he had "perhaps another small Matisse you could consider parting with." Invariably, Elmyr would consider it. Sometimes the checks came from a private party for drawings sent to a museum. "They wrote me saying how happy they were with the drawing or painting and if you ever come by Philadelphia, or Brooklyn, or San Diego, or wherever it was, please do visit us. I had a nice list of people I could have sold to, personally and privately, but I never used it."

He was most pleased and flattered, however, with the sale of a Matisse—*A Lady with Flowers and Pomegranates*—to the Fogg Art Museum at Harvard University. The Fogg was considered the outstanding art school in America; if you had your training at Harvard, every door in the American art world was open to you. It was the midpoint of Elmyr's career and for him, as an artist, the pinnacle and climax of recognition.

Much later, when the jig was up in Europe and his name was about to make international headlines, Elmyr boasted that the Fogg had asked him—had written and sent daily telegrams—to lend part of his collection, at least five drawings and paintings, for an exhibition of French Post-Impressionist art. He had, he said, accepted the honor and complied with the request.

But this was not true, and the statement throws an interesting light on the artist's shadowy, necessarily throttled need for recognition. In fact, after his initial success with the Fogg, Elmyr sent the museum a number of Modigliani drawings and a Renoir, which he offered to lend them for possible purchase and exhibition—as he put it in his letter, "to show my appreciation." One of the Modiglianis and the Renoir, however, aroused the immediate suspicions of Agnes Mongan, the museum's Assistant Director. The Fogg held the drawings over the summer, believing that their owner probably had them and had offered them in good faith, but recognizing, as they so delicately put it, "that they were not of any significance"—i.e., they were probably out-and-out fakes.

The museum told Elmyr nothing of their suspicions; never having met him, they didn't know whether or not he himself was aware

Henri Matisse:
*A Lady with Flowers
and Pomegranates.*
Drawn by Elmyr in 1955
and sold to the
Fogg Art Museum at
Harvard University.
Shortly afterward, the museum
began to doubt the
authenticity of the work,
and the drawing was
never exhibited.
(Courtesy of Fogg Museum.)

of the doubtful value of what he had. He had not asked for opinions; the museum knew about defamation of title, and had offered none. But by Christmas of 1955, when Elmyr sent her a holiday greeting card, Agnes Mongan was sufficiently uneasy to have a note put in the file which said: "Keep this name and address."

The Fogg eventually returned the Modiglianis and the Renoir, still believing that the original Matisse was genuine. But as time went on Miss Mongan began to have the uncomfortable feeling that it, too, might be wrong. One of her assistants compiled a list of drawings attributed to Matisse; she also assembled a batch of photographs of Matisse drawings from various private collections and museums. These were then divided into two categories: those they were sure were Matisse, and those where there might be doubt. So many of the doubtful drawings resembled Elmyr's that the Fogg eventually came to the painful decision that they had bought a forgery.

This investigation and analysis actually covered several years, and during that time the museum spoke to hundreds of collectors and dealers about the situation. "At one point," Miss Mongan said later, "we were in touch with a dealer in New York who told us that Raynal had turned out literally hundreds of Matisse drawings, mostly in series, the various series based on authentic drawings in many cases. The New York dealer also told us that Raynal went by several names, and that he had been picked up by the Paris police, but not for forging. What he didn't know was that the forger was still alive—it was the belief of the New York dealer that he had recently died. A Chicago gallery had in all innocence handled many of the drawings. So had Knoedler's, as well as the Museum of Modern Art. They were all pretty well taken in, as we had been. In fact, in making our list we came upon false Matisse drawings scattered across the country from the east coast to the west coast."

What Agnes Mongan and her associates had uncovered, of course, was just the tip of the young iceberg that was to reach its maturity ten years later. In this golden age when he lived and worked in Florida, before the blow struck which was to end forever his peaceful sojourn in paradise, Elmyr did perhaps seventy drawings and paintings—for which he received, in cash, a little more than $160,000. He had not only reason to be proud of the success of his labors, but to be grateful as well for their rewards.

It was a prolific and profitable period in other respects, too. Shortly after his settling down in Miami Beach he met a man named George Alberts, who worked in a local establishment that Elmyr describes as "one of those tourist traps for which Miami Beach is justly famous. The shop was a complete bazaar: porcelain that wasn't really porcelain, silver that wasn't really silver, lace, paintings that looked like antiques but weren't and so forth. They worked on rich suckers. People didn't walk in, they were lassoed in. There was always someone hanging around on the street ready to grab you if you even poked your nose in the direction of the plate-glass windows. Later on, when I got to know them better, they hired Jimmy Damion as a combination salesman and shill. There were six or seven salesmen and partners who kept coming in and going out all day long. You were never sure who owned this shop. But they loved Jimmy. George Alberts said, 'He has such a straightforward, beautiful face, such an honest face—we *need* someone like that. You know how many we are involved with in the shop—we need one person we can trust, because none of us trust each other.'

"That was Jimmy. He was the only one allowed to go to the cash register."

Somehow in the first weeks Elmyr met Alberts, who was evidently impressed by the Lincoln Continental, and the next day, with Jimmy happily playing the role of chauffeur, Elmyr pulled up to the curb with a load of paintings—his own—and Alberts bought some to decorate his windows, took others on consignment and then proceeded, with considerable success, to sell them to the tourists. Elmyr, when he had occasion to do so, remembered him fondly. "He was a very kind and goodhearted person—a crook who wouldn't hesitate to cheat anyone, but somehow when it came to a human motive there was something serious. Later he went to prison. I don't know exactly for what, but it could have been any one of a dozen things."

Settling down in Florida also made it possible for Elmyr to turn his attention properly—and profitably—to the medium of oil on canvas. He had realized several years earlier in New York, when he sold his first major Modigliani, that not only did oil paintings offer a broader opportunity and more complex challenge to the artist than drawings or watercolors, but they also fetched considerably higher prices.

The realization, however, had been difficult to implement, since the problems for the wandering forger were formidable. A watercolor or gouache dried quickly under a hot hotel lamp, and a line drawing didn't need to dry at all. An oil painting, while it appears to dry within a matter of days, in fact can stay technically wet for years: the point of a needle drawn lightly over the surface will cut or drag rather than slide freely, and a bit of cotton soaked in turpentine will remove the faintest tinge of color. Fortunately, when Elmyr was so much on the move during the first decade of his career, he chose to work with men like Modigliani and Matisse, who for the most part did a drawing directly on the canvas, thinned their paint liberally with terps and often just rubbed it into the canvas with their brushes. The fuller treatment of Braque and Picasso had to wait until Miami, and the rich impasto of a Vlaminck or Derain oil until years later when Elmyr had settled down even more permanently in Europe.

Drawings were also easier to do than oils because, in America, old paper was more susceptible to clandestine private manufacture than old canvas. In New Orleans Elmyr had managed to find an art supply store where he bought several blocks of *papier d'arche,* an expensive French make much favored by Picasso and Dufy. To age it he tried various methods. Then he remembered reading somewhere that the Chinese had artificially aged their ivory by cooking it in tea. He lightly swabbed the paper with cotton dipped in yesterday's tea, and it yellowed the paper very nicely. For the sake of variety—and for Modigliani, who was too poor to buy anything but odds and ends of the cheapest stock available—he also kept cutting out the end pages of old French picture albums (*Châteaux of the Loire; Battles of the Great War*) hauled down from the dusty shelves of secondhand book stores.

Old unpainted French canvas, however, simply didn't exist, and

French oil paintings from the correct period (from which the paint might be soaked off down to the priming, as Elmyr did later in Europe) were far too expensive. Stretchers—the wooden frames on which the canvas is stretched taut before painting—with the distinctive joinings and wedges used in France were also rarities in Hollywood, Kansas City or Dallas.

In America, prior to 1954, Elmyr had solved the problem by an imaginative use of American canvas and American stretchers. When his painting was dry he took a razor blade and carefully cut the canvas away from the stretcher. Then he glued it to the front of a second stretched canvas of identical size. It was not uncommon among professional restorers—in which capacity, one may recall, Elmyr had faithfully served the city of New Orleans—to use a similar procedure when a valuable old painting had to be removed from its original stretcher because of warping, fraying, or the natural decay of age.

Later, when he had settled down in Florida and gone into the lucrative mail-order business, Elmyr imported one genuine French stretcher from Paris and put a puzzled Miami carpenter to work making several dozen exact copies. He aged the wood himself with a mixture of terps, dirty linseed oil and brown color, then stretched some new French canvas and repeated the procedure on the back side, using a Flit gun. When the painting was finished he sometimes sprayed it again, more delicately, with a mouth atomizer containing a thinner mixture of the same stuff. "I did rather enjoy all that," he said, with a professorial air.

A few years later he read an article in which David Stein—the young English forger who had made several Chagalls and Picassos and was caught soon afterward (and whom Elmyr considered something of an *arriviste* in the profession)—told how he preferred Lipton's tea to age his paper and a sun lamp to dry his watercolors. "I did get a little bit annoyed," Elmyr admitted. "I thought, that's very indiscreet to give away so many trade secrets. Now everybody's going to jump on the bandwagon!"

It was a good life in Miami Beach—too good to last, it seemed to him. There are, again, two versions of what happened to signal the beginning of the end of Elmyr's career in America. One of them is

Elmyr's. The other is that of a prominent Chicago art dealer named Joseph W. Faulkner, the owner of the Main Street Galleries on North Michigan Avenue.

Elmyr's tale is as follows:

"I had been to the Main Street Galleries a year or two before then—let's say 1954. They had a bookstore, too, and they dealt in small Picassos and Braques, nothing spectacular, and I had sold them something in person in the past. I wrote them from Miami Beach and told them I had a Matisse drawing for sale. Oh yes, they said, we'd be interested in the Matisse, but do you have anything else? I mentioned Modigliani drawings. I sent them a batch, they telephoned me, we argued price and made a deal on the phone. Two days later they wired the money."

" 'Do you have any more?'

" 'Yes, I have a fairly large collection, but I don't intend to sell them right away, just little by little.'

" 'Oh, please do, we have excellent clients and it's spring and people are in the mood to buy. Next year there might be a recession.'

"Terrific pressure on me," Elmyr related. "So I sent a few more and right away got a phone call, how much?—Oh, that's too much—Well then, all right, I'm in no hurry to sell—can't we compromise at $7000? And okay, right away I got a check.

"Then one day I got a phone call from Faulkner that he's coming to Miami for a vacation and he hopes to meet me. He arrived, stayed at the Fontainebleau Hotel in a luxurious suite and came with a friend to see me. He looked around. He was very impressed. He wanted this one and that one—they were very well framed and discreetly hung—and there was again a small painting by Matisse: a woman sitting next to a table, with a bright red background. He wanted it badly. I asked $10,000 and he said he couldn't make a decision then, but could he take it back with him to Chicago? We had so much dealing already that I thought there's no reason not to trust him. I handed over the painting and three drawings. About a week after he left Miami I got a call from Chicago and he said: 'The painting is okay. I have someone interested in it, but I'd like to make a quick deal, I can sell it with a little profit. I can't get as much as you want, I couldn't pay you more than $7500.'

A photograph of
Elmyr de Hory
taken in Miami Beach
in 1955.
It was in Miami
that Elmyr went into the
"mail-order business"
and sold a number of
drawings to Joseph Faulkner,
owner of the
Main Street Galleries
on North Michigan Avenue in Chicago.
Faulkner was later
to accuse Elmyr of forging and brought
charges against him.

"With the other two or three drawings he'd taken with him it came to a total of $10,000. So I was cagey—'Well, I don't know, it's not very much . . .' but finally, naturally, I agreed. A week later I got my certified check. I felt rich, I had maybe about thirty or forty thousand dollars then, so I went out and traded in the old Lincoln Continental for a new 1956 Cadillac convertible. That was a mistake—it was a beautiful car, but I had all kinds of trouble with it. I heard later that '56 was a bad year for Cadillacs. For Hungarians, believe me, it turned out to be even worse."

Faulkner's statement to the authorities, two years later, was different and rather more specific:

"I received a letter," he wrote, "in March 1955 from Mr. E. Raynal of 1443 West Avenue, Miami Beach, Florida, offering to send for my inspection some Matisse drawings. Since I was surprised that such things would be in Miami Beach, and a little suspicious, I contacted Mr. Karl Schneidwind, Curator of Drawings at the Art Institute, who told me that he knew of Mr. Raynal, that his reputation was good, and that he had already sold Matisse drawings to various museums."

Faulkner wrote to Elmyr and asked him to send on the drawings, which, on arrival, looked "very good." He bought two of them for $700 each. After further correspondence and perusal he bought a number of Modigliani and Matisse drawings, paying for them with certified checks of $250, $1200, $1000 and $2200.

"Some of the Matisse drawings in earlier purchases," Faulkner continued, "were sold to a dealer in New York who later sold them to Bergruen in Paris, and all concerned were satisfied with their quality and authenticity. One Matisse drawing went to the St. Louis Museum. Pleased with this progress, I bought a Matisse oil painting from Raynal for $7000 and have his receipt for the purchase and statement of authenticity. This painting was accompanied by a photograph certificate of authenticity signed by Matisse, and it was subsequently sold by me in October of 1955. Later I bought a second Matisse painting for $5500, and paid for it by certified check at Raynal's request. This painting was not accompanied by a photograph certificate of authenticity but did have the working drawing with Matisse's handwriting all over it, which made it seem authentic.

"In February 1956 I was in Miami Beach and met Raynal for the first time. Prior to this all our contacts had been through correspondence and long distance calls. He showed me some drawings and watercolors by Modigliani, Matisse and Renoir. I bought one Matisse drawing for $300, one Modigliani for $400, one Renoir for $600 and another Renoir for $900."

Before he bought any of these, Faulkner said later, he showed them first to the Art Institute of Chicago, who gave him their opinion in each case that the work was genuine. But later that month he shipped a large collection of drawings, including six or seven bought from Elmyr, to the Delius Gallery in New York for an exhibition. He also sent the second Matisse oil painting.

Two weeks later he received a letter from Delius informing him that the exhibition had been canceled because, according to Delius, "the two Renoir drawings were reproductions, not originals." Delius also distrusted the authenticity of the Modiglianis. As for the Matisse oil, he had sent a photograph of it to Matisse's one-time secretary in the South of France, who had cabled back that the painting was a fake.

Faulkner had recently received a letter from Elmyr, replying to his request for background information and provenance of the two Renoir drawings, which certified that they had originally been part of the Paul von Majowsky collection in Budapest and that he, Raynal, had bought them long ago through a Paris art dealer. The Paul von Majowsky collection of Renoir drawings was in the permanent collection of the Budapest Museum, but the bulk of it had been reproduced in facsimile on drawing paper and bound into portfolios; each plate was embossed in the corner with the printer's stamp. They were of such superb quality that only the stamp differentiated them from the originals. A little stunned and fearing the worst, Faulkner went immediately to the Ryerson Library of Chicago's Art Institute and checked the two large portfolios of the facsimile reproductions of the von Majowsky collection. Delius was correct. The two drawings were there. "The ones Raynal sold me," Faulkner explained, "had the right-hand margins skillfully cropped so as to remove the printer's stamp."

This is the only known instance of Elmyr's ever having sold a fake that was not of his own creation, and why he did it that way, instead of rendering his own versions of the von Majowsky Renoirs, remains something of a mystery. Taking the most simple explanation, one can only guess that he came upon a copy of the facsimile reproductions, understood their exceptional quality, doubted that American dealers would know of the Budapest collection, saw the opportunity of a quick sale, and said to himself—as of old—"Why not?"

Faulkner, in any event, knew there was nothing to be done about the Renoirs; he had been had and that was that. He could only hope for the best concerning the Modiglianis and, in particular, the second Matisse oil. Gritting his teeth, he telephoned Elmyr in Miami Beach and asked him to send at once a bill of sale for the Matisse. Also, did he have any papers of authentication and provenance? The dealer's voice, Elmyr remembered, was "vaguely unpleasant."

"I definitely don't have any papers of authentication," Elmyr replied, "but I'll certainly look around, and if I find one I'll mail it to you."

He looked around, and then prudently decided not to find. Instead he sent a telegram to Faulkner which read IF IT APPEARS NECESSARY I WILL COME TO CHICAGO BUT PLEASE REMEMBER I HAVE ALWAYS GIVEN YOU ALL THE TIME YOU ASKED FOR AND NEVER PRESSED OR URGED FOR DECISION. I HAVE TO SPEND THE NEXT TWO OR THREE DAYS WITH A FRIEND JUST ARRIVED FROM EUROPE. RAYNAL.

The next day Elmyr left Florida.

Faulkner in the meantime notified his clients who had bought the forgeries and, ultimately, despite the fact that several art experts stated to FBI investigators that the paintings and drawings sold to him by Elmyr were genuine, he reimbursed the buyers the full amount of each purchase. His personal losses on the various transactions amounted to $18,500. "The excuse I make for myself," he said later, "is that I would never have had any dealings with Raynal/de Hory if I had not checked him out first with the Art Institute."

He eventually obtained a judgment against Elmyr in the Dade County, Florida, circuit court, with an attachment of his bank account and safe deposit box. The checking account contained only a few hundred dollars and the safe deposit box was empty but for the $1000-printed bands that had encircled bundles of notes. This gesture Faulkner considered evidence of a certain "malicious humor." Although other art dealers urged him not to do it, warning that publicity would help neither him nor the art world in general, Faulkner instituted a federal case in Chicago on the grounds that mails, telephone, and telegraph had been used in the perpetration of fraud. "Since I had reimbursed *my* clients," he explained, "I had nothing to fear. I went ahead."

But it was too late, and the nimble Hungarian was long gone. Soon after his hasty exit from Miami he telephoned from Atlanta to find out how the wind was blowing in his absence. Jimmy Damion, who had the job in the curio shop and had stayed behind, informed him that two FBI men had already visited the apartment. They didn't search it, but they took a good look around and wanted to know when Elmyr would be back.

Elmyr sighed.

"I put two and two together," he says, "and it made five. I couldn't fight the charge because I had no passport and I was in the country illegally. In the least, they'd deport me. Right or wrong, I couldn't afford to get involved with the FBI.

"So, once again, I was a fugitive."

7.

in which Elmyr
flees to Mexico,
becomes a
suspect in a
murder case, and
paints a famous
Matisse.

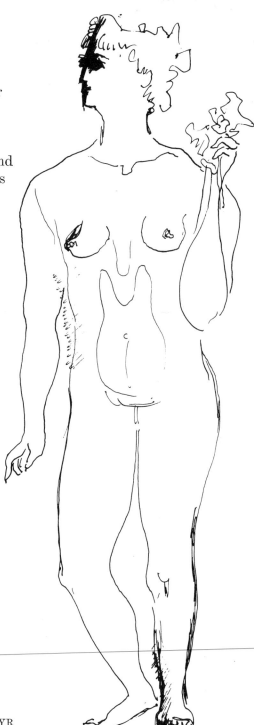

BRAQUE BY ELMYR

lmyr headed westward in his Cadillac, which broke down twice en route. The second time was in Little Rock, Arkansas, where through a happy coincidence he had an introduction to a hotel owner who in turn introduced him to the owner of Little Rock's only expensive art gallery. There followed the sale of two Matisse drawings which, according to Elmyr, then went to a high political figure in the state. The price paid by the dealer was $1800. Elmyr felt better already; if he was a fugitive, rudely ejected from his nest by the beach in Miami, at least he would make fugitivism pay.

"I proceeded slowly, I don't remember what route, back to Los Angeles—my old hunting ground. With the difference this time that I had a lot of money with me and my style of living had definitely changed. I drove a Cadillac down Hollywood Boulevard, not a beat-up old Chevy. I stayed first in a rather chic apartment in the hills and then moved out to Bel Air, where I rented a house from a young actor friend. I never changed my name, I was still Elmyr de Hory. This actor knew everyone in Hollywood and so I met a few celebrities. I became very friendly with Lady Lawford, Peter Lawford, and Nina Anderton—but I never sold them anything because they weren't the least bit interested in art. I once did ask someone—a young Canadian friend—to take to the Hatfield Galleries, where I'd sold my famous Modigliani self-portrait three years ago, a sort of semi-cubist still life watercolor by Derain and a watercolor landscape by Vlaminck. I said, 'I know I can sell them to him, to Hatfield, but I'm not on good terms with him.' The friend left the work with Hatfield and some days later got the money, about $1000 for each. Also I went several times to Santa Barbara, where I sold some Matisse drawings to the museum."

But then Elmyr learned that Frank Perls, the Beverly Hills art dealer who of course knew his identity as a forger, had discovered that he was operating again in his West Coast precinct. One may well wonder how Elmyr had had the nerve to return to Los Angeles in the first place, after his rude eviction from Perls' gallery in 1953. But his sense of self-preservation was minimal, and he all too often operated out of the forlorn hope that other people's memory was as short as his own. He often took risks without the slightest realization that they were risks; and this blind bravado, in many cases, accounted for his astonishing ability to repeat his successful forays. Military historians such as C. S. Forester like to point out that extraordinary opportunities in war are often missed because generals overestimate the resources of the enemy. If this is true, Elmyr might have made a great field commander: he marched bravely and blithely forward into the teeth of the enemy's defenses. Or, as he once put it, in all innocence and modesty: "I thought then that I was such a small fry—I did rarely think that they would be on the lookout for me." It was all part of his ingrained belief that he had done nothing *really* wrong, that he had committed no crime. Also, in the case of Los Angeles, he explained: "I hated to give it up as a market. It was the easiest place in the United States to sell something."

But, sadly for him, in 1956 Elmyr realized that once again it was time to go. After half a year of drifting and looking warily over his shoulder for the FBI, he decided to get away from it all for a while and have a vacation—if possible, out of the country. Since the southern border could be crossed without a passport by United States citizens, he chose Mexico City. However, he needed some sort of official identity paper, such as a birth certificate. He telephoned George Alberts, explained his problem, then sold the Cadillac and flew back to Miami, reluctantly abandoning his little library of art books and portfolios in Los Angeles. He wanted to travel light; and they could be replaced. In a week or so, Alberts was able to provide him with the necessary document, under the name of Louis E. Raynal. But Elmyr's luck—that is to say, the sudden lack of it—followed him even to Mexico. He rented a spacious five-room apartment not far from the new Mexico City Hilton, and promptly hung what he considered a splendid little collection of Matisse, Chagall, Marquet, Renoir, Derain and Modigliani all throughout the apartment. He may have abandoned his library, but he never for a moment considered jettisoning his inventory; he had carried it with him from Miami Beach and added to it in California. The work was quickly and expertly framed at minimum cost in Mexico City. It took a week or two to make connections in the local art world, and soon afterward a wealthy young gallery owner named Antonio Souza y Souza inspected the collection at one of Elmyr's cocktail parties and invited him to make an exhibition.

"I was a little leery about that," Elmyr recollected. "I'd never done that kind of thing before—hang a whole exhibition of fakes in a gallery. But there was terrific pressure put on me. Souza was then having an exhibition of Rufino Tamayo, the great Mexican painter, and Tamayo himself came to me and said, 'Elmyr, you must do it, if only for the benefit of the public.' So, reluctantly, I said okay. They covered all my costs and printed a beautiful catalog. The museum wanted to make an exhibition also, but they had at the time another exhibition of earlier French works. They asked me to wait, but I told them, 'Well, I'm here today, gone tomorrow.' So I went to a lot of trouble and didn't sell a thing. A few people at the opening inquired about prices but they were so high there was no question of sales. In Mexico those sort of paintings, and their prices, were absolutely new to the general run of collectors. Anything above two or three thousand dollars had to be a Rembrandt. There were a few rich families, of course, who did know what was what, but they naturally went to New York or Paris to do their buying. The exhibition was a failure except that I got a lot of publicity as a rich collector, which turned out later to be the worst thing that could have happened."

A little hungry then for cash sales, Elmyr went—as L. E. Raynal —to Señora Montes de Oca Quijada, owner of the Galeria Proteo, and offered to sell outright to her gallery a part of his collection, consisting mostly of Modigliani drawings. He had dropped his price spectacularly to an average of $350 apiece. Suspicious that there could be so many rare drawings in one private collection and at such cheap prices, Señora Montes made some inquiries by mail to various American gallery owners and was told that the drawings sounded very much like a series of fakes that had recently turned up in the market around Chicago and New York. Joseph Faulkner of the Main Street Galleries, the Perls brothers and the FBI had not been entirely inactive. Señora Montes turned Elmyr down flat.

Business was bad south of the border, Elmyr decided, and the trip turned out to be something less than a vacation. Two months after his arrival he found himself in the hands, never famed for their soft and gentle qualities, of the Mexico City police. This time it was not fake Matisse oils they wanted to discuss with Señor Raynal—it was murder.

The murdered man was a rich sixty-year-old Englishman, a homosexual who lived in a villa in one of the more lush suburbs of Mexico City. He had had a companion, but they had parted and at the time of his death he had been living alone. He liked boys in the eighteen to twenty-two age group and it was his habit at night to cruise the gay bars of the city. He had no servants who slept in the house and one morning he was found dead—strangled—in his bedroom. The police naturally began to investigate the homosexual world of Mexico City.

Elmyr at the time spoke no Spanish at all and so heard almost nothing about the case, until one evening someone casually mentioned at a cocktail party that a young middle-class Mexican boy named Carlos had been apprehended and jailed on suspicion. Elmyr's French art collector friend, Jean-Louis, was visiting in Mexico City at the time. "You know the boy," he reminded Elmyr; "we met him a few weeks ago at a party." Elmyr only shrugged; he didn't remember.

A few days later Elmyr gave a cocktail party of his own, and after it was over and he was gossiping with Jean-Louis and the maid was cleaning up the debris, two men rang the doorbell and asked to speak to Señor Raynal. They were detectives. Elmyr identified himself and they said, "You will please come with us to the police station."

He went, accompanied by Jean-Louis, and he was a little bit upset because of his false identity papers. He soon learned, however, that it had nothing to do with his papers—it had to do with the murder. More than a little upset then, Elmyr swore that he'd never laid eyes on the Englishman.

"And the boy, Carlos?"

"I never met him, either."

"Then why," asked the police, "did we find in the boy's room a little notebook which contained a small list of names and telephone numbers, including that of the man who was murdered, and including yours, Señor Raynal?''

After a grim pause Elmyr realized what had happened. He had met the boy at a cocktail party, they had chatted amiably in a group of people, and then Elmyr had given him his name and telephone number and said, ''Do give me a ring sometime.''

''I'm innocent,'' Elmyr gasped, and tried to explain.

The police seemed to believe him. But after several hours of questioning they suggested—an idea not exactly uncommon south of the border in such circumstances—that Elmyr pay them 1000 pesos (about $90) for their trouble, and they would let him go. He was furious, but with the help of Jean-Louis the best he could do was argue the price down to 500. It seemed wise to pay. The detectives very kindly drove him home and said goodnight.

A week later, however, they bagged him again. Jean-Louis had gone back to Paris and Elmyr, on his own and looking rather haggard under the cruel unshaded bulb of the station house, agreed to pay a second installment of 500 pesos. The police knew that he was probably a homosexual and certainly a rich and important art collector; in short, a pigeon. But when he was called in a third time for questioning and payment, Elmyr decided he'd had enough. He had met Sir Andrew Noble, the British ambassador, and Sir Andrew recommended a lawyer—William O'Dwyer, former Mayor of New York City and ex-American Ambassador to Mexico, who had just gone into private practice in the capital. O'Dwyer had been to the exhibition, too.

''Don't get excited,'' he said, after Elmyr had poured out his tale of harassment. ''It's always the same story. They find out some *gringo* has money and they try to squeeze him. I'll take care of it.''

A week later the lawyer called to tell him all had been arranged, the authorities were never going to bother him about it again. Delighted, Elmyr asked how much he owed. O'Dwyer suggested he come down to the office to discuss it and, when Elmyr arrived, handed him a bill for $1000. Elmyr's eyes widened with shock.

For that kind of money, he squawked, at the going price of 500 pesos a bribe he could have paid off the cops twenty more times.

For exactly what specific services, he demanded to know, did he owe his lawyer $1000?

"I'll tell you the truth, Baron Raynal," O'Dwyer said. "I had to give the chief of police $500 to promise to leave you alone, and I think I deserve at least $500 for being able to have that kind of leverage with the Chief. That's just the way it is in Mexico. You have to learn to watch out for yourself."

Elmyr nodded, then sighed grievously. "Tell me," he asked hesitantly, "would you consider accepting, in lieu of cash payment . . . a small Renoir drawing?"

O'Dwyer was delighted. It was delivered the next morning with Elmyr's apologies for the fact that it was locally framed.

While he was in Mexico, to add to his increasing burden of woes, Elmyr met a man named Oscar Herner, an Austrian refugee with an art gallery on the calle Iturbide. He came to Elmyr's exhibition, became interested in Elmyr's collection, and began to invite Elmyr often to his house. Oscar Herner had owned an antique shop in Vienna and now in Mexico City had a gallery, as Elmyr put it, "like a *salade niçoise,* a little bit of everything, mostly for the American tourists.

"He was a very shrewd businessman, and I think he suspected something about me. A few remarks he dropped gave me the impression that he was not quite convinced that all the paintings were genuine. Not because he was a connoisseur or knew anything about art—my butcher in Ibiza knows more than Oscar Herner knew—but, because he was an Austrian refugee, something about my story didn't click. He realized the trouble and ordeal I would have had getting all that art work out of Communist Hungary. We never discussed it specifically, but he knew, and I knew he knew, and he knew that I knew that he knew. He put two and two together, like me, and it came out five."

At first, after this bit of Central European mathematics, Oscar proposed that they go into partnership with a second gallery, but when Elmyr showed Oscar's draft of a contract to a lawyer—not O'Dwyer—the lawyer said: "But, Señor Raynal, he has all the profit and you have all the work."

Elmyr de Hory
in La Falaise, 1968.

Amedeo Modigliani:
*Portrait de
Jeanne Hébuterne.*
Painted by
Elmyr in 1964
and sold the
following year to
Algur Hurtle Meadows.

Henri Matisse:
Femme aux fleurs.
Painted by
Elmyr in 1963.

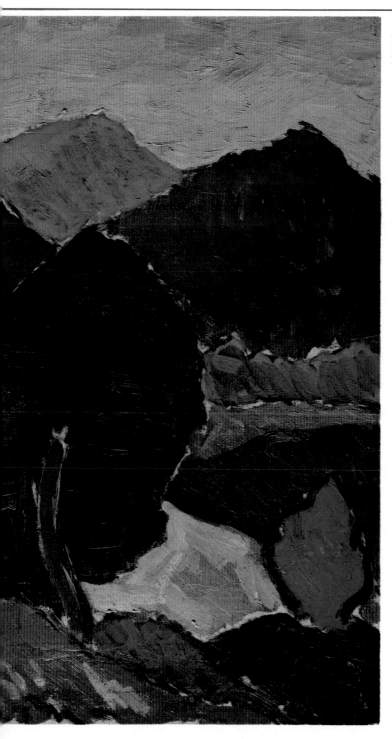

André Derain:
Les arbres.
Painted by
Elmyr in 1964.

Kees van Dongen:
Portrait of a Woman.
Painted by
Elmyr in 1965,
this oil received
van Dongen's expertise.

Henri Matisse:
*Femme dans
un intérieur.*
Painted by
Elmyr in 1965.

Raoul Dufy:
Promenade des
Anglais, Nice.
Painted by
Elmyr in 1962.

"You see," Elmyr explained recently, "I have no head for business. In fact, after all these years I've decided I'm not even an intelligent man."

He seemed bent on proving this, for when he finally quit Mexico he left with Oscar a half-dozen paintings on consignment, including a Matisse oil—a girl seated at a table on which stood a vase of mimosa, a subject Matisse had painted often—for which Elmyr wanted $10,000. It was from Matisse's later period, around 1948, and Elmyr had painted it in Miami Beach, so that it was already perfectly dry and presentable. He had had it framed in Mexico City.

"I know it's worth more than $10,000," he told Oscar, "but I'm not sure how much more. It's a bargain."

Beyond that figure, they agreed, was profit for Oscar, who was sure he could sell it and backed up his optimism with an advance payment of $2000. Elmyr had hesitated at first, but, spending heavily, running out of cash again, the $2000 convinced him.

Six months later, standing in the mild winter sunshine on the corner of Hollywood and Vine, he opened the 1958 issue of the *Art News Annual,* and there, filling the whole of page 22, was an advertisement featuring a reproduction of the Matisse oil, now titled *Figure with Flowers.* Above the reproduction it said: KNOEDLER GALLERIES, NEW YORK. Elmyr hurried back to his hotel and telephoned Knoedler in New York. He was a collector, he explained, and he had seen the Matisse advertised in *Art News.* Could the gallery quote a price?

No, they said, they were sorry, but the painting had been sold. Next month, however, they might possibly be getting another Matisse oil, somewhat smaller and perhaps not that high in quality. Elmyr inquired the price and was told "In the area of $60,000."

His voice rising in astonishment, Elmyr asked: "The *Figure with Flowers*—the one you advertised in *Art News*—sold for *more* than that?"

"It was a very unusual painting," Knoedler's representative explained patiently. "A Matisse of that quality, you know, rarely comes on to the market."

Henri Matisse:
Figure with Flowers.
Painted by Elmyr
in 1956 and sold
that same year
by M. Knoedler & Co. in New York.
The price paid for
the painting was reportedly
more than $60,000.

Giving his name as Josef du Pont, Elmyr promised to drop by when he passed through New York. Then he called Oscar Herner in Mexico City. "*Buenos días.* Here is Elmyr de Hory," he announced, "who has seen *Art News* and would like to timidly inquire, señor, where is my money?"

Oscar claimed he knew nothing about it.

"What do you mean you don't know anything about it?" Elmyr shouted. "Where is the painting?"

"I was in Switzerland a few months ago," Oscar explained, "and I left it with an agent in Geneva."

"And you mean that agent sold it to Knoedler in New York and didn't tell you anything about it? You don't know anything about it at all?"

"Yes, I give you my word—"

"Are you *serious?*" Elmyr ranted and raved but Oscar remained adamant: he knew nothing. Finally he calmed Elmyr down, promised to call Switzerland immediately and then fly to Hollywood to meet Elmyr the next day. True to his word, he arrived and told Elmyr he had tried a dozen times, but he "couldn't get in touch" with his Swiss representative.

"Call from here," Elmyr suggested.

"Don't get excited," Oscar said.

"So what's with the other drawings I left with you, the Modiglianis and Renoirs? I want to know."

The Renoirs, Oscar went on patiently, were still in Mexico, and the Modiglianis had been entrusted to the same man in Geneva. "But don't worry, we'll clear it up very shortly. I feel very badly about this. I'll give you $3000 right now."

"Okay," Elmyr said, figuring that he was on the right track. Oscar paid in cash and promised to meet him in New York in two weeks' time, after which he would continue on to Geneva to unravel the mystery. Elmyr flew to New York. He was afraid to check personally with the management of Knoedler & Co. to discover who had sold them the Matisse, so he waited in New York for Oscar to appear. Incredible as it may seem to an observer uninitiated in the gullibility of those whose business is trading upon the gullibility of others, when the two met, Oscar talked Elmyr into giving him a large Modigliani oil portrait, two more Renoir pastels and some drawings, and another little oil by Matisse. The potential market value of the lot, even at that time, was in the area of $300,000.

Oscar collected the paintings in Elmyr's room at the Waldorf-Astoria prior to having them crated and sent to the airport. He studied the Matisse for a while and then said, with some annoyance, as if Elmyr had been trying to trap him in a particularly nasty way: "Don't you think you ought to put the *e* in Matisse's signature?"

"Then," Elmyr later recalled, with deep regret, "I was sure he knew something wasn't kosher. It put me at a great disadvantage, that little mistake. I don't know how it happened—maybe the telephone rang in Miami just as I did finish painting it. If so, it was an expensive telephone call. I fixed it while he waited and then Oscar left for Switzerland."

The arrangement was that he would cable Elmyr if anything sold, but in any event he would surely be back in New York within two weeks. Elmyr heard nothing. He finally tracked down the elusive Austrian by telephone a month later in Mexico City. Oscar, according to Elmyr, said: "I have nothing to report. I have sold nothing. If you want to talk to me, come down here," and then hung up.

When Elmyr frantically rang him back, Oscar had changed his mind. "You know, it's not healthy for undesirable aliens to come to Mexico. *Pistoleros* you can hire cheaply."

However, the *Figure with Flowers*—the first Matisse that Oscar had taken on consignment from Elmyr—was doomed. Oscar, it seems, had initially sold it in Mexico to an American collector named G. David Thompson, who left a deposit on it and took the painting home to Philadelphia. Within a short time he learned the painting was fake; when Oscar came to collect the rest of the money he had a deputy sheriff waiting, and threatened to arrest him. Oscar returned the deposit and left with the painting. Soon afterward it was sold to an agent in Switzerland, and somehow from there it wound up in the hands of another, more reputable Swiss dealer, who contacted E. Coe Kerr, Jr., of Knoedler in Paris, showed him a color transparency of the painting and offered to buy it in partnership with Kerr. After this was done the painting was sold by Knoedler and advertised—strictly for prestige purposes—in the *Art News Annual*. Thompson, the Philadelphia buyer, saw the advertisement, called Kerr (whom he knew) and informed him that it was the same painting he'd bought in Mexico. Kerr was told shortly thereafter by the new owner of the Matisse that it was his wife's favorite painting and, as he says, "I didn't have the heart at first to inform him it was a fake." But when the client found out, Kerr had a refund check ready and waiting for him.

The painting was returned to Switzerland, only to turn up again three years later and become internationally famous when Matisse's daughter, Mme. Duthuit—who had inherited most of her father's archives and sketchbooks—condemned it. Again, as with the oil previously sold to Faulkner in Chicago, she had no record of the painting. "But," says Elmyr, "numerous experts came forward at that time and said 'Absolutely no doubt that it's genuine.' There was a great battle by correspondence, with insults shouted backwards and forwards across the Atlantic between Paris and New York. The French and American art dealers did never have any love lost between them, and this was a fine *cause célèbre*. It finally petered out—Mme. Duthuit did not want to go too energetically against Knoedler, who were involved up to their ears, because it's like a banking house in the art world and they handled too many other genuine Matisses."

At present, according to Kerr, the painting is probably confiscated in the vaults of the Paris police; but other sources of information, including Elmyr, state that by 1962 the picture had been privately sold three more times and was last seen with a reputed price tag of $165,000 on the yacht of a famous Greek shipping tycoon. The explanation may lie in Kerr's wistful memory of the Matisse itself. "It was a great painting," he said recently—"just great. You could never *dream* it was a fake."

Ready to leave Mexico in late 1956, Elmyr faced the problem of how to gain entry once more to what was obviously for him the land of milk and honey, the United States. "I didn't see myself as a wetback, swimming across the Rio Grande with my Matisses and Modiglianis strapped on my back, so I decided to get into the States as unobtrusively as possible. I flew first to Canada.

"I stayed in Montreal for a while and I was running out of money. I discovered a lot of Hungarian refugees who were sitting there, just after the revolution in '56, waiting to get into the States. Through one of them I met a very pleasant couple who owned a jewelry store. I mentioned that I had a small Post-Impressionist collection. They told me they had a cousin who was a great collector—a Canadian, the head of an enormous corporation, who had a big house in Palm Beach and a huge fortune. (In fact, it was on my recommendation years later that Fernand Legros contacted him in Chicago.) Anyway, I had an appointment with him and I showed him a small collection of drawings, unframed, in a portfolio. He said he can't make a decision, he had to show them first to experts. So, four days later I phoned him and he said the experts liked them and assured him they were genuine. I think I asked $15,000 and he argued the price down to $12,000.

"That was that for Canada, except there were also two or three galleries in Montreal, one of them run by a Frenchwoman. I showed her a Modigliani portrait, an oil, and she was very excited about it, and she said she had a sure buyer, a man who owned a big Canadian whisky company. I handed it over to her because he wanted an outside expert to see it, too. It stayed with her a while and then she told me that this whisky king had taken it to New York for an expertise, but naturally I had nothing to worry about. Then something happened to him in New York—he got sick, had to go to a hospital there for treatment of some kind, couldn't get back —and I was waiting and waiting. Finally I didn't want to wait any longer. I wanted to get back to the States. It was March. I was cold. I called the woman at the gallery and said I'd be in touch with her—I was a little leery about giving forwarding addresses, since I didn't feel very secure at the time, after my experience in Florida and then in Mexico. I had to play it very cool. The FBI had been to Zsa Zsa and several intimate friends, even Jolie Gabor, Zsa Zsa's mother, asking about me. I saw these people here and there on my travels and they told me. So I left Montreal . . . and to this day I never found out what happened to that Modigliani oil.

"I decided to cross from Windsor, Ontario, into Detroit. Someone told me there was lots of traffic and only a superficial border control. I shipped all my things via Railway Express and took a taxi from Windsor to Detroit like a French-Canadian sightseer. The taxi was stopped at the border. They asked me for my I.D. card, and then began to thumb through their very thick books. Nobody smiled. I had a bad ten minutes. I must have been white as chalk. I was sure that somewhere in those books would creep up my name. Finally they asked me what I wanted to see in Detroit.

"I couldn't think for a minute, and so I said, 'The art museum.'

" 'Have a pleasant visit,' the guard told me. I thanked him and then nearly fainted in the taxi. I was so upset I didn't say anything to the driver and he took me right to the museum. I dismissed the taxi and I went inside and wandered through the halls like a zombie. The only thing that snapped me out of it was the shock, walking through the French collection, of suddenly coming face to face, on one wall, with my own Matisse. I remember, it said it was a gift to the museum from some foundation of sorts.

"I felt a certain sense of satisfaction—you might even say, of welcome."

8.

in which we meet
Fernand Legros;
and in which
Elmyr plays
midwife in
Washington and
tries to do away
with himself.

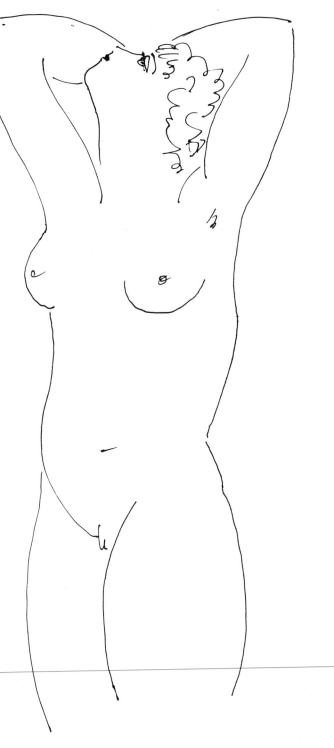

PICASSO BY ELMYR

n the midcentury boom for French Impressionists and Post-Impressionists the price on all of Elmyr's work was skyrocketing, and as the paintings moved from gallery to private owner to museum, their dispersal grew wider and their authenticity continued largely unquestioned. A few weeks after his return from Detroit to New York, in Brentano's bookstore on Fifth Avenue he casually picked up a volume of Modigliani drawings edited by Arthur Pfannstiel, quickly leafed through and found three of his own works (there were two more that he thought might have been his as well, but he had done so many by now that he couldn't be sure), including the Melrose Avenue self-portrait. The commentary after another of Elmyr's forgeries called it "the first masterpiece" of a particular period in the artist's life. Again Elmyr felt some sense of satisfaction, but he was also peculiarly upset.

"I can't explain exactly in which way. But I felt very odd. It just made nonsense out of everything. Perhaps because I'd had so little money for it, and now it had such a fantastic value."

Wherever he looked after that he seemed to see examples of his work. It started abruptly, with books published from 1957 onward. He didn't search for them, but he would open a new $15 coffee-table volume on Matisse and there would be a drawing he had sold for $300 in Seattle, or glance through the most recent catalog of Parke-Bernet and spot a Renoir pastel he'd sold for $800 that had reached $5000 in auction sale. Once in the barber shop of the Hotel Pierre he opened a popular American weekly magazine to be confronted with a photographic layout of a Venezuelan oil baron's luxury home in Caracas. On the living room wall, over the massive stone fireplace, was a Modigliani portrait Elmyr had sold to a New York gallery—he could no longer remember which one—in 1953. The article related that it was the pride of the oilman's art collection, which was "worth millions." He must have bought it, Elmyr reckoned conservatively, for at least $50,000.

Such revelations began to depress him more than elate him. He was completely discouraged, too, with the idea of ever again trying to sell his own paintings. The dealers wouldn't touch them. They were strictly in business, he decided, and if they had to choose between remaining rich men or becoming patrons of the arts—why, it was no choice at all. With time he had developed a dislike for art dealers that bordered on a passion. He had no regrets now for what he had done. Whatever moral handicaps he may have had at the beginning had slowly but finally vanished, like falling leaves in autumn. He knew that virtually all of his forgeries would go ultimately from the dealers' hands to museums or private collections. In either case, if it ever came out that they were fake or even disputed masterpieces, the dealer would have to pay back the money. And that, Elmyr told himself, was the best thing that could happen. Indeed, the idea gave him genuine pleasure. It was quite beside the point that whoever had bought or was going to buy his Modiglianis and Renoirs would derive esthetic enjoyment from them. The fact, he thought, that if ever there's any trouble the dealers have to peel out their checkbooks and give up a fraction of the tremendous profit they were making from art—from the labors of great and gifted men, who all too often had died poor, disappointed, and unknown—and from *him*—filled him with a deep, bittersweet satisfaction.

But his private banishment from Mexico set the tone for the year to come, from both a personal and professional point of view the worst of Elmyr's life. It began with the unfortunate affair with Oscar Herner and ended with Elmyr's trying to kill himself. It was the year, also, that he became friendly with a man named Dr. Josue Corcos, an M.D. from Morocco and then a resident of New York. Elmyr had taken an apartment in Murray Hill and thrown a lavish housewarming party—"Marilyn Monroe was there, but to give you a better idea of what the party was like, downstairs in front of my door were standing *three* Rolls-Royces"—when Dr. Corcos arrived late, in company with a young man who, according to Elmyr's description, "hadn't shaved in at least two or three days. He had a long narrow nose, thin black hair, a suit and shirt that wasn't just not soigné but looked like he'd slept in it for three days on Washington Square. He looked like a Bowery bum and I gave him my usual stare that I reserve for such types."

He grabbed Corky a few minutes later and said, "Who's that?"

"I'm sorry," his doctor friend said. "I see you don't like him."

Amedeo Modigliani:
Portrait de jeune fille.
Drawn by
Elmyr in 1955.

"What you mean, I don't *like* him? He's unwashed, unshaved. He stinks! What's he doing here?"

"Well, he just arrived in the States. He's an unhappy boy, half Greek, half French. He's just had an unhappy love affair. And," Corcos confessed finally, "I didn't know how to get rid of him."

"So that means you have to bring him here?" Elmyr waved his hand just as Marilyn Monroe went by. "To this sort of party?"

"Calm down," Corky said. "We'll go." And fifteen minutes later they did.

The young man's name was Fernand Legros.

"The summer passed," Elmyr related, "mostly on Fire Island, where I stayed usually as a guest of Peggy Fears at The Pines and sometimes at the Boatel in the Pines Yacht Club. In those days, if the FBI was looking for me they could have found me easily—it was like the time toward the end of the war when I was in Budapest, after I'd escaped from Berlin, and the Gestapo were supposed to be hunting for me. If I was in Manhattan I was every evening at seven o'clock having a drink in the bar at the Plaza. On Fire Island I was very well known. I never bothered to hide. Maybe I was just careless, but basically I think I just didn't give a damn any more.

"I did none of my own painting now. People assumed I'd given it up and was living on maybe some small inheritance that had come my way. None of my friends in the States had ever seen me absolutely poor, so I had not to explain the ups and downs of my affluence. In any case, if you move in those circles people just assume, without ever asking, that you have an inexhaustible supply of money, or maybe even a family that pays you to stay away from wherever you come from so as not to embarrass them. It's a hectic and very costly life."

But Elmyr had no inexhaustible cash reserve and no family. The money, as usual—even the large sums he had made during his two-year stay in Miami Beach—had gone on boys and the keeping up of appearances. Worse, his good luck seemed to have deserted him. Too many rumors were beginning to circulate throughout the American art world since the Chicago dealer's complaint to the

FBI, and the market grew both narrower and tighter. For the first time, Elmyr had trouble selling. This was the time that he began doing his lithographs, which he could sell easily to small art dealers who ordinarily didn't handle expensive paintings and therefore wouldn't have been warned, through the grapevine, to "watch out for a suave fifty-year-old Hungarian with a monocle in his eye and a Matisse under his arm."

The lithographs, of course, weren't lithographs at all, but drawings done on paper with a lithographic crayon, then sprayed with a fixative so they wouldn't smear. They were signed and marked in pencil, for example *16/75*—which meant number sixteen of a series limited to seventy-five. Elmyr's favorites were heads and figural drawings by Braque, Picasso and Matisse, for which he got without any trouble in the neighborhood of $200 to $300. Before his career was finished, including the period when he worked with —and later, for—Fernand Legros, he was to do over two hundred of them, the best of which are probably in the Picasso *Tauromachia* series. It was a modest and original concept in forging and to date a surprisingly small percentage has ever been challenged by expert or dealer. But it was essentially door-to-door selling, hard on the shoe leather, so that in the summer of 1958 Elmyr elected to try his hand once more at bigger things.

He was in Washington, D.C., staying in the apartment of a friend, when he met an art dealer named Charles Ouriel, who had no gallery but sold out of his Georgetown apartment.

He was Elmyr's first "salesman" since young Jacques Chamberlin in Paris in 1946. Elmyr's business sense had not improved—the denouement was even more of a disaster.

The partnership flourished only briefly. Peter Deitsch, a New York dealer in rare prints and drawings, had recently discovered that some Matisse drawings he had bought from another New York dealer were, as the trade likes to say, "wrong." Tracing the history of the drawings, he found out they had all been bought originally from Ouriel, and he thought, too, that in the work he detected the fine hand of the elusive Hungarian, known to him as L. E. Raynal, the perpetrator of the Chicago forgeries.

Deitsch then got together on the telephone with Joseph Faulkner, owner of the Main Street Galleries in Chicago, the man who had lowered the boom on Elmyr in 1956. In the midst of some confusion (for a long time the two art dealers believed that Ouriel and Raynal were probably the same man, since not only did the physical descriptions tally, but Faulkner also suggested that Ouriel was a false name and could be an anagram of the names Raynal and Von Houry, which he had been told was Elmyr's real name), Deitsch was personally approached by Ouriel himself, up from Washington to sell some Matisse lithographs. Deitsch recognized them instantly as carbon-pencil forgeries. He asked Ouriel to leave his gallery and then quickly spread the word among New York art dealers. Ouriel's second major market dried up overnight.

At the same time the two partners had been embarked on an even more ambitious project. Several months previously, Ouriel had made Elmyr an interesting proposition. He had in his possession two paintings—an interior "that could have been attributed" to Pierre Bonnard and a landscape that "looked like a Sisley." Both were oils. The former was an interior with a woman standing next to some coats that hung on a rack, the latter a landscape with a flowing brook and a grove of trees. If they were reborn as a genuine Bonnard and a genuine Sisley, they would be worth a great deal of money. Ouriel wanted to know if Elmyr could play midwife.

"Retouching isn't faking," Elmyr explained. "You know it's a very difficult job. Very complicated."

"Too difficult for you?"

"I didn't say *that*," Elmyr replied huffily.

He worked on them for several weeks, and then they were allowed to dry for another month.

Then, despite Elmyr's insistence that the paintings were unsaleable for years—"the old and the new color," he explained, "take a terribly long time to 'fit' together"—the Bonnard interior was brought to one of the directors of the Phillips Memorial Gallery in Washington, who examined it and said (in front of Elmyr, introduced as the owner): "If ever I've seen a Bonnard, that's one." Ouriel in the meantime had sent a color transparency and a black-and-white photograph of the newborn Sisley to Rome, to Lionel Venturi, author of *Painting and Painters: How to Look at a Pic-*

ture and recognized as one of the several great experts on Impressionist masters. Venturi wrote back that he had no doubt it was a genuine Sisley; and to Elmyr's surprise, he enclosed a certificate of his expertise written on the back of the black-and-white photograph.

Ouriel was delighted. Elmyr, who was broke, two weeks later asked for an advance on his fee, which was meant to be a stipulated percentage of the final sales price.

But in the interim Ouriel had had his run-in with Peter Deitsch in New York, and had found the New York market abruptly and unpleasantly closed to him. The interest of the FBI had been mentioned, as well as the names Raynal and de Hory, and suddenly Elmyr had become a distinct liability to the Washington art dealer. So instead of a check Elmyr received a chilly look, and then a suggestion that he leave town within a week—since Washington, if he didn't know it, happened to be the national headquarters of Mr. Hoover's dreaded Bureau. "Get lost," Ouriel said, in case the message wasn't clear.

There was no public protest Elmyr could make without implicating himself. This was it—the end of the road. Where could he go now? He was, in his own words, "broke, tired, depressed, sick of hiding and always doing something that had to be hidden. My so-called crusade against museums, art dealers and art galleries was finished; I had proved my point. What had it got me? Now it was a matter of survival, like a fox that's being run to earth by the dogs, and I really wasn't interested in that.

"I went to raise some money in New York and couldn't do it. I have a weak, perhaps oversensitive, character. It was all too much for me—first Perls in Los Angeles, then that man in Chicago who hounded me, then my troubles in Mexico and Oscar Herner, and now this. It was all too humiliating. Back in Washington, I left my car in front of the apartment, went upstairs and took about fifty sleeping pills."

Ever a survivor, he was found thirty-six hours later, barely breathing but still alive, and taken to a hospital. His stomach was pumped and he then spent four days on the critical list. This was followed by the complication of pneumonia, necessitating three more weeks in a recovery ward. After that he was at the mercy of his old New York friends, including George Alberts, the curio dealer he had met in Florida and who had since moved to a penthouse apartment at 55th Street and Second Avenue. Alberts offered him some money and the use of his apartment while he was away on a European buying trip.

Elmyr, who had passed the crisis—and, as is usual in such cases, having purged himself of his misery through the aborted act of suicide and the subsequent rallying of friends to his aid, had also decided that life was once again bearable—accepted Alberts' offer. Corky, his doctor friend, proved to be his principal nurse. A conference of well-wishers soon decided that the best place for complete recuperation was Florida, since the availability of the New York apartment was on a short-term basis. Also, George Alberts had a small apartment in Miami Beach and a Cadillac he wanted driven south in a few weeks. The immediate problem was to find a congenial driver; Elmyr was down to 110 pounds and so weak he had trouble holding a knife and fork.

One day Corky came to visit and feed him. "You know who just arrived on a Greek freighter from Europe?" he asked casually.

"No," Elmyr said gloomily.

"Fernand Legros."

It rang only a dim bell. "And who is Fernand Legros?"

Corky reminded him.

"That horror?" Elmyr protested, remembering the unshaven, badly dressed, half-Greek, half-French, beady-eyed, long-nosed, balding young man who had crashed last summer's chic party in his Murray Hill studio.

"Listen, Elmyr, he's an old friend of mine and he's in a tough situation. He got off the boat this morning with exactly five dollars in his pocket and nowhere to stay. He's got a wife, but for private reasons he doesn't want her to know he's here. You know I haven't got the room to put him up—but I can lend him some money, and there's an extra couch here in your living room——"

"I don't want anything to do with him," Elmyr said. "He's dirty. He left a very unpleasant impression with me."

"He's intelligent," Corcos said, "and he'll keep you company.

He could even drive you to Florida. You need someone to take care of you until you're strong again. He's a very unhappy boy who—''

"I've heard this story before," Elmyr sighed. But Corcos argued, and finally Elmyr agreed.

"Okay. Call him. Where is he staying now?"

"It seems," said Elmyr, recounting the tale, "that he was waiting outside the front door of the apartment. Corky let him in and I made, as they say, a good face to a bad joke.

"Fernand slept on the couch and became right away very friendly with George Alberts, whose permission at the beginning wasn't asked and who came back a few days later from Europe. Alberts was a Syrian by birth and Fernand, it turned out, had been born in Egypt. They spoke Arabic together—it was a new United Arab Republic. Fernand turned on all the charm. He took a bath, and the second day George Alberts was back, he borrowed fifty dollars from him.

"And then a week or so later we left New York together, in the Cadillac, for Florida. That was the beginning of everything."

9.

in which
Fernand
becomes a
partner;
and in which
Elmyr flies
to Texas to
visit the
Princess of
Prussia,
decorates a
cattleman's
ranch and
makes
good his
escape to
Europe.

MODIGLIANI BY ELMYR

Fernand Legros had been born in Ismailia, Egypt, where his father had been an employee of the Suez Canal Society, and at the age of eighteen had begun a career as a dancer —not with Roland Petit in the Ballet de Monte Carlo and on The Ed Sullivan Show, as later reported by the French press, but in the male chorus of a Paris theater similar to but not quite so chic as the Folies-Bergère. The same French newspapers also parroted as fact Fernand's oft-repeated boast that he spent his twenty-fifth birthday at Delmonico's in New York, celebrating his advent to the rank of millionaire. He may well have been at Delmonico's for that specific anniversary, but if so it was more probably at the invitation of the Spanish marquis who picked up the tab in those days, and whom Fernand served, as the jargon goes, in the capacity of "traveling companion and personal secretary."

Someone who knew him fairly well in those early years has since described him as "a drifter. One of those shadowy people you meet around Saint-Germain-des-Prés and Piccadilly Circus and Times Square—you don't know where they're coming from the night you meet them and they know even less where they're going the next morning. He was half-Greek, so naturally he had a relative in the South of France who was in the shipping business. That's how he managed to get back and forth across the Atlantic so frequently."

After the war, which he spent in Cairo, Fernand was sent to France at the age of twenty to do his compulsory military service. But for reasons never publicly explained, he was almost immediately discharged from the Army. He was a student for a while in Paris, and then in 1952 he picked up his first Greek freighter from Marseilles to the United States. Somewhere along the line, too, in the following years, Fernand picked up for himself an American wife (with whom he never lived after the first few months, but who was convenient for several reasons, including the eventual acquisition of an American passport) and a card which attested to his having studied art history at L'Ecole du Louvre in Paris.

"Whether for a week or a year," Elmyr said later, referring to these studies, "one never knew, because at the time I met him he didn't know a watercolor from a gouache, he couldn't recognize a

Cézanne from a Matisse or a Raphael from Titian. And he remained in complete abysmal ignorance until the last day of our relationship. He always had to look first at the signature before knew who did the painting. He had no powers of observation—he could pass by the same painting every day for six weeks and if you showed it to him a month later he wouldn't recognize it. He was a man totally without taste. But he developed an incredible veneer which completely covered up his coarseness—he had the cleverness of the Oriental people, that Eastern sense of humbugging. He could get power over you. He was a juggler with a talent for selling and for seducing people."

No one could bear better witness to this than Elmyr de Hory. When they arrived in Miami Beach, he and Fernand Legros moved into George Alberts' little apartment. Elmyr found himself paying the bills and in a few weeks, by the time he had gained back some weight and recovered his health, he had also very nearly spent his last dollar.

"How are we going to live now?" Fernand demanded.

"Go out and get a job," Elmyr told him.

But this was utterly distasteful to Fernand. He had once worked briefly as a ticket agent for an airline company in New York, and as far as anyone knew this was the only honest labor he had ever done in his life. "It didn't suit me," he explained, tossing his head.

He had another idea now. Through the indiscretions of their mutual friends he knew something about Elmyr's history and the way he had made his living. He began to pressure Elmyr. "Why don't you just do one little drawing? It won't take you more than a day, and we could live for a month on what you get for it."

"It would take me only half an hour," Elmyr corrected him. "But that's not the point. I had a little trouble once here in Miami. I can't go out and sell to the galleries here. And where," he added, frowning imperiously, "did you get this idea that *we* could live for a month on it?"

Fernand ignored that.

"Then how will we eat? What happens when George Alberts wants his apartment back? Why don't you give *me* the drawing to sell?"

Faced with the prospect of real poverty and Fernand's absolute refusal to go out and work, Elmyr gave in. It was a curious decision in one sense, considering his unfortunate past experiences with Chamberlin in London and Ouriel in Washington, but it was testimony to Fernand's extraordinary powers of persuasion as well as Elmyr's weakness in the face of repeated demands. The situation was to repeat itself many times in the future, with exactly the same results. There were no sexual overtones to the relationship, but Fernand, for all that Elmyr considered him a man "totally without taste," was a shrewd and powerful personality, relentless in his pursuit of whatever he wanted; whereas Elmyr, under pressure, would give in rather than fight, if only to preserve his superficial peace.

"Yes, yes—okay," he said at last, with a weary sigh. "I'll make some lithographs. I'll tell you what to say when you try to sell them. But first you'll have to shave. And before you go into an art gallery you'll have to change your socks. You'll never look like a gentleman, but at least you won't smell like a bum. Here—let's see if my blue suit fits you. Take a bath and then try it on."

The suit fit. Fernand went forth with the brashness of youth, the look of a parvenu and the natural confidence of a born con man; and he sold three Matisse lithographs, all that Elmyr had given him. It was the beginning of a three-way business relationship that was to last, with one intermission, for more than nine years.

The third member of the trio seemed at the time an unlikely candidate for such honors, but he was already on the scene in another capacity. The first week in Miami, ambling along the beach, Elmyr had struck up a conversation with a good-looking, bushy-haired, freckled nineteen-year-old named Réal Lessard, who had hitch-hiked down to Florida from Montreal. "When I first met him," Elmyr remembered, "he was a simple boy with a sixth-grade education, and really rather a sweet person. He was sitting all day on the 18th Street beach in Miami. That's what he liked—to lie around all day on the beach and get brown. He had simple tastes. An average kid, not especially bright, not especially stupid. He grew up fast. Three years later he was having his suits custom-made in Paris, at *my* tailor."

Elmyr was attracted to Réal, but had no choice other than to introduce him to Fernand. Times were tough in Miami and Réal still had about twenty-five dollars cash left in his jeans.

"So Fernand turned on the European charm—they spoke French, of course—and took it away from him—I mean literally. He asked him how much cash he had, and when Réal said 'Twenty-five dollars,' he said, 'Let's see it,' and when Réal pulled out his wallet, he just literally took it away from him. Then he laughed and patted Réal on the cheek and told him he was a very sweet boy. And somehow the two of them wound up sharing the same hotel room. I was a little annoyed, but there was nothing I could do."

A week after the first successful sale Fernand said: "We'll never make enough money with these lithographs. Why don't you do some beautiful drawings and watercolors and we'll take a trip someplace where there are really big galleries?"

Elmyr thought it over and decided to try out the idea. They would "test-market" the product, and the business arrangement, on a brief trip to a single city. He chose Chicago and flew there with Fernand for five days, leaving Réal behind in Miami Beach. The deal, after travel expenses, was 60 per cent for Elmyr and 40 per cent salesman's commission for Fernand. In Chicago, with careful instructions from Elmyr on what to say and how to act, Fernand sold two Matisse drawings, a Picasso lithograph and a watercolor by Braque to three different galleries.

When they got back to Miami, Réal told Elmyr that a man from the FBI had been to the apartment, inquiring after a certain L. E. Raynal.

"He described you perfectly. I didn't know what to say, so I told him I thought you'd gone to the Bahamas on a fishing trip. He said he'd be back."

"Those son-of-a-bitches want my blood. I've got to leave town," Elmyr announced grimly.

"We'll go together," Fernand said.

"No, that's too conspicuous. I'll fly to New Orleans. You fly to Atlanta and then take the bus to New Orleans. We'll meet there"— and he named a time and place.

Thus began the American road tour of the new partnership. Fernand had already announced that he wanted Réal to go with them; he was particularly fond of the young Canadian, and Réal himself had been so thoroughly seduced, body and soul, by what he then considered an older and sophisticated European man of the world, that he was willing to go to Siberia and eat bread and water if Fernand so willed it. Again it seemed to Elmyr that he had relatively little choice, and he agreed on the one condition that Réal was to know nothing of the business dealings other than what he might guess—and there he was to keep his mouth shut.

"Let's not involve him," Elmyr said forcefully. "He's only a kid and he might be indiscreet"—so that wherever they traveled Elmyr lived and worked in a separate hotel room or apartment. It was a useless precaution. Without bothering to tell Elmyr, Fernand explained everything to Réal in the most abundant detail; a future business partnership was already being forged between the twenty-eight-year-old ex-cabaret dancer and the nineteen-year-old Canadian boy who had quit school and gone to Florida "just to sit in the sun."

Rising to the surface now in Fernand's character were two dominating traits—ambition and greed—with which Elmyr, for better or for worse, had never been cursed. By the time they left New Orleans he had wheedled from Elmyr a small portfolio of a dozen drawings and several Fauve watercolors. These vanished in Houston, Dallas, St. Louis and Denver, and before they reached Los Angeles Fernand was demanding small oils. Elmyr of course suspected that Fernand was getting higher prices than he would admit, but he couldn't prove it. He could only notice that in Denver Fernand on his 40 per cent salesman's commission stayed with Réal in the Brown Palace, the best hotel in town, while he, Elmyr, on his 60 per cent and with no companion, could only afford a good businessman's hotel. This extravagance, which was constant, did not impart to Elmyr a great sense of trust in his partner's accounting.

In most places, however, Elmyr was too frightened to go out and sell on his own; his spate of recent troubles had made him aware that not just his name, but his face and personality were too well known in the art world.

"And when I did get some courage to sell a Modigliani drawing on my own, all hell broke loose. In Houston I met a French art dealer I knew who was doing some business in Texas. He said that he's looking for a Modigliani drawing representing the painter Soutine. I said, 'I think I know a drawing like that in Chicago, and it's for sale.' 'How much?' I told him, 'I don't know, I'll have to telephone and find out if it's available.' So I went to the library in Houston, got out some art books and found some portraits and photographs of Soutine, and then went back to my hotel and sat down and in half an hour I made it. I called the dealer and told him I'd have it in three days and it would cost $1500. We agreed on $1250, and when he saw it he was very pleased and paid up immediately. But when Fernand found out he let out such a shriek that I did nearly go deaf. He claimed I had to give him 40 per cent of it because we were partners. I hadn't known that so explicitly before he told me, but I knew it then.

"In California, too, I was a little short of cash. I'd met a young man whom I liked, and he needed a few hundred dollars to repair his car. So I made one or two lithographs and sold them on my own in Laguna Beach and La Jolla. I went by bus, and no one knew me down there. Fernand somehow found out—there came a frontal attack on me, accusing me of selling behind his back, and I never intended to give him any accounting. He made such a scene that I was nearly ill. By then our sixty-forty arrangement had become fifty-fifty. He yelled: 'The money you gave to that boy is money *stolen* from me!' He had what I later realized was a terribly twisted mind."

In Hollywood, where he stayed in a small apartment with Réal, Fernand fell ill with a serious attack of infective hepatitis. He was confined to his bed for four weeks. It was during that time that Elmyr, sitting by the sick man's bedside, imparted so much of his knowledge of the art world and the craft of forgery to Fernand Legros. He loved to gossip and reminisce, and he entertained Fernand with tales of the painters' lives and loves and indiscretions back in the heyday of Montparnasse.

"Do you know how Matisse and Derain and Vlaminck and the others got to be called Fauves? It was during the Autumn Salon in

Paris in 1905, and all their new paintings, with those brilliant colors, did get hanged in one room. In the same room did sit a rather old-fashioned but simple piece of sculpture, which one critic preferred to all the paintings. I think the critic was supposed to be in love with Vlaminck, too, but Vlaminck wasn't interested. So the critic said very loudly, about the sculpture: 'Such a pure work of art in the midst of such an orgy of color, it is Donatello among the wild beasts—*Donatello chez les fauves.*' "

He talked at length about dealers to whom he had sold, and methods he had used. He analyzed art, artists and techniques. Vlaminck, he explained, often worked with colors squeezed directly from the tubes onto the canvas. ''That's why his oils are difficult to fake. The fat slabs of paint take twenty years to dry to the core.''

He also talked about other fakers of the century, like the German Otto Wacker, who confined himself exclusively to van Gogh before he was unmasked in 1928; and Jacques Marisse, the Paris art dealer who was supposed to have sold scores of fake Utrillos; and the famous Dutchman, Hans van Meegeren, who just after the war had caused the greatest sensation ever made by an art forger with his two Pieter de Hoogh forgeries and seven fraudulent Vermeers. ''It's a beautiful story,'' said Elmyr, ''and he was a great craftsman—but he made many, many mistakes. He did a de Hoogh where he had a woman holding a glass in a way that looked very unnatural, because the glass had no stem and the detail was actually taken from a Vermeer. He had got his two painters mixed up. No one noticed until much later, when van Meegeren was caught. Hindsight is easy, but with the knowledge that they're fakes, I don't see how he was able to fool such a number of grand connoisseurs. I didn't thought the big Vermeers were that good. They looked too mundane. His faces didn't have seventeenth-century expressions, they were modern neurotic faces. I heard a story later he used the heads of Valentino and Garbo for models. That's always a temptation, to be cute, but it's always a mistake.''

Fernand asked questions all day long, and Elmyr answered.

''In effect,'' Elmyr realized later, ''to keep him cheered up and amused, I told him everything I'd done and everything I knew. For once he was a sharp listener. And, as the years to come would show, he remembered almost everything.''

It was also during that time of Fernand's illness that Elmyr had a preview of the jealous rage that was to lead eventually not only to the breakup of the triangular friendship but also to the destruction of the most profitable swindle in art history. Réal, who had been cheerfully tagging along on the journey as chauffeur and general handyman, now played nurse and sat up with the sick man day and night. One afternoon, however, when Fernand's fever had abated, Réal went out before dinner for a walk and didn't return until nearly 10 P.M.

''When the boy finally got back,'' Elmyr recalled, ''Fernand had worked himself into such a fury that he broke nearly every plate and window in the apartment. He screamed like a wounded animal. He was half-dead with hepatitis but he tried to hit Réal with a milk bottle, he tore the bedclothes, he fell on the floor like an epileptic. It was a terrible, frightening sight. I myself felt sick. Poor Réal, he wept with fear. He was only a kid of nineteen—he'd stopped off on the way home to see a movie!

''That's when I made the decision that I can't stay with this man any more. We'd been together six months. After all, I hadn't signed a contract, I'd never intended it to be a lifelong partnership. I was getting more and more nostalgic for Europe, and we'd often talked, the three of us, about going there together. Réal thought he knew a way that for about $2000, through a lawyer he'd once worked for in Toronto, he could get me a Canadian passport. I said okay. I would somehow come up with the money. Fernand, of course, meant for us to do business together over there in Europe. We went back to New York together and they went up to Toronto to see if they could arrange things. All I had to do was to find the $2000, which, naturally, I didn't have at the time.

''I checked into the Winslow Hotel on East 55th Street, sat down in my little room and quickly put together a small collection of things: some Degas pastels, a Renoir watercolor and a group of various drawings. It took me about three days—it was all work I had done before, I knew the subjects so well I didn't even have to look at the books any more to get what you might call 'inspiration.' In one sense, perhaps unconsciously, I was even copying my own earlier fakes—that is, without having them in front of me to refer to, except that I could see them in my mind's eye. It's something every artist does, of course: going over old subjects from a fresh point of view. I did it at the time so that I could work fast, because I had to sell fast.

"I also had a beautiful watercolor by Cézanne that I'd done in Miami—it was very expensively priced. I had an idea. I'd just heard that a good friend of mine, the Princess of Prussia—the granddaughter of Kaiser Wilhelm II—had married a Texan and was staying in San Antonio. I knew that people in Texas were getting more and more interested in fine art, so I called her. She said, 'El–*myr?*'—and then, 'Yes, of course, come!' I gambled everything and flew out to San Antonio. Just before I got there, for some reason or other, the Princess had to fly suddenly to Europe. A matter of hours. I was in San Antonio without knowing a soul. I was terribly upset.

"But I had to do something quickly. I met a dealer there who had an art gallery and he saw my little collection and said: 'Why don't we hang an exhibit and I'll invite a few people?' That's exactly what happened. He sold one or two things and then a very rich cattleman and his wife said, 'Could you bring the Degas pastels and the Renoir out to our house? We want to see how they look in our living room.' The exhibition had only lasted a few days. I went out there with some misgivings—I felt like a furniture salesman. But they had a magnificent ranch and they put the paintings, all beautifully framed, on the walls of their living room and den. They looked marvelous. I myself was impressed. And two days later, in San Antonio, I got a check for $30,000. I was stunned."

It was a completely unexpected bonanza, and by far the most money Elmyr had ever collected at one go. Suddenly, however, he felt uneasy, for it presented a new problem; he had told the dealer and the cattleman that he was an expatriate Frenchman who was thinking of settling in the San Antonio area, and he didn't want to make it too obvious that he was skipping town instantly with all of the cash. He had a vision of being stopped at the airport by the sheriff; or worse, hauled off the plane by a posse of vigilantes led by the cattle baron. To take even a certified check with him to New York was too risky, since he well knew that even in a few days anything might happen. He presented the $30,000 check at the bank and asked for cash, which took a little time.

"I have to fly to New York for a few days, so I'd like a safety deposit box to put the money in."

He packed all the money in the box. The bank manager suggested the possibility of investment and Elmyr said, "Yes, that's an excellent idea. Perhaps you'd be kind enough to prepare a small list of stocks. Then I'll make a decision." The next morning he returned to the bank, ostensibly to leave some valuable drawings in the safe deposit box. He carried a large portfolio, which he quickly lined with twenty- and hundred-dollar bills; in their place, in the box, he stuffed a wad of newspaper. Then, with beating heart, he took a taxi to the airport. There was no posse.

"I flew to Chicago, stopped off for a few days, bought traveler's cheques, cashed big bills, and suddenly decided to buy a car. I missed not having a car. I didn't really know for sure where I'd go next. I bought a beautiful blue Corvette convertible and drove off to New York."

In New York he stayed again at the Winslow Hotel and made his final decision. He was tired of looking over his shoulder for the FBI and the vigilantes. He would return to Europe.

He told Fernand and Réal that he had sold "a few small drawings" in Texas; and now he had the money to pay for the Canadian passport. Pleased, they flew back to Ottawa. Elmyr shipped the Corvette from New York to Paris, and his luggage with it—except for one cabin trunk which he left in storage at the Winslow Hotel. It contained, as a kind of farsighted American insurance policy, the unsold Cézanne watercolor and a number of drawings. He had no idea that it would be Fernand Legros, not himself, who would be the beneficiary.

"Then, a week or ten days later, I went to Ottawa. As usual, I had no papers. I walked across the border from Niagara Falls without luggage, without even a brief case, like a sightseer. As usual, I was half frightened to death. I had more than $20,000 in my pockets, and if they'd searched me they would have been terribly suspicious. But, as usual, I made it. Fernand and Réal were waiting for me—I handed over the $2000 and their plane tickets to Paris, which was all part of the deal, and they handed over the passport.''

It was a genuine, brand-new Canadian passport in the name of Joseph Boutin, with Elmyr's photograph in it. Boutin was a real person. What they had done was scout around until they found some unassuming little man, an insurance clerk about Elmyr's age, married, with children, and with very little money, the sort of man who would undoubtedly never leave his home town, much less Canada. They then secured a copy of his birth certificate and had a lawyer apply for a passport in his name. Like so many schemes that looked foolproof, it turned out in the end—in a way that no one could possibly have anticipated—to be a disastrous mistake.

At the time, however, Elmyr was delighted with his new identity.

''Fernand and Réal took me to the airport. Réal wanted first to visit his family in Quebec and then they were going to fly over to Paris a week later and meet me. I said okay. We spoke about continuing our business in Europe, but no definite arrangements were made. I was cagey. Fernand tried to pin me down but I kept saying, 'We'll look around first. I'm tired, I want to rest up a bit in Paris.'

''My secret thought was, 'Good riddance to bad rubbish. I don't ever want to lay my eye on Fernand Legros again.' ''

10.

in which, after a
lady and a movie
director have
their say, Elmyr
gives Fernand
the slip and
settles in Rome;
and in which is
related the
mysterious
affair of the
Winslow trunk.

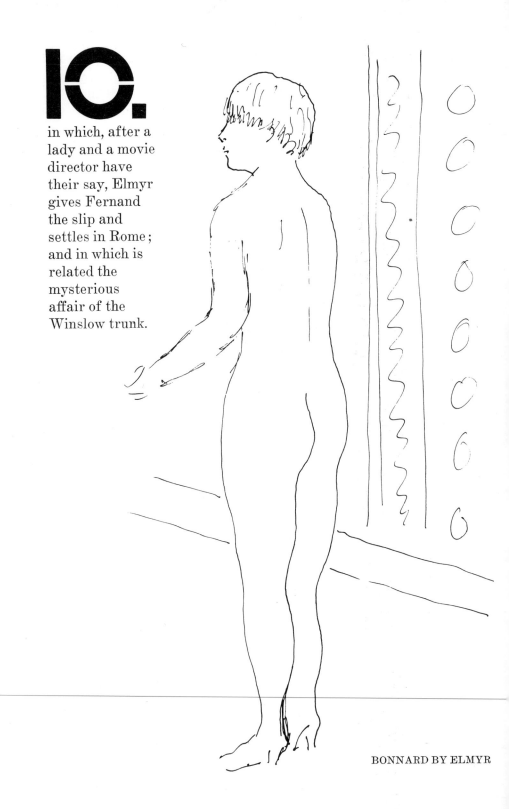

BONNARD BY ELMYR

f Elmyr had stopped work at this natural crossroads in his career, he would already have been the most prolific and successful art forger of all time—perhaps a dubious honor, but still one he might have secretly relished and then in his old age shyly revealed to an incredulous public. Despite the unpleasant brushes with astute dealers like Joseph Faulkner and Frank Perls, he had in the previous thirteen years turned out a body of work of astonishing magnitude, and undoubtedly most of it still hung unchallenged on the walls of museums, art galleries and blue-ribbon private collections. The art establishment was a close-knit international club, with an excellent intramural communication system, but Elmyr had traveled so much and used so many pseudonyms as to ward off the admittedly difficult conclusion that one man was responsible for so much skulduggery. With but one exception—and there Faulkner and Deitsch were only operating on a hunch they were unable to prove—none of the experts who had detected single forgeries were able to link, for example, the Elmyr de Hory who had sold to Klaus Perls in 1947 and blanketed the San Francisco galleries in 1949, the Baron Herzog who had traveled throughout the Midwest in 1951, and the L. E. Raynal who had fled down Brighton Way from Frank Perls in 1952, then sold by mail to the Fogg Art Museum in 1955 and finally been detected by Joseph Faulkner in 1956. Elmyr's very weaknesses—his illegal presence in the United States, his clandestine personal life and his general restlessness, which caused him to hop erratically from city to city —had been the unwitting weapons which secured his anonymity and baffled the hunters. He was also aided by rumors that he was dead or vanished from the scene. As late as 1967 Klaus Perls believed that the man he had known as de Hory had been "in jail in New Orleans, and quite sick. After that, I lost track of him." Stephen Hahn, at first associated with the Niveau Gallery and later the owner of his own establishment on Madison Avenue, said that same year: "De Hory had some talent, but the outstanding forger of our time was Raynal. He was a magnificent forger, a true genius. I had heard he died in France around 1960."

Elmyr himself, when he left for Europe in 1959, had no clear idea of how much work he had turned out, or that he had already earned himself a major chapter in the annals of crime. He kept no records, took no photographs and made no lists of work sold either by himself or Fernand Legros in their thus-far brief partnership. To do so would have forced him to face the fact that forging was his career, his life's work. He stubbornly refused to believe it. He considered himself a painter who had fallen on hard times and occasionally forged a few small things in order to eat. Despite his scorn for the art establishment and his claim that he "had no regrets," his moral sense was not entirely paralyzed. More important, his ego was rampant, and that ego would not permit him to believe he had done anything "wrong." He saw himself rather as an unappreciated artist—a victim. He blamed the war for his poverty and lack of scruples, he blamed the art establishment and the philistines for his failure to become a known painter in his own right. He was a sensitive man who had learned to live in a world of shadowy half-truths, and if they were challenged he could not survive. He never fought back; he simply turned his back on the challenger and walked away, head held high. He quickly forgot the humiliation he had suffered at the hands of Frank Perls, who had thrown his portfolio at him and chased him down the block; instead, Perls had simply "hinted" that he leave town. Faulkner was the villain of the piece in 1956; he had "persecuted" Elmyr and lied to the FBI that the paintings had been sent through the U.S. mails. With time and enough repetitions, his own version of the tales became the indisputable truth for him, and he could be shocked and genuinely hurt if anyone suggested the opposite. The definition of a disloyal friend was anyone who laughed at him or didn't believe him. He held his head high.

His memory of Mrs. Lilienfeld—the wife of the gallery owner who gave him his first exhibition in New York in 1948—is a perfect example. "A rather unpleasant woman," he recalled. "She gave me a very hard time afterwards about my show. It had something to do with money she claimed I owed her."

Lilienfeld is dead now, but his wife, who ran the gallery with him back in 1948, tells a more expanded version of that winter's tale. Even today, twenty years later, her anger is close to the surface—as she recalled the incidents, it boiled over more than once.

It seems, according to Mrs. Lilienfeld, that Elmyr agreed to pay the gallery $300 as costs for his show, and was then in such financial straits that he promoted an additional $75 in cash to meet his living expenses while waiting for "a large check from South America." He skipped town without paying a dime. Then, "all sorts of people" began calling the gallery. He had promised to do a portrait of Magda Gabor and convinced her to buy an expensive dress for the sitting. Not only did he neglect to do the portrait, but the dress went with Elmyr when he left New York. Then, the accusation continued, a man from Dunhill, the quality men's tailor, telephoned. Some months ago his father had died and he had shortly thereafter commissioned Elmyr to do a portrait of the old man from some photographs. For this, as payment in advance, he made Elmyr a suit and a yellow double-breasted cashmere overcoat. Elmyr never found sufficient time to do the portrait. Finally, Mrs. Lilienfeld related, he was thrown out of his hotel after running up a bill in the thousands of dollars. Detectives tracked him down after the exhibition and caught up with him one sunny winter morning on Fifth Avenue in front of St. Patrick's Cathedral. (Here, in her narrative, Mrs. Lilienfeld uses gestures and plenty of body English to give a picture of a very debonair, outraged Elmyr.) "But there he was with his cane and his yellow Dunhill overcoat and his aristocratic manners. They were afraid to arrest him."

That week, too, the check he had been waiting for "did finally arrive" from South America, and got shown to all pressing creditors. No cash was available, however, and even the check, according to the indignant Mrs. Lilienfeld, turned out to be a phony. After the incident in front of St. Patrick's Cathedral, Elmyr left town.

"He's a charming man," she concluded, "and a good painter, and he can smile right in your face and tell the most awful lies. He's also a crook, and I've never said that about anyone else I've ever shown in this gallery."

She had no idea, of course, to what extent he was "a crook." But then, neither did Elmyr.

One of the most extraordinary illusions that he entertained during all the years of his career as an art forger was that what he was doing was not a crime, and therefore he was not in any sense a criminal. He knew, of course, that it was *against the law*—but so was jaywalking, running a stop sign on a deserted street at night, smoking marijuana and minor income tax evasion. Who in the sophisticated world hesitated to do these things, provided reasonable precautions were taken against being caught? They were against the law; therefore, technically, "crimes"—but they did no harm to others. That was the important distinction in Elmyr's mind. Forging a Matisse or a Modigliani harmed no one. Had he stolen from a poor man with a wife and six children to support? Had he killed anyone? Was he an extortionist, a member of the Mafia? Certainly not, and accordingly he held his head high.

One of the more poignant tales to illustrate this attitude came from a well-known French movie director, who became friendly with Elmyr during a visit to Miami in 1956. Despite his claims that he never sold to private persons, Elmyr did in fact sell him two drawings by Modigliani. They met again in New York in 1958. During the interval Elmyr had evidently been seized by an attack of conscience, and he said to the movie director: "François, I've discovered that those two drawings I sold to you were not authentic Modiglianis. I've been bothered about it ever since. I'm leaving town in a few days and I want to give you back the money."

The French director naturally accepted the offer. He deposited the check the next day. It bounced. The account had just been cleared out.

Years later, in Spain, the movie director was working in Pamplona during the annual fiesta of San Fermín, where the bulls run through the streets of the town behind the crowd of *aficionados*. He was shooting on the edge of the bullring during the *corrida* when suddenly, out of the stands on the shady side, anxiously calling his name, descended his old friend Elmyr. With some show of annoyance the Frenchman turned his back, but Elmyr was not to be denied his moment of auld lang syne. "François," he said, "I know what you think. But you must let me explain. I did forget completely about the fact that I'd closed the account when I gave you that check in New York. I have no head for financial matters. Please, meet me this evening at my hotel, let me buy you a drink. I live now in Spain and I'll give you a check in pesetas for what I owe you.''

They met, they had several friendly drinks, they reminisced, and Elmyr gave him a check on his bank in Ibiza. The movie director cashed it through a Spanish associate. It bounced.

This story was told by the director in 1968 to a close friend of Elmyr's, who then said: ''But you must really be furious at him after that.''

''Strangely enough,'' the director replied, ''not at all. He is what he is, and there's something wonderful about a man like that. He's a charming crook. I wouldn't be surprised if he really believed on both occasions that there was cash in the bank to cover the checks. No, I still consider him a friend—if I saw him walking down the other side of the Champs-Élysées right this minute, I'd run across the avenue and embrace him.''

Returning from Paris to Ibiza, the friend repeated this whole tale to Elmyr, verbatim, thinking he would be pleased at such an expression of loyalty in the face of insuperable odds. Elmyr was anything but pleased. His face assumed a deeply wounded expression, the corners of his mouth turned sharply down and he sniffed disdainfully.

''Well,'' he said, ''I wouldn't run across the avenue to embrace *him*. I don't think that's a pleasant story at all. How dare he call me a charming *crook?*''

After an absence of nearly thirteen years, Elmyr returned to Europe—to Paris first, which he knew so well and which he felt, within hours of his arrival, had changed so little in those many years. It was early September and the city was just coming alive after the hot summer slumber and the tourist invasion. He walked the streets of Montparnasse, where he had lived as a young man. He sipped an apéritif at the Dôme. There, at that table, more than thirty years ago, he had been introduced to André Derain and Kees van Dongen. A few blocks away had been the studio of Léger, where the young Hungarian *bon vivant* had sat at the feet of the great teacher. It was a warm but mild afternoon, with a welcome breeze that ruffled the leaves on the trees that lined the boulevard. It was home—all of Europe was home—and here, Elmyr swore to himself, he would live. He would begin again the life that had seemed such a failure and a travesty after the war. What had happened in America was unreal, a nightmare. It had to be pushed into the shadowy recesses of his mind, forgotten and finally obliterated. He would begin again. He would become the painter he had always dreamed of being. In California, once, he had tried and failed, but California was another world, too lush with its promises, too new, too cruel in its demands. Europe was older and would be more gentle with him.

He had already begun to look up his old friends and search for a studio when, a week later, Fernand and Réal arrived from Canada and checked into the Hôtel Pont Royal, where Elmyr too was staying. Fernand soon announced that he had no money.

"Listen," he said to Elmyr, "I know you too well. I know you sold more on that little trip to Texas than you told us. We're partners and I have a percentage. So you will kindly pay the hotel bill and advance some cash until we get started."

Confused and apprehensive, Elmyr paid. The Corvette arrived and Fernand saw it parked on the quai by the Seine in front of the hotel. "What is this?" he demanded.

When Elmyr blandly replied "My new car," Fernand became enraged. He danced up and down in the street, waving his hands. "How could you do such a thing? How could you be so stupid? How could you buy a sports car that doesn't have room for the three of us?"

Elmyr muttered his apologies.

"Remember," Fernand warned, "I know all about you. I know who you are and what you've done. And you are," he added, "the most inconsiderate and thoughtless man I have ever met."

A few days later Elmyr announced that he was driving down to Cap d'Antibes in the South of France to visit some friends. He would be back within a week or two, he promised. Fernand complained bitterly, but had little choice.

Elmyr left, murmuring, *"Au revoir, Paris."* As long as Fernand Legros was there, he had no intention of returning.

In early October, after a swing along the Riviera to visit old friends and make new ones, Elmyr reached Rome.

This is it, he told himself. Here I stay—and he took an apartment on the Via Boncompagni near the American Embassy. It was the season: the Matarazzo girls were in Rome, throwing parties; and Eva Bartok, an old friend and compatriot; and the Borgheses and Elsa Maxwell; and Crown Prince Constantine of Greece and the Aldovrandinis. The social whirl for Elmyr was exhilarating, and at the same time, somehow, squeezed between other people's parties and the ones he gave himself, he found the time to paint. A few months after his arrival he was introduced at a luncheon to the owner of the Galeria Monte Napoleone in Milan, one of Italy's best galleries for contemporary figurative art. The gallery owner visited his apartment the next day, saw Elmyr's work and offered him a one-man show.

It was a modest success: the critics were kind to "Joseph Boutin, a new painter who exhibits brilliant colors and a fine sense of composition," and Elmyr sold three landscapes. Several of his pals from Paris came down for the opening and the subsequent parties in Milan and Rome.

"Your old friend Fernand Legros keeps asking for you," Jean-Louis said.

"For God's sake," Elmyr replied, "whatever happens, if you bump into him again don't tell him where I am. That man is an absolute pest."

In the summer, however, a rumor reached him that Fernand had put Réal in school in the South of France and had himself gone to live for a while with his parents in their home near Nice. Rome was hot, and crowded for the 1960 Olympic games, and Elmyr had a yen to visit Paris. Off he went, and two days after his arrival he was sipping his morning coffee at a brasserie near the Gare St. Lazare, when a familiar figure, tieless, wearing a shabby brown serge suit, emerged from the Métro and minced across the street, hips gently undulating, directly toward where he sat. Elmyr tried to duck his head and register a blank stare, but there was no avoiding him. *"Mon cher Elmyr!"* Fernand cried. *"C'est vraiment toi?"*

"Yes, it's really me," Elmyr answered unhappily. He could think of no excuse, so he offered Fernand a chair and invited him to a coffee.

"Where are you living now, my dear?"

"Madrid," Elmyr said promptly.

"And are you painting?"

"Not at all," said Elmyr.

"Then you have money?"

"Not a dime."

"You're such a liar," Fernand said, but not unpleasantly. "And it was very naughty of you to run away from Paris last year. Réal was terribly upset. And I, naturally—" he smiled thinly— "was very disappointed."

He tried then, without much preamble, to make Elmyr a business proposition. Europe was a virgin market, waiting—no, fairly begging—to be sold. Elmyr shook his head. He was finished with all that, he explained. He had sold nothing since he had left the States.

"Then why not give me some of the things you had left over when you were in New York? I have contacts, I can sell them easily. Where is that lovely little Cézanne I liked so much?"

He was referring to a Cézanne watercolor that Elmyr had painted just before they left Florida in the spring of 1959. The asking price had been $20,000, but the best offer en route from Florida to California was $8000 from a dealer in Houston. Elmyr had turned it down. He had then taken the painting with him on his flying trip to San Antonio, but it remained unsold.

"I don't even have that any more," Elmyr said truthfully. "I left it in storage with all the other things, in my trunk at the Winslow in New York." He spread his hands apologetically; he failed to notice the sudden spark of light in Fernand's solemn brown eyes. They talked a few minutes more, then Elmyr glanced at his watch and explained that he had an appointment for which he was already late.

They shook hands coolly and said *au revoir*.

If anything, Fernand Legros was a gambler, and a daring one. He guessed that Elmyr had been telling the truth about all except his personal whereabouts and his financial situation. He hurried back to his hotel in Saint-Germain-des-Prés and placed a long-distance telephone call, in the name of Elmyr de Hory, to the Winslow Hotel in New York. He demanded to know if his trunk was still safely stored away in the hotel baggage room. The management, after a rapid inquiry, replied, "Of course."

In that case, Fernand explained, a young man named Fernand Legros, bearing proper identification and a letter of introduction from him, Elmyr de Hory, would be picking it up within the week.

Two days later, with a one-way ticket and $100 of borrowed money, Fernand was on an Air France jet bound for New York.

Checking into the Winslow Hotel, he produced a paper with what seemed certainly an authentic signature of Mr. Elmyr de Hory. The trunk was brought up to Fernand's room. The padlock presented no problem to a man who had traveled three thousand miles to deal with it. The contents, a modest treasure of twentieth-century French drawings and watercolors, spilled out on the bed—and Fernand Legros was ready to launch himself in what was to be perhaps the zaniest career, and certainly the most profitable swindling enterprise, in the history of art.

"I didn't know it for years," Elmyr said, "that he'd got my trunk. The first clue I had was in 1961. I was in Hamburg, visiting Arthur Pfannstiel, the authority on Modigliani who had previously bought several drawings from me mailed from Los Angeles under another name." Pfannstiel was pleased to meet a man who was almost as knowledgeable as himself on the subject of Amedeo Modigliani's life work, and they were sitting in his living room, drinking coffee and discussing the sad state of contemporary art, when the German expert suddenly said: "*Mein lieber Baron*, look at these. They've just been mailed to me from France by an art dealer who wants an expertise. What do you think of them?'' He then produced from a folder three drawings by Modigliani, which Elmyr instantly recognized as his own. He broke out into a light sweat. He couldn't remember to whom he had sold them. He replied, casually: ''Well, they look all right . . . I guess.'' A little later he asked Pfannstiel the name of the dealer who had sent them, but Pfannstiel for some reason elected not to answer.

Elmyr left Hamburg, a little disturbed. He was almost positive the drawings were his, and from a recent period in his career, since he had recognized the paper—a fine old French paper from the first decade of the century that he had discovered in a New Orleans bookbinder's shop around 1956. But where he had sold them, for the life of him he couldn't remember.

It took him a further five years to find out. Toward the end of his relationship with Fernand and Réal, when things were in a very bad state indeed, he and Réal met in a Madrid hotel suite to discuss strategy. Réal quit the room for a few minutes to make a telephone call. As was customary among the three partners when any one of them left his luggage unguarded in the presence of any of the others, Elmyr dove for the briefcase on the bed and began rifling its contents. Before Réal returned he had discovered a set of photographs and Kodachrome transparencies, as well as a 1965 catalog from the Galeria de Arte Solarium of São Paulo, Brazil; all reproduced one of the three Modigliani drawings shown to him by Pfannstiel and several other paintings that had been left behind, safely stored for his old age, he had reckoned, in the trunk in the Winslow Hotel.

At last Elmyr understood how Fernand had made his start in the international art market. The Cézanne watercolor, he learned later, had first been offered to Galerie Hervé in Paris. Hervé, one of the most sophisticated and knowledgeable young art dealers in the business, took a quick look at the Cézanne—''which,'' he said, ''was good enough''—and a long, hard look at the man trying to sell it.

''Get out,'' he told Fernand. ''You're a crook. I never want to see your face again.''

Fernand got out, walked down the Avenue Matignon to still another gallery and, undaunted, sold the Cézanne to a less discriminating dealer.

Réal, accused by Elmyr in the Madrid hotel room of being partner to the foul deed, claimed he knew nothing about it. ''That was 1960,'' he explained. ''I was just a kid.''

II.

in which, growing
tired and older,
Elmyr makes a
fatal bargain.

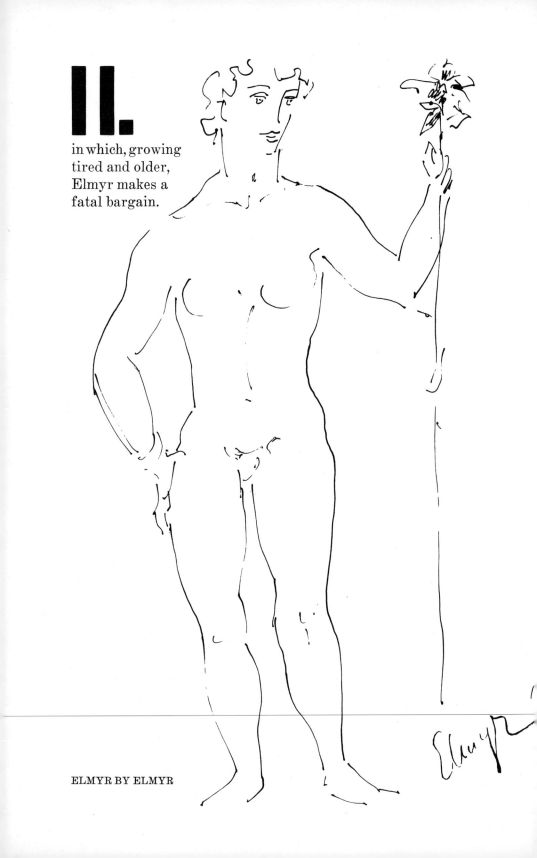

ELMYR BY ELMYR

While Fernand was in Paris setting himself up in business with the contents of the Winslow trunk, Elmyr was doing a little business of his own. His good intentions—to begin life again, to live as a painter of his own work and obliterate his past existence as a forger—turned out to be intentions and no more. They vanished with his bank account. He had discovered that even in the enlightened, cultured Europe of the 1960s, he couldn't make a living from his own painting. After the show in Milan he made the rounds of the Rome galleries, but they were interested only in commercial work or abstract art. The latter would have been a completely false move on Elmyr's part, and he was determined to paint no more palm trees and pink poodles. Once again, naturally, he was nearly broke; life in a city like Rome, wining and dining with the upper classes and buying drinks for young men on the Via Veneto, was not cheap. It was a familiar dilemma and he wasted no time dangling painfully from its horns. With his by now customary sigh, he bought a fresh set of art books, French paper, canvas, ink, pastels, watercolors and the correct oils, and set to work in his studio. He had hardly lost his touch; if anything, it had improved. After a month's labor he had a collection of some twenty-five Renoir and Degas pastels, Chagall and Derain watercolors and Matisse drawings.

"I'd outlived my time in Rome, and I decided to leave. I couldn't seem to stay very long in any one place, I always did become too terribly restless. I went here and there—Holland, Germany, Switzerland, London—still with the Corvette, selling this and that to dealers and art galleries. In that period I concentrated on Renoir. Somehow, no matter what I sold, I never could accumulate money, so in the winter I decided I'm going to make a tour of South America, selling. I realized I wanted to live in Europe and it might be better in the long run not to sell, so to speak, in my own backyard. And then I thought, maybe I'll even live in Rio or Buenos Aires. Who knows? I really didn't know what I wanted to do—it was a confusing time in my life, a period of great indecision. I sold my car in London and after the taxes I still got more than $2000, and off I flew to Brazil."

But the South American trip proved a disappointment. Despite a number of sales to the museum in São Paulo and dealers in Buenos Aires, including a Chagall watercolor and a colored drawing by Léger, the market in general was poor; after a stay of nearly two months Elmyr had cleared, after expenses, less than $5000. That would last him no time at all. And where to go now? Europe was the answer, and he flew back this time to Madrid, a tired and disconsolate man. Sitting in his hotel room at the Ritz he pondered his situation, and realized that somehow it wasn't working out the way he'd planned when he left the United States two years ago, full of hope and resolve. His try at painting his own works had failed to bring him even a measure of fame or success, and his recourse to painting and selling fakes had failed to bring him security. As usual, when he had money he spent it, on hotel suites, on air fares, on young men, on gifts and good food, on any form of diversion that presented itself. Although it took a considerable effort for him to face this truth squarely, he was in reality a fifty-five-year-old indigent, the quintessence of the twentieth-century expatriate, the wanderer. Again, and more sharply than ever before, he felt the pangs of loneliness that accompanied an oncoming old age with neither a mate nor a family nor a home. He had friends, yes, but they were scattered throughout the world; he saw them only from time to time and then briefly, when he was passing through some place like Paris or Madrid or Biarritz. He was always welcomed as one appearing from the dead, but then he moved on. What he desperately missed was the companionship, the comfort of routine, that came from living in one place among a circle of people who didn't fade with the seasons toward greener pastures. He remembered with nostalgia the little apartment in Miami Beach that he had shared with Jimmy Damion. He even longed for his boyhood in Budapest, a city to which he could never return. Perhaps, he thought, he had come full circle, yearning for the lost security of a child, wanting precisely that bourgeois existence he had scorned as a young man in search of adventure in Munich and then Paris. How he would support himself he didn't know, didn't care—that was beyond the scope of his introspection and desires. But what he needed, he decided, was a kind of nest somewhere, away from the distractions and the whirl of city life, a quiet place to work and live more modestly than was his custom. It seemed his only hope. Perhaps an island—cheap, still undiscovered. Did such a place exist outside his daydreams?

He turned his nose toward the Mediterranean, the perennial haven of expatriate artists and writers; if he could find a home anywhere, it would be there. Because he was already in Spain, and because he had heard it was cheap, the first place he investigated was the Balearic Islands. Majorca, he thought, was too big and would be already overrun. The island that attracted him, and which in fact a friend in Paris had mentioned to him years ago, was called Ibiza.

The guidebook said: "Ibiza was truly made for Man. It is not vast or spectacular but just of the right size and contours for the human eye to roam restfully over its quiet landscape. Here all is noble, calm and serene." Lying only a hundred miles off the Levantine coast of Spain, the island had been discovered by Phoenician traders in the ninth century b.c., invaded and raped in subsequent epochs by Chaldeans, Egyptians, Carthaginians, Romans, Vandals, Byzantines, Arabs, Spaniards, and finally the international tourist traffic, led as always by the intrepid English, of the 1950s. By the time Elmyr reached Ibiza in 1961 the boom was in high gear, and yet to anyone coming there for the first time—the airport, with links to London, Paris and Frankfurt, still looked like a bush station serving some remote African province—it could well appear a relatively untouched paradise. It was an island, then and now, which seemed to attract beautiful young people. The foreign community was friendly and closeknit. There were beatniks, potheads, artists, writers, actors on holiday, escapees from New York advertising agencies, a couple of Canadian ex-con men who had sold shares in a nonexistent asbestos factory and beat it from Montreal only one step ahead of the Mounties, longhaired wives with daddyless babies, German land speculators, a few rich men, many more poor ones, and even a reported Nazi war criminal whose bull neck, beady eyes and kindness to children made him a caricature of what he was supposed to be. Life was strictly on a first-name basis. In case of duplication, people received names like Wanted John and Spade John, Pretty Pat and Hairy Pat, Danish

George and Fat George, Eduardo's Karen and Carl's Karen. Elmyr, of course, was an original—"Man, dig *that* cat!"

Still, after two months on the island he wasn't quite sure—"I had a slight fear that in such an out-of-the-way place, which Ibiza really was in the early 1960s, I might be, in a sense, 'burying myself.'" However, it was cheap enough for him to rent a small house, called Villa Platero, which he could either return to or abandon as he chose; and at the end of the summer he decided to try Greece and the Aegean.

Not far from Athens, already well known for having served as background to the film *Boy on a Dolphin,* lay the island of Hydra. Elmyr stayed six weeks. Jules Dassin was there, filming *Phaedra,* and Elmyr met Melina Mercouri. They became friendly and Dassin soon offered him a walk-on part in the film—"I need a lecherous old man," he said, "who hovers in the background"—but such mini-stardom was not enough to keep Elmyr in Greece or tempt him to pursue a new career, so that in October 1961, once again hunting for money, he went back to Paris to sell something. En route he stopped off in Vienna, where he took to his bed in the Bristol Hotel with a bad cold and fever. It was not debilitating enough to prevent him sallying forth in the Viennese rain to the art galleries and disposing of two Matisse drawings. Then, red-eyed and still sneezing, he continued on to Paris.

The first evening, as if on cue, Fernand Legros and Réal Lessard were standing outside the Café Flore in Saint-Germain-des-Prés, apparently waiting to bump into him as Elmyr emerged from a taxi.

"It seemed unavoidable," Elmyr said later. "Maybe even, in one way, it was Fate."

Fernand seemed terribly pleased to see him, and Elmyr immediately noticed about his erstwhile partner what he later recalled as "a certain air of prosperity."

Fernand, of course, had by then parlayed the contents of the Winslow trunk into a burgeoning business and a steadily growing reputation as an art dealer specializing in French Post-Impressionist masterpieces. He had always had some wit, and now he had added a cultivated charm to his arsenal of weapons. Nor had his years in America been wasted; he had become a devotee and now a specialist of the hard sell. Through his connections in the homosexual establishment of Paris he was able to meet a good many dealers and collectors—the rest was a question of coming up with the goods. This, somehow, he always managed to do, snaring this and that on consignment and occasionally offering things even before he had been commissioned to do so. With the profit from the Winslow trunk he had also bought three genuine Dufy watercolors from a Dr. Alexandre Roudinesco, who had been a close friend of and physician to both Dufy and Vlaminck. Queried some years later, Dr. Roudinesco said: "I didn't want to part with them, but he was a terribly persistent young man. He kept pestering me and in the end I was worn out and agreed."

Fernand was not yet rich and he was not yet famous, but he was on the road to a kind of prosperity, as Elmyr had seen at first glance; although Elmyr knew nothing about the origins of Fernand's good fortune. He still wasn't absolutely certain about the Modigliani drawings Pfannstiel had shown him earlier that summer in Hamburg, whether he or Fernand had sold them two years ago in California or what, and when he questioned him now Fernand's eyebrows shot up in puzzlement; he shrugged broadly and said: *"Mon cher,* that was so long ago! If *you* don't remember, how should I?"

Upon the occasion of this, their second meeting in Paris, Fernand wore a new dark suit with what appeared to be a red silk lining, had a two-year-old Cadillac and a pleasant though not ostentatious apartment on the rue de la Pompe which he shared with Réal. Réal, now twenty-three years old, had taken on the duties of junior partner and confidential secretary as well. He looked, Elmyr thought, just a little pale and a little unhappy.

"How are things between you?" Elmyr asked when they were alone for a minute.

"The same," Réal said, sighing.

Fernand asked of course where Elmyr was living and what he had been doing in the year since they had last met near the Gare

St. Lazare. Elmyr had made more than twenty watercolors of his own when he was in Ibiza and Hydra, and he showed his friends the portfolio.

"Oh, they're beautiful!" Fernand exclaimed. He turned to Réal. "Don't you think we can sell them easily to our customers?" Without waiting for an answer he asked Elmyr: "How much do you ask for them?"

"Well, I, ah, I don't really know—usually about fifty dollars each——"

"I'll buy them all," Fernand said, with great enthusiasm, as if the price were dirt cheap. "Cash."

He did. "And I have to admit it," Elmyr said later, recalling the incident which was to precipitate one of the major turning points of his life—"I was a bit impressed."

What impressed him, of course, was the gesture of friendship and forgiveness as well as the casual affluence that apparently lay behind the purchase. In some obscure way he felt he had treated Fernand shabbily by running out on him after their return to Europe in 1959. Now, once again, the magic of Fernand's flamboyant personality was at work, exactly as Fernand intended. Throughout his life Elmyr had steadfastly refused to accept the fact that certain people, like Fernand Legros, instantly recognized him as a "mark," a willing victim to be flattered, used, and then discarded when the risk overwhelmed the potential profit. To have accepted this would have been a blow to Elmyr's ego too cruel to suffer; he wanted to be flattered, fawned upon, loved—even by Fernand.

They saw each other several times in the next few weeks, during which period Elmyr brought some Modigliani drawings to the representative of Mlle. Modigliani, the painter's daughter, secured an affidavit that they were genuine and then sold them to a prominent art dealer on the Avenue Matignon. For a reason which is not clear, but most probably just to impress his old friends and because he couldn't resist puffing up his image in a situation where he saw no danger as a result, he told Réal about the sale. Fernand came immediately to see Elmyr in his hotel. "It's so dangerous for you to sell your own work, *mon cher*," he explained, his face graven with a deep frown. "Why do you take such foolish risks?"

"Well . . ." Elmyr hesitated.

Fernand looked serious, genuinely concerned. "You are a *maître* now," he went on. "A master. You shouldn't expose yourself that way. Réal and I are getting to be known in the art world; people are starting to give us very fine things on consignment. It was bad of you to run away from us," he chided—while Elmyr blushed —"but we forgive you, and now we can start all over again. We'll take all the risk, and you can live quietly on this little island you talk about."

He referred to Ibiza, for by then Elmyr had made up his mind to return to his dream island off the coast of Spain. Hydra, near Athens, had been the alternative, but when he was there Elmyr had discovered there was no airport and in bad weather the boats didn't run. In his profession, with or without partners, he needed more mobility.

Fernand's offer, of course, was no surprise to him; he had anticipated it and been tempted by the possibilities ever since their second chance meeting. He wanted badly to settle down, to build his nest, and he was not displeased with the idea of someone else taking the risks of selling. He would never again have to face humiliation at the hands of people like Frank Perls, Faulkner and Ouriel. That would be Fernand's problem now. And Fernand seemed so calm, so reasonable, so suddenly chic, completely unlike the wild man Elmyr had glimpsed in Hollywood when Réal had failed to announce that he was stopping off on the way home to go to the movies. He's grown up, Elmyr thought. He's found a sense of responsibility, he understands my needs. It never occurred to Elmyr that Fernand was playing a rôle; he wanted to believe, so he believed.

"You'll have security," Fernand explained smoothly. "That's the main thing. We'll send you a few hundred dollars every month. You'll have a regular income, like clipping coupons off a General Motors bond. And every time we make an important sale you'll have a share in it, after expenses. You'll live like Robinson Crusoe in your little Mediterranean island paradise. We'll take all the risk. I think we'll start with a series of Dufy watercolors."

"I've never done any Dufy," Elmyr protested. "I don't know—"

"Well, if you have a chance now, try something. You have the touch, the hand of a master. Study him a bit. I *know* you can do it."

Elmyr browsed through galleries and museums and bought some Dufy portfolios at secondhand bookstores. Still, he hung back; he painted nothing while he was in Paris. Fernand already knew that whatever Elmyr did he could undoubtedly sell, since he had foisted off the entire contents of the Winslow trunk with no trouble whatsoever. But he tried not to press too much. "I was the goose that would eventually lay all the golden eggs," Elmyr realized later, "and he didn't want to kill it."

One day Fernand said: "After the Dufy series I think we should try a few small oils by Matisse and Derain—"

By then Elmyr was hooked. He cautioned that oils had to dry for a long time, at least two years, before they could be sold, and Fernand said: "Exactly. That's a very good point. So if we have to wait that long, perhaps you'd better get started right away." In the meantime, while the paintings were technically wet, he would hang them on the walls of his apartment in Paris. He explained to Elmyr that if he had an important painting hanging on the wall, "all the buyers get excited—I wish you could hear it, they twitter like birds in the springtime—and sometimes I'm able to sell something unimportant because they're so impressed. They're hoping that if they buy a little watercolor from me today, I'll break down and sell them the big oil tomorrow."

He had also bought a good copy of a Toulouse-Lautrec oil, a woman sitting at a table confronting a glass of absinthe, her hair hanging bedraggled in her face, which he suggested that Elmyr touch up for him to metamorphose into an original rather than a copy. But he particularly wanted the Matisse oils. Gradually, in discussion, they became "large" Matisse instead of "small"— which made Elmyr turn a little pale. He warned Fernand that his Matisse shouldn't be sold as long as Mme. Duthuit was alive; her expertise would be necessary, and since the day Joseph Faulkner of the Main Street Galleries had contacted her she was all too aware of Elmyr's existence and his forging style. Fernand solemnly promised.

The final financial arrangement was that Fernand and Réal would pay Elmyr, through his Swiss bank, a "salary" of about $400 a month, which would be more than enough for him to live comfortably on Ibiza. They would pay his expenses: canvases, colors and shipping, and he would also receive "bonuses" from time to time whenever a major sale was made. Fernand had been doling out pocket money thus far in Paris. Now he provided a cash advance of $500 and saw Elmyr off on the plane to Madrid.

"It all happened so quickly," Elmyr later recalled. "I felt like Faust must have felt after he'd sold his soul to the Devil. A little bewildered, a little frightened. At the same time I breathed a sigh of relief, because I thought: *At last, my worries are over.* I didn't realize they were just beginning."

12.

in which *le maître* finds a home in Ibiza, Réal visits Kees van Dongen, and Fernand becomes a millionaire.

MATISSE BY ELMYR

t was January 1962 when Elmyr returned to his first house on Ibiza, and there, on his "Robinson Crusoe island," he decided that he was content and he would stay. The last thirty years seemed to have been an endless succession of furnished apartments and hotel rooms; the little Villa Platero was the first home he'd had since he was a youth in Budapest. He had someone to share it with him, which made life all the more sweet. He had met a young man on the mainland of Spain, a Canadian who was traveling through Europe for the first time; he had been attracted to him, had found him pleasant and undemanding and had invited him to stay. The relationship was to last for nearly two years and give to Elmyr's daily life an emotional stability it had lacked since he had lived in Florida with Jimmy Damion.

He liked the Ibizencos, too, a friendly and dignified island people, and he found the resident foreign colony amusing, easygoing and nicely permissive. You couldn't beat your children, starve your dog or abuse your mate too fiercely in public; but beyond that, moral censure was not encouraged. You did as you pleased and you paid the price privately.

"It was my kind of place. People seemed to live on terribly small incomes in those days," Elmyr said, casting his eye back on a happy time in his eventful life. "Anyone who had $200 a month was considered rich. I became friendly with some of the up-and-coming young artists like Edith Sommer, Clifford Smith and David Walsh. They had great talent, I had a little more money at my disposal than they did—I wanted to help them, so I bought their work. That's why I called myself an art collector. I myself, when I first arrived, kept working on my own paintings. I still had hopes that one day I would be a success. I made a series of watercolors of the port and some views of the Old City. But as I got more and more involved with Fernand and Réal, I more and more hid the fact that I was an artist. They were furious when I told them I'd spoken to Ivan Spence, the Englishman who ran the local art gallery, about having a show of my own. Finally, I stopped doing my own work altogether."

For the first half year or so the $400 arrived regularly each month, and once Fernand sent him a bonus check for $1200. In return Elmyr did the Dufys and some Derain watercolors, rolled them in a cardboard tube and sent them to Paris by registered airmail. He marked the tubes PRINTED MATTER: POSTERS, and all arrived safely.

"To protect myself from any possible future trouble," Elmyr claims, "I decided not to do any of the work in Ibiza—or for that matter, Spain—so I used to take quick trips to Tangier or Estoril, in Portugal. I took a large room at the old Estoril Palace Hotel and I worked there. People on Ibiza thought I was either terribly restless or a compulsive traveler. But all the time I was off the island I was painting."

The oils were superficially dry by June and Réal flew down to Spain to pick them up. "I knew from the beginning," Elmyr later confessed, "that he was a full partner. They had their fights and personal jealousies, but they were in the business together. Réal rapidly was learning and already then, in 1962, I had the impression that very quickly he's going to know much more than Fernand about art and the art business."

By the time they had left for Europe, in fact, Réal had been tutored to the point where he knew the whole operation. Completely under Fernand's influence and spell, deeply involved with him emotionally, he had lost whatever scruples and fears he might have been burdened with as a young boy fresh out of provincial Canada. At first, in the States, it had been a lark for him. Later it became a way of life. Like so many pupils who begin young and have an abundance of energy and natural talent, he was eventually to surpass his master.

"When they got to Europe," Elmyr recalled, "Fernand took him down to his parents' house near Cannes and put him in school there, but it didn't last long and to this day Réal can't write either a proper French or English. Réal was very unhappy at the time, because he was so much in love with Fernand and he knew that Fernand constantly chased after other boys, and yet demanded that he be absolutely 100 per cent faithful. He *was* faithful, too— then. He matured somehow into a clever young man with expensive tastes, but as the years passed I felt more and more sorry for him. Everything he knew in life since the age of eighteen he'd learned from Fernand, in bed and out. It was a strange education. The relationship was in some ways like Pygmalion and Galatea—in other ways, as it turned out, like Dr. Frankenstein and his monster."

The two dealers in Paris continued to supply Elmyr with the best Lefranc colors, as well as old canvases that they picked up in the Flea Market. These had to be from the correct decade, thinly painted, and still mounted on the original stretcher. They left it to Elmyr to clean them. He would soak the canvas with an alkali solution, leave it for half a day, then gently scrape off the paint with a palette knife. Great care had to be taken not to destroy the original priming or cut into the canvas itself. This happened once: the knife slipped, the canvas tore and had to be written off as a total loss. If all the paint wasn't removed the first time, the process had to be repeated. "Not a big job," Elmyr explained, "but a dirty one. And very boring."

Réal brought him art books and color transparencies, greatly enlarged, of certain paintings that they thought might serve as "models." He also showed Elmyr a special restorer's varnish which copyists often used to induce a surface that has a peculiar golden glow, sometimes called a "Rembrandt patina." The varnish made the surface dry more quickly and produced a natural *craquelure,* the tiny veined cracks that appear in oils with old age. Réal, who was learning both sides of the business all the time and assuming more and more of the responsibility of liaison between Fernand and Elmyr, did the spray job himself. "He liked that sort of thing," Elmyr said. "He used to put some of the signatures on the Vlamincks, too, though not very well."

The special photographic enlargements gave Elmyr a good chance to study brushwork and technique. "I hadn't been in French museums for so many years that I was out of touch with the originals. What you see in a second-rate reproduction in a book is just useless. If you don't examine the brushwork and the building up of the color, the subtleties, in a way you miss the whole idea of the painting. I learned new things all the time. There are certain characteristics of brush strokes peculiar to every painter. For example, I noticed that Dufy created thickness through the addition of white paint. I experimented with various different whites and matched them up against the original Dufys, and that way I eventually found out that it was zinc white he used. So I did use it, too. In copying oil paintings you must observe texture and thickness very carefully. Also, you must be aware that styles and techniques changed for each artist with time—they were always experimenting with new or old methods. I made my basic notes in the margins of my books in Hungarian, so that if anyone by chance picked up the book, unless they were Hungarian they wouldn't have the faintest idea what I'd written. There weren't too many Hungarians in Ibiza. It was a useful language to know.

"So I painted, and my friends in Paris sold. I had no idea what they were doing up in Paris or how they were doing it. If they sold a drawing or a painting, I had no way of checking on it. I thought, naturally, that they would start slowly, that it would take a while to build a reputation for themselves and find a good clientele. In that way, I underestimated Fernand's ability."

Whatever Elmyr had taught him in America about selling, Fernand had now added some refinements to the business that smacked of his own brand of genius. He soon moved from the rue de la Pompe to a small but more elegant apartment in the Avenue de Suffren. The first batch of Dufys were sold for an average of $8000 each, and soon the walls in the Avenue de Suffren were covered as well with Derains, Vlamincks and three large Matisse oils. He also had a real Vlaminck and a fine genuine Renoir oil. Thanks to the Winslow trunk, Fernand was already known in New York and Paris as a *courtier,* a private art dealer, and now that he was once again in active business with Elmyr he swiftly became, in that stylish world of art buyers and dealers, mildly famous—or infamous—as both a personality and a get-rich-quick young businessman.

Today most reputable art dealers admit to having been approached by him. The majority say: "Legros? Yes, he's one of the few people I've ever thrown out of my gallery." Such an astonishing number of dealers claim to have thrown Fernand out of their galleries that one wonders to whom he ever sold. Michel Strauss of Sotheby's, London's great auction house, met him for the first time in the summer of 1963. Legros came to Sotheby's with a pair of

Maurice de Vlaminck:
Scène de neige.
An oil painted by
Elmyr in 1963.

Dufy watercolors. "I didn't like them," says Strauss—which is a dealer's prudent way of intimating that the work is wrongly attributed or an outright fake—"and Legros very nearly had a fit in my office. He got furious. I wouldn't say I threw him out, but he was most definitely shown the door." The two Dufys then were sold at auction elsewhere in London.

Visitors to the Avenue de Suffren were impressed when they saw Fernand's collection; obviously he was a dealer of some stature. As a result they gave him paintings on consignment. A good fake hanging next to a genuine painting rarely suffers by the comparison—on the contrary, it gains in stature by the company it keeps. With time, when enough people have seen it and fixed it in their memories, it tends to assume the authority of its more venerable partners. Even then, as early as the fall of 1962, Fernand was offered $75,000 for one of the Matisse oils—which unfortunately couldn't be sold without an expertise from Mme. Duthuit, the painter's daughter.

"If I could find someone to bring that woman a box of chocolates filled with arsenic," he said wistfully to Elmyr, "that would be the day I'd become a millionaire."

But unknown to Elmyr that day had already arrived, and without the aid of arsenic. The operation had expanded and succeeded in a way that he had never dreamed possible.

Throughout 1962, their first full year of operation, Fernand and Réal had confined their selling activities to Paris, New York, Chicago, Switzerland and the South of France, but in the next four years they traveled practically every place a major art market—or for that matter, a well-known, wealthy and potential buyer—existed. In 1963 alone they hit Rio de Janeiro, Buenos Aires, Capetown, Johannesburg and Tokyo. Between these jaunts they never failed to stop off for a week or two in New York, where Fernand took a suite at the Hotel Delmonico and paid his customary visits to the Parke-Bernet Galleries and the better art dealers on 57th Street and upper Madison Avenue. He put drawings and paintings up for auction at Parke-Bernet in his own name, Réal's and later in the name of a gallery they controlled in Paris. Whenever it was possible, Fernand and Réal appeared at the auction itself; they would make careful note of who bought their paintings, and then later approach the buyer privately to offer him or her something more of the same at a reduced price. By 1963 Réal had also met and been befriended by a couple named Rose and Edwin Bachmann, private art dealers on Manhattan's East Side, who introduced him and Fernand to art collectors of the metropolitan area. The same pair, a few years later, were also to offer their assistance and connections to David Stein, the young forger who afterward pleaded guilty to six of ninety-seven counts of counterfeiting (Chagall, Picasso and Matisse) and grand larceny. Besides the Bachmanns, Fernand also found a book in New York which was of great help to him: a thick volume, privately printed and distributed among international art dealers, listing every American art collector's name, special tastes, address (summer and winter) and private telephone. With this, he rarely made the mistake of trying to sell a Degas to a man who collected Mondrian or cubistic Picasso.

From the very beginning, since he was in the business of selling high-priced goods, Fernand's technique relied on the concept of the expertise—a proof of one sort or another that what he was offering for sale was the genuine article. The French government recognizes certain individuals as experts *auprès du tribunal,* which means they have the legal right, gained by years of study and superior knowledge, or their relationship to the deceased artist, to provide for a specific work a certificate of authenticity. In return for this they receive a small fee. Fernand, who appears to have been gifted with a nose for the weakness in systems as well as people, went right to the heart of this one. He simply raised the fee. He said later to a friend: "I wasn't trying to bribe anyone. I just dropped a thousand dollars on the table. If the man didn't pick it up, I dropped a second thousand dollars. I found that people preferred round numbers."

He received expertises without any trouble from Mmes. Vlaminck, Marquet, Dufy and Alice Derain, and Mlle. Jeanne Modigliani. Some of the popular experts like André Pacitti, Maurice Malingue and Paul Epstein were beyond corruption, but here Fernand counted on the quality of the work itself; and they gave their expertises usually without undue hesitation. Pacitti, for one, was so charmed by Fernand and so admiring of his art collection that he provided his signature time and again on the Dufy watercolors. He was completely convinced they were genuine.

After a while the story was told that he refused to give his expertise to two genuine Dufy paintings. He had become so used to seeing Elmyr's "hand" that it was "right" for him, and the hand of poor dead Dufy looked suspect.

When Elmyr heard this tale, he glowed. "From a man as knowledgeable as Pacitti," he said, "that's a very nice tribute."

Growing even bolder with time, Fernand sent Réal to the South of France to visit Kees van Dongen, one of the few famous Fauve painters still alive. The old Dutchman, a naturalized French citizen since 1929, lived quietly with his wife in the hills near Monte Carlo. Réal brought him an Elmyr oil portrait of a beautiful woman with sculptured lips and a necklace of blue pearls; it was simply another version of a 1908 van Dongen called *Woman with Hat*. Van Dongen, nearing the age of ninety, had earned a widespread reputation in his youth as a sensualist and ladies' man. He studied the portrait carefully, then smiled wistfully with remembrance of things past. Yes, he said, of course it was his. He had a particularly vivid memory of the model, and he even recounted to Réal how many times he'd had to interrupt his painting to make love to her.

"You know," he mused, "she must have posed for me a dozen times, and I haven't the faintest idea where half the paintings are." Then, on the back of a photographic reproduction, underneath where Réal had typed: *Le tableau reproduit ci-contre mesurant 62 × 52, est une oeuvre de moi, peinte vers 1907–1908,* van Dongen scrawled his shaky signature. Réal dashed back to Paris with the news. It looked as if the partners had struck gold in Monte Carlo. Fernand excitedly snatched up the telephone to Elmyr and cried: "Do more!"

"You push me too hard," Elmyr complained, the next time they met. "You get here on Monday, you tell me you're leaving Thursday evening and you need five Vlamincks, three van Dongens, two Bonnards, and they *must* be ready. You're out of your minds."

Later, whenever he needed cash in a hurry or the painting he was trying to sell might be of questionable authenticity, Fernand dispensed with the bother of a genuine expertise. It was just as easy, he decided, to provide his own. He had copper plates made by a young Japanese engraver that perfectly reproduced the official stamps (*Expert auprès des Douanes Françaises*) used by Pacitti, Epstein, Malingue and the late M. André Schoeller. Réal himself, after a few tries, learned to reproduce the shaky van Dongen signature.

Another element in the "pedigree" of the painting was a certificate from a prior owner, usually one of several fairly well-known collectors who might have fallen on hard times and were among Fernand's coterie of friends in Paris. Again it was cash on the table, and for $2000 Fernand would receive a bill of sale for ten times that amount. The next step was to get the expertise. Then, if it was a major work and destined to bring a major price—say, $50,000—Fernand would put it up for auction at one of the better establishments, like Hôtel Drouot in Paris or Parke-Bernet in New York. From 1962 through the end of 1965 some forty-five paintings belonging to Fernand were sold at Parke-Bernet. Since auction house principles forbid disclosing the name of the consignor or seller, there was no room for suspicion or even wariness on the part of the prospective buyers. They trusted Parke-Bernet's excellent reputation. All but a few of the forty-five paintings were of course fake. If the particular work couldn't be knocked down at auction for the desired price, Fernand or Réal would buy it back for themselves and forfeit the 10 per cent commission. That 10 per cent they considered a cheap price to pay for the illustration and entry in the Parke-Bernet catalog and the subsequent official record of sale.

Armed thus, with documents stuffed in all their pockets and bulging out of their expensive Italian pigskin brief cases, Fernand and Réal had little trouble selling their wares. The argument was never one of authenticity, merely of price. But to insure themselves against any unforeseen resistance, and to provide a testimonial which not only appeared unimpeachable but was also so classy that it hiked the price to its limit, they hit on a scheme which for its

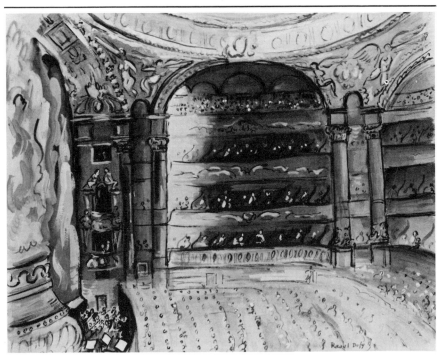

Raoul Dufy:
This gouache was
painted by Elmyr
in 1962
and was accompanied by
a forged
André Pacitti expertise.
Elmyr also received
a number of authentic
Pacitti expertises for
other fake paintings.

La gouache reproduite au verso, - mesurant:
haut.,0m50; larg., 0m65,- signée en bas à droite ,
est une oeuvre authentique du peintre Raoul Dufy.

A Paris, le 12 Juin 1962

André Pacitti

bravado, ingenuity and simplicity of thinking should have earned them some sort of rascality prize.

Like all great swindling gimmicks, it was obvious—once you thought of it. It traded on the fact that large color reproductions in many fine art books and portfolios, so that they can be removed and individually framed by the buyer, are often only lightly glued to the center of the page. Fernand and Réal searched the Paris bookstores for rare and out-of-print books with such detachable reproductions, sometimes called tip-ins. If, for example, they found two different books—a 1940 Modigliani portfolio and a 1934 volume titled *Nudes by French Masters*—both of which offered tip-ins of one particular Modigliani painting, they were in business.

Under the reproduction it might say: "Modigliani, Reclining Nude, 1918 oil on canvas, 92 × 118, signed lower left corner, Private Collection, Paris." Fernand would then place his order with Elmyr for "one Modigliani reclining nude, 1918 oil on canvas, 92 × 118, signed lower left corner." After the new painting was dry and delivered, Fernand had it photographed and the color transparency enlarged and printed on the same paper stock as the tip-ins in the genuine portfolio. He then removed the lightly glued genuine reproduction and inserted the fake, gluing it and all the other reproductions in the book firmly to the page.

What buyer could resist? Not only did the painting possess a pedigree, but also a certificate of fame that could be left out on one's living-room coffee table for all one's friends to see. What buyer could check? Even in New York, much less Houston or Johannesburg, out-of-print French art books from the thirties were almost impossible to come by. It was such a brilliantly conceived system that if Fernand had enough copies of a specific portfolio to leave with his customers, he could dispose of the same painting—for example, half a dozen versions of the Modigliani reclining nude—to half a dozen scattered collections. In this way he sold at least four Dufy views of *The Reception at Elysée Palace;* one went to Meadows in Dallas, one to Chicago, one to Atlanta, and one to São Paulo, Brazil.

During their 1963 trip to Japan, he and Réal added yet another gimmick to their swindler's kit—a set of false customs stamps. A valuable painting, which might be considered a national treasure, when it leaves France needs a "permit to travel." The previous year Fernand had run afoul of the Swiss authorities by taking several fake Vlaminck gouaches out of the country on a one-way three-month permit. When the Swiss customs demanded the return of the paintings, Fernand realized he had fouled up his bookkeeping and sold them elsewhere. This, he quickly learned from his lawyer in Geneva, meant not only the elimination of the lucrative Swiss market, but the possibility of prison. In a slight panic he called Elmyr and told him to get busy and quickly paint some Vlamincks similar to the missing ones. Elmyr did so, and these new fakes soon replaced the old fakes, and everything was okay in Switzerland again.

To avoid a repetition of the incident, Fernand found a man in Tokyo who made him a complete set of Swiss and French customs stamps. In later years Réal carried them with him from country to country in his suitcase, wrapped in brown paper and Scotch-taped together like an ordinary parcel. He showed them once to Elmyr, who said, amazed: "How can you take such a risk? Suppose they open it at customs somewhere?"

"They once did," Réal said, laughing. "In South Africa. And I told them, 'I'm taking these stamps to my nephew. He collects stamps.'"

"He has the blood of a fish," is Elmyr's grave comment today.

In Tokyo, in 1963 and 1964, Fernand found customers in dealers and private collectors, and also sold to the National Museum of Western Art a large Derain oil, a Dufy gouache and a Modigliani drawing. By coincidence, André Malraux, the French Minister of Culture, happened to be in Japan at that time, and Dr. Hidaya Sasati, the curator of the museum, asked Malraux to have a look at the paintings before the deal was consummated. Malraux obliged. When he heard the prices he gratuitously offered his opinion that they were quite reasonable for work of such high quality. Later, in 1967, before an inquiry of the Japanese Diet, the Minister of Culture quoted his French counterpart as having said, back in 1963, that he was "really surprised how these paintings ever got out of France."

Fernand and Réal, in any case, got out of Japan with over $250,000. They also took with them a six-inch portable Japanese television set which they presented to Elmyr as a gift. That was his "bonus."

13.

in which
Fernand tries to
burn up Réal's
Alfa Romeo,
homage is given
to Raoul Dufy,
and Elmyr
unwillingly
builds a palace.

DERAIN BY ELMYR

ernand's personal habits since returning to Europe and striking it rich had undergone a significant change. He had begun to live on a grand scale, to spend money like the proverbial drunken sailor on shore leave. He rebuilt his parents' house in a small town near Cannes in the South of France, he bought jewelry and a mink coat for his mother, and at home, in Paris, he cultivated and finally established a small male harem. An obsessive homosexual, he demanded at all times to be surrounded by obsequious boys and good-looking young men. He paid handsomely for their favors—not with outright cash, but with gifts and luxury maintenance, buying them clothes and cars and taking them with him on trips to Spain and South America. All he asked in return was constant adoration and absolute fidelity. The great sufferer in the arrangement was Réal, who loved him and had to participate. But if Réal ever looked at another boy, or a girl, Fernand would fly into a rage.

"The things that man did," said Elmyr, "would curl your hair. He used to cruise around schools. Once, in Switzerland, he was accused by the Lycée Jacard of trying to importune two boys, and he was brought before the police. There was one little boy in his harem later on, I don't think he was more than twelve years old."

"Underneath that ooze of charm," Elmyr later tried to explain, "Fernand was a hysterical personality—a paranoiac. Violent, vindictive and insanely jealous. A kind of madman. He was never put in jail or in an asylum because the minute he got in trouble or damaged some property he reached for his wallet—where he never carried less than several thousand dollars in cash—and started paying out right and left, to hotels, waiters, police, shopkeepers, witnesses, everybody and anybody. He spent a small fortune to stay out of trouble."

Whatever Fernand's problem may have been from the point of view of a psychopathologist more qualified than Elmyr, it manifested itself as intense jealousy and intense distrust, and the object of both these tendencies was always his closest friend and partner, Réal. Once aroused, the slim, balding, debonair art dealer invariably lost his cool, and then violence was *de rigueur*. If they were talking business in the bar of the Plaza Hotel and Réal happened to glance too lingeringly at a pretty girl sitting nearby, with or without a client present Fernand would either flounce off from the table or pick up his whisky glass and throw the contents in Réal's face. If he chose to leave, the scene would follow later in their suite, where accusations were followed by tantrums, and tantrums by action, with mirrors and glass tabletops the favorite objects for Fernand's flying feet.

Any description of the fights during these years reads like the shooting script for a slapstick black comedy, a cocktail composed of the Keystone Cops, Grand Guignol, a Tom and Jerry animated cartoon and Fellini's *La Dolce Vita*. On another level it can be interpreted as the tragedy—or pathetic history—of two young homosexuals swimming for all they were worth against the mainstream of their environment, driven to excess and absurdity (in the existentialist sense) for lack of an emotional anchorage, living a bizarre professional life that perfectly matched their private tastes and peculiarities. Although the more liberal morality of the mid-twentieth century allowed them to flaunt convention and ward off isolation by running in a pack, they were still essentially outsiders in both their sexual and their public lives. Privately they lived from day to day, affair to affair, never knowing when the axe of the outraged bourgeois community might fall on their heads; so it was not difficult, as Jean Genet has pointed out in the literature of the criminal homosexual, to live a professional life that involved the same risks. Fernand's flamboyance—his madness, as Elmyr believed—can easily be seen as an unconscious protest against a world that had always hemmed him in on all sides, an attitude of "I don't give a damn because there's no hope for me anyway."

The first major freakout had taken place in California in 1959, when Réal, without bothering to announce his plans in advance, had stopped off on the way home to Fernand and gone to the movies. Elmyr had witnessed that incident, and later heard graphic descriptions from both participants of a dozen more.

"They were in New York once," Elmyr recounted, "around the summer of 1962, in the Adams Hotel on upper Fifth Avenue. Fernand went up to Boston on business, to sell something, but he hired a private detective to follow Réal while he was gone. Réal realized he was being followed so he deliberately spent the night at another hotel, I think the Pierre. When Fernand got back from Boston he was enraged. They had a terrible fight. They were in the suite at the Adams on the twentieth floor. Fernand probably wanted to throw Réal through the open window, but he settled instead for Réal's clothes. Everything he could grab he flung out of the window —every shirt, every tie, every single handkerchief. On Fifth Avenue people were holding out their arms and waiting for all those Cardin shirts and Sulka ties to come floating down in the middle of the day. Réal rushed down in the elevator. But nothing was left in the street, naturally, except maybe a pair of socks with holes in the toes.

"Once I met Réal in Lisbon—I'd gone to Estoril to work, and my car, the new Mustang they'd bought for me as a gift, was just arriving in Lisbon from New York. Fernand began telephoning from Paris, but Réal wasn't in the hotel room. It was two o'clock in the morning—'Where is he?' Fernand shrieked. There was never anything of a sexual nature between myself and Réal, so Fernand expected me to be a kind of chaperon for him. I said, 'Don't scream at me,' and I hung up. I had some experience with this situation before, so I told the hotel operator, 'No more calls.'

"So three days later, we had driven to Valencia, when who appears at our hotel around midnight—Fernand Legros. How he tracked us down, I don't know. He attacked Réal in the street outside the hotel, screaming like a lunatic, calling him a dirty little peasant, kicked him in the face like a dancer and then chased after him through the alleys and boulevards of Valencia. He jumped on my Mustang, too, and tried to destroy it. He tore off the antenna. I left. The whole disaster ended in the hotel, and Fernand wound up paying about $500 in damages.

"There was another famous fight. Réal had a brand-new cream-colored Alfa Romeo convertible which he adored, and they were driving along the Champs Élysées and started to argue about something. Fernand smoked—he was a chain smoker, and Réal never smoked—and in the midst of the argument he put out a cigarette beneath his shoe on the carpet. Réal said 'Stop that!' and then Fernand started burning the seats, deliberately punching holes in the red-leather upholstery, and Réal screamed at him to stop, and Fernand kept on trying to burn up the Alfa Romeo. Réal started to hit him—I guess it was in light traffic. And they got so mad at each other that suddenly Réal pulled up at the Rond Point next to the *gendarme* and said: 'Officer, this man sitting next to me has made me not only an improper proposition, but he was trying to molest me sexually in my car.' They were both taken into the police station, and a few hours later they apparently kissed and made up and Réal finally dropped the charges.''

It often puzzled Elmyr why Réal still stayed with Fernand under such circumstances, and the only satisfactory answer he could give himself was that Fernand had some kind of extraordinary magnetic power—which was something Elymr could readily understand in the light of his own experiences in Florida and Paris. If he, a grown man in his fifties, could be so easily swayed and dominated, what chance was there for a young man of twenty-three who was emotionally involved as well? Fernand's mood could change from minute to minute; he might try to incinerate Réal's car in the morning, and then in the afternoon declare his undying love and present him with a pair of diamond cufflinks from Cartier. And of course they were making a small fortune together, which was something Réal could not entirely ignore. No matter how they bit and scratched privately, business was still business; and its machinations bound them together as securely as the emotional tie—for a while.

Until recently Elmyr had only a limited understanding of their business practices and the resultant fortune. In 1963 all he could find out about the junket to Japan was that they had gone, as Fernand said, "to establish connections for the future." Later Fernand admitted to Elmyr that they had sold a few watercolors cheaply, and that "the Japanese were very slow payers. Very cunning. Very cautious." But that year, for $350,000, Fernand bought a floor-through apartment on the Avenue Henri-Martin in Paris. The previous owner had been King Hassan of Morocco. It was furnished after the Tokyo trip at a reported cost of $160,000, which included gold faucets in the three bathrooms. Fernand lived there with his so-called adopted son, a boy named Patrick Bucque (whose mother had been the *femme de ménage* on the Avenue de Suffren), Réal, and various intermittent guests such as a trio of brothers from New York, the Urbach boys, one of whom was to play a key role in the 1967 *débâcle* in Ibiza. There were rarely less than four cars haphazardly and illegally parked on the pavement outside the front door: Fernand's red Cadillac, Réal's Alfa Romeo and usually a pair of matched Corvettes for the use of the other current residents.

Elmyr knew of the apartment's existence but didn't see it until the summer of 1965, when he made a brief and unexpected visit to Paris. He was shocked. All the walls were covered with red brocade or red velvet and inlaid with strips of gilded baguettes; there were glittering crystal chandeliers, gold-leafed ceilings and giant silver candelabra on an immense Italian marble dining-room table. Amid this carnival of opulence hung the art collection, looking, thought Elmyr, rather pale in comparison.

He tried to explain to Fernand that the great art dealers showed paintings against neutral velvet backgrounds in the most somber of rooms.

"This is all so—so *nouveau riche,* my dear."

"So are my customers," said Fernand, vastly amused by Elmyr's disapproving attitude.

But, in essence, Fernand was telling the truth. He was a new breed of art dealer in a new kind of art market that had begun to take shape in the early 1950s, gained momentum in the latter part of the decade and by the early 1960s had reached gigantic proportions. Before the war great art was bought primarily by knowledgeable collectors and a few very rich people whose buying was done for them by a comparative handful of knowledgeable and established dealers. With the postwar economic boom, there were more people with money than ever before. What Texas was in 1949, the whole Western world had become by 1959. At first it was enough to own two Cadillacs and travel to Europe every summer, but these status symbols paled, and the new symbol was a Matisse or a Picasso on the living-room wall. If you had arrived, you owned a fine painting. If you had *really* arrived, you had a modest but valuable collection of Impressionists. "You *can* afford it," was

Fernand's spiel to oil company executives and the wives of bank vice-presidents. "And look! So-and-so bought a Chagall from me in 1955 for $5000. Today it's worth $30,000. It's not only a beautiful painting, it's a fantastic investment. How can you lose?"

With that kind of eager and ever-growing clientele, scattered throughout the United States, Europe, South Africa and the Far East, Fernand was constantly on the move—he flew back and forth across the Atlantic at least half a dozen times a year, to ferret out new buyers and pick up new paintings to sell to them. It should come as no surprise that the whereabouts of the great majority of the paintings is still unknown; they hang on the walls of living rooms and board rooms from Los Angeles to Johannesburg, and there are few brave men today who will say "I bought my collection from Fernand Legros."

Elmyr had never kept records of any sort, and had habitually lost track of his work. Who the new customers were, specifically, no one bothered to tell him. Fernand explained: "The less you know, the safer you are. It's true that you don't make as much money as we do, but you live quietly on Ibiza and no one is ever bugging you. You'll never have any trouble. We do all the running around, we have to keep up a big front, we have terrible expenses, and we take all the risk."

It was a convincing spiel, but it didn't pay Elmyr's bills. In the first year or two when he needed money badly he raced up to Paris twice to pound on Fernand's door. The first summer he arrived without sending a telegram to put his partners on their guard.

"I went by train because it was cheaper, and walked in on them unexpectedly, early in the morning. Réal let me in and Fernand was in bed with somebody who scampered quickly out and into the bathroom. (I just stared. At first sight I thought it was maybe a white puppy dog, but then I looked twice and I realized it was a pale little boy—a *child*. He looked maybe seven or eight years old. I was horrified, I couldn't believe my eyes! But we had lunch together afterwards and he turned out to be older, just small for his age.) I made a big scene then about money and Fernand said, 'Oh, we sent it . . . wrong address . . . came back'—the usual bullshit story. 'Then we forgot about it.' I said, 'You *forgot* about it? I sent you fifteen telegrams!' He produced a few hundred dollars in cash right away and said, rubbing his hands together, 'Did you bring us something?'

"They didn't want me to stay in Paris, and later I found out why—because Réal had just got as a gift the new Alfa Romeo convertible, cream-colored with red-leather seats, a special design. They didn't want me to see they'd made so much money so they pushed me out in two days. My Dufys had been sold for as much as $11,000—but I only learned that later. I found out he paid nearly $8000 for Réal's car and got himself a big Renault limousine and bought a mink coat for his mother, that dragon."

To supplement his income that first year Elmyr went off on several selling trips of his own to Germany and Austria. He sold a batch of drawings and lithographs each time, until he had picked up a quick few thousand dollars, then returned to Ibiza. When autumn arrived, in a fit of pique that Réal was tooling round in the Alfa Romeo while he, Elmyr, was still driving a miserable little Fiat, he told them what he had been doing. They were most upset.

"*Mon cher!* You'll get into terrible trouble," Fernand explained, tapping his fingers nervously on the table.

"Then send me my money on time," Elmyr retorted.

He understood, of course, that what upset them most was their realization that if he could sell successfully on his own he might break up the partnership. That was when they brought him the Mustang and suggested building the house, La Falaise. During the first six months of the construction work a joint account in the names of Fernand, Réal and Elmyr was opened at the Credito Balear bank in Ibiza to pay for the labor and materials. Fernand transferred dollars from New York and Elmyr signed the peseta checks. "But they suddenly took it out of my hands," he said, "because I used some of that money for my living expenses. Not much, but a little. It annoyed them. From then on their lawyer in Ibiza paid the bills."

"We had to keep him poor," Réal explained later, "or he'd have quit. He needed incentive. Whenever he had money he didn't see why he should work, so we decided rather than give him large sums of cash we'd bring him gifts—like the portable TV set, or a red sports car. That sort of thing always made him happy. He was like a child.''

To Elmyr's regret, his companion in the Villa Platero had long since returned to his home in Canada, and Elmyr was living alone and not liking it. Ibiza, however, was a popular stopping-off place for young people, beatniks, hippies and bourgeoisie of all nationalities, who were traveling or bumming their way through Europe; it was cheap, it was warm, it was beautiful, and it was on the well-traveled route from Paris to Tangier. Elmyr could cruise through the cafés and bars on a spring or summer evening, sit down with many friends and meet whoever he liked. Unfortunately, the relationships that developed out of these encounters were rarely satisfactory. For one thing, although Elmyr liked young men who were, as he put it, ''undemanding,'' he himself made more demands than were to most people's liking, and in his house he tended to treat his companions—unless they bore a title before their name or had money—more as servants than as guests. For another, his taste often ran to types who in any other kind of community would have been labeled as juvenile delinquents, and for this he paid the price. He was even more of a natural victim in his personal life than in his profession.

He would meet someone and invite him to stay in his guest room. He would pay all the expenses. A week or so later, whatever the result, the young man would usually announce that he was leaving the island, or had met a girl and wanted to stay with her, or would simply pack his bags and vacate the premises without giving any reason at all. All too often he would leave owing Elmyr money, or take with him some sort of souvenir from Elmyr's wardrobe or collection of *objets d'art*. On one occasion two German boys appeared one night at 4 A.M., drunk, to smash the plate glass windows of his living room. Another time, something even more serious happened. Pale and trembling, Elmyr raced round one morning in his car to the house of his painter friend, Edith Sommer, to tell her that a Swedish boy had vanished from Villa Platero, and apparently from the island, with a suitcase full of silk scarves, cashmere sweaters and, he added dramatically, two Picasso drawings from his private collection.

Picasso:
Femme.
Painted by
Elmyr in 1964.

"But I didn't know you had any of your collection here," Edith Sommer said. "You never showed them to any of *us*."

"I will one day. I meant to. I'll show you marvelous things. I kept them locked away in a closet in the back room," Elmyr explained. "He broke in."

"How terrible. We'll go to the police. They'll contact the Guardia Civil on the mainland, and they'll stop him when he tries to leave the country."

"No, no," Elmyr said. "I can't do that."

"But they're Picassos," she protested.

"No," he said nervously. "I can't. The boy is liable to make up some lie about me, and they'll ask what he was doing in my house, and I'll get into trouble."

In the beginning Fernand and Réal had suggested that Elmyr rent a room somewhere in Ibiza, far enough away from the Villa Platero so that people wouldn't know of its existence, and that he should paint there. But Elmyr patiently explained: "That's not only difficult, it's impossible. Ibiza is not that sort of place. People here have nothing to do but watch where you're coming and going so that maybe they can guess who you're sleeping with. Two weeks after I rented such a place the whole island would know it, and they'd be creeping all over the rooftops and peering in at the windows to find out what's going on."

It was Elmyr's alternative idea then to spend the winters working in Austria, somewhere in the Tyrol, an area that he knew and remembered fondly from vacations in his youth. In November 1963 he went with Réal to the ski resort of Kitzbühel and rented a large chalet in the mountains above the town. In December they met again in Munich—Fernand was delayed in New York and would join them as soon as his business was finished there. Elmyr and Réal were to drive to Kitzbühel in Réal's Corvette, but there was some trouble getting proper chains and snow tires for an American car, and for several days they stayed in a suite in Munich's Hotel Bayerischerhof. The second night, around one o'clock in the morning, Fernand telephoned from Orly Airport in Paris. Elmyr, reading in bed, answered. Réal was out on the town.

"What is that boy doing out at one o'clock in the morning?" Fernand demanded angrily. "Who is he with?"

"How should I know?" said Elmyr. "I'm not being paid to spy on him. Ask him yourself."

Fernand was enraged, he began to shout, and finally Elmyr hung up on him in disgust. Five times in the course of the next two hours Fernand called back, hysterical, shrieking curses and threats and insisting that Elmyr tell him who Réal was with. Each time Elmyr hung up.

When Réal finally came back he wasn't alone; he had brought a young American friend with him. Ten minutes later Fernand called again. "Don't lie to me," he yelled over the telephone to Réal. "I know exactly who you're with! He's American, he's blond, and he's wearing a red sweater. If I were there I would kill you both!"

He had previously telephoned the night reception clerk in the hotel lobby, promising him $100 if he would call Paris when Réal returned, furnishing Fernand with all the details. This time it was Réal's turn to hang up in fury; and this time he left the receiver off the hook.

"I was so embarrassed," Elmyr said later, "that I never went back to that hotel again. Early the next morning we got our snow tires and drove to Kitzbühel. Our house was in the mountains, somewhat isolated, and hard to find. When we got there we saw a taxi out in front, and there beside it in the snow—wearing only a sweater and the trousers of his business suit, his face the color of a tomato and stamping his feet to keep from freezing, shrieking and ready to strangle us—was that man, Fernand Legros. It's hard to believe it, but it's true. The taxi driver, thank God, helped me to pin down his arms before he could do any damage. He had flown straight from Orly Airport on the first flight to Munich and gotten there just after we'd checked out of the hotel and gone to the garage. There were no flights to Kitzbühel, so he hired a taxi to drive him there. It's a long ride, you know, across the frontier from Germany to Austria, about a hundred miles and right over the Alps. He didn't care. He had no luggage and no money. I had to pay the taxi driver for him."

Somehow, after that shaky beginning, the three partners managed to settle down to a bloodless winter in the mountains. The *maître* installed his easel in a breakfast room on the second floor, packed Fernand, Réal, and their various houseguests off to the ski runs, locked the door and spent the day painting. Fights were kept to a minimum. It was a productive winter and the faster Elmyr painted, the faster his partners sold. For the end of November they had organized a show at the Galerie Pont-Royal Hôtel in Paris. Called *Homage to Raoul Dufy,* it comprised thirty-three Dufy watercolors and oils—twenty-six of them by Elmyr. The French critic, Gérald Messadié, contributed some flowery praise for a catalog featuring on its cover a color reproduction of *Les Courses, Deauville 1925,* a reputedly genuine Dufy oil owned and lent by Fernand's lawyer at the time, a prestigious collector named Roger Hauert. Sales in the show were excellent. Elmyr, carefully cut off in Kitzbühel and Ibiza from the world of art, knew nothing about it.

That spring the two dealers came to visit Ibiza. They brought fresh colors, paper and canvases, some needed art books, and told Elmyr in turn what they wanted from him in the months to come. He had thought it unwise for them to stay in his house, the Villa Platero, and had booked them into the nearby Hotel Marigna. The Marigna stood across the road on a hill in the Figueretes suburb of Ibiza, looming directly between Elmyr and the sea. That winter the management was adding a second floor which, when finished, would completely cut off Elmyr's cherished view of the blue Mediterranean. He was complaining about it when Fernand said, ''Well, you want to live here, and you really should have a decent studio. Why don't you buy land and build a house?''

''With what?'' Elmyr replied sardonically. The tourist boom had begun; land was no longer cheap. He had only a few dollars in the bank, and he still knew nothing about such things as the Dufy show in Paris.

''I'll advance you the money,'' Fernand said. ''Call it a gift. The house is for you, *mon cher.* We want you to be comfortable.''

Elmyr remembered then an American doctor who owned a piece of land on the cliff of Los Molinos behind the city walls. The doctor had bought the land sight unseen from a promoter in New York; when he arrived on Ibiza he found that there were open sewage drains in the town and the electricity sometimes failed. Discouraged, he was willing to sell it for what he had paid. It was a beauti-

Raoul Dufy:
Reception.
A watercolor painted by
Elmyr on Ibiza in 1962
and featured in the
exhibition, *Hommage à Raoul Dufy,*
given by Fernand Legros

at the Galerie Pont-Royal Hotel
in Paris.

ful site for a home, and nobody could ever cut off the view: the cliff dropped steeply to a magnificent expanse of blue Mediterranean, and on the horizon lay only the primitive, neighboring island of Formentera. "Let's buy it," Fernand said immediately.

The doctor's lawyer was in Barcelona. Two days later the contract was signed and notarized—in Fernand's name.

"You're a refugee," he told Elmyr. "You have no status, the name you use isn't your real one—it's not a good idea for you to own land or a house. Suppose there's a revolution? Who knows what might happen to you?"

"I let him have his way," Elmyr lamented afterwards, "and it was one of the biggest mistakes of my life. Again, because I have no sense of the future, no foresight. If only later, when he asked me for paintings that he badly needed, I had had the sense to say, 'Okay, but first I want the house in my name.' I might have gotten it and saved myself all the trouble that was to come. He needed the paintings to pay for his apartment on Avenue Henri-Martin, to pay for the servants, the boys, the parents of the boys, the relatives of the parents to keep them quiet about these boys of fourteen, fifteen, sixteen. He had to keep whole families quiet. That's why he was always broke. He paid them all. And he paid them generously. He sent some of the boys to school in Switzerland so they would be properly educated young gentlemen. That much credit I must give him. It was my money, money he made strictly off my labors, but he was generous with it."

"You should have a large bedroom with a studio attached," Fernand suggested when it came time to meet with the resident American architect. "And it should be built in such a way that people can't burst in on you accidentally. And a nice landscaped garden, and a big barbecue pit. And let's also make a second small apartment, in case we come down here we don't have to be cooped up in a hotel. We'll decorate it all in red, because that's my favorite color. You can use it for guests."

All this sounded reasonable, except that Elmyr thought the house was getting far too grand. Fernand wanted three stories; Elmyr wanted one. They compromised on two. But what kind of money would he have to make to keep up such a palatial establishment? Fernand told him not to worry.

"I do worry," Elmyr grumbled. "I don't get enough money as it is now."

"But we take all the risk," his partners reminded him.

In the middle of construction, Fernand ordered the architect to put in a swimming pool with a modern imported filter system on the edge of the flower garden, and Elmyr blew up. Who was going to pay for the upkeep of *that?*

"*Mon cher,* that's not your concern," Fernand said, patting him on the head like a child.

It was then, for the first time, that Elmyr began to suspect that his partners were becoming rich. A thought occurred to him.

"You're sure you haven't sold any of the big oils yet?" he asked suspiciously.

"I swear to you on the head of my mother," said Fernand, sounding a little aggrieved.

By the time the house was finished it had become the island's showcase luxury residence—so much so that a year later Elmyr almost found himself playing host to the daughter of the President of the United States. When Lynda Bird Johnson, then unmarried and touring Spain, expressed the thought that she might like to visit Ibiza, the American Embassy in Madrid put through a telephone call to the island to check on the possibility of discreet private accommodations. Local Spanish officials suggested La Falaise. The Embassy telephoned Elmyr, who was delighted to oblige. But the visit fell through with a bang when he learned that the entourage would include a quartet of Secret Service men.

"What do they think?" Elmyr exclaimed to some young friends —with *hauteur* proper to a Hungarian baron and lingo appropriate for a man who had been wanted for ten years by the FBI— "I am running here on Ibiza some kind of flophouse for the fuzz?"

14.

in which, after
Fernand strikes
gold in Texas
and pays $30,000
for a genuine
Rouault, Elmyr
is banished to
Australia.

DUFY BY ELMYR

That summer Elmyr had other troubles to keep him occupied. His Canadian passport under the name of Joseph Boutin was about to expire, so that Réal, passing through Rotterdam on a selling trip, brought it in to the Canadian Consulate in that city. A clerk checked the files and found something which changed the Consul's bored accommodation to a sharp frown.

Joseph Boutin, it will be remembered, was the supposedly nondescript, married, middle-aged Toronto insurance clerk whose birth certificate Réal had procured in 1959 to secure a genuine passport for Elmyr under a new identity. Stranger things happen in life than in fiction, and Elmyr's ill-starred life was certainly stranger than most men's. There was indeed a file on Joseph Boutin, and the Royal Canadian Mounted Police had been looking for him for some years. He was wanted in Ontario for possession of stolen property, and—an irony that no one who knew Elmyr could have foreseen—for bigamy. *Caveat emptor.* Let the buyer beware.

"Where is this man?" the Consul demanded.

For once, Réal lost his cool; he turned and raced out the door, down the steps and into the street. He never looked back.

That was the aborted end of Joseph Boutin's career in Europe, and Elmyr found himself once again without a passport. He was feeling more and more unhappy until he hit on the idea of applying, as a stateless person, for a Spanish residence permit. Some influential Hungarian friends in Madrid vouched for his identity and bona fides; and Elmyr got the *residencia,* this time under the double-barreled compromise name of Joseph Elmyr Dory-Boutin. With it, he was entitled to carry a passport guaranteed by the Spanish government. Things were looking up. He had a new identity and he would soon have a new home.

The oils, of course, were being sold almost as fast as Elmyr could paint them, and for prices that started at $20,000 and ranged as high as $115,000 for a large Derain that was sold through a major New York gallery some five months after Fernand had carted it away from Kitzbühel.

"I told him, always," Elmyr says, "if there's any trouble with a painting, anything doubtful about it—if it's questioned in the *slightest*—you must bring it back. It has to be destroyed. We agreed on it. I never got a single one back.''

Fernand had already scented gold in the rich Texas oil fields and it was then, around April 1964, just after construction of La Falaise had gotten underway, that he was introduced in Dallas to a genial multimillionaire oilman and art collector named Algur Hurtle Meadows. Meadows had already bought, in Madrid, a million dollars' worth of doubtful Goyas and El Grecos from such sources as the ''Infanta collection of Isabel de Borbón,'' and had endowed Southern Methodist University in Dallas with an art museum and sculpture court; he was certainly fair game for the likes of Fernand and Réal. In the course of the next two and a half years they unloaded on him no less than fifteen Dufys, seven Modiglianis, five Vlamincks, eight Derains, three Matisses, two Bonnards, one Chagall, one Degas, one Marquet, one Laurencin, one Gauguin and a Picasso—all painted by Elmyr. About half of them were oils. Meadows thus became, according to one reporter, ''the man who owns what may be the largest private collection of fake paintings in the world.''

Once the scandal had become public Meadows quickly became the symbol of the dupe, the accumulator, the rich philistine who buys for prestige rather than for love—or, as a critic put it, ''to circumvent oblivion and the Collector of Internal Revenue at a single stroke.'' His motives and his gullibility concerning the prices offered him are perhaps suspect, but his esthetic taste can hardly be faulted. The same paintings had been selling for years—''like hotcakes,'' as Elmyr said—to so-called experts, dealers, galleries and museums. It was not just a trusting Texas oil millionaire who was taken for a ride, but the entire worldwide and supposedly knowledgeable art establishment.

''Because,'' Elmyr explained, ''the establishment knows nothing. A college art student knows easily as much about modern art as the best dealers in the best galleries. The dealers know one thing very well: to buy cheap and sell dear. That's the extent of their expertise. I long ago realized that if I do commercial things in painting I got such a minimum that it was barely enough to hold me alive—not enough to live on, but just too much to die on. My better work, I couldn't sell to the galleries at any price. But if I brought them the same drawing with the signature of Picasso they were ready to peel out any amount of money. I found the whole thing so incredibly—how to say? . . . partly funny, partly sad, partly disgusting.

"I remember the last time I brought a few Matisse lithographs into a very good gallery in one of the big cities in Germany. The dealer thought they were fine but he didn't want to buy them without the okay of the museum. We went to see the museum director, there came also a professor of art from the university, and they opened about ten books and God knows how many portfolios all filled with Matisse reproductions and originals. These big fat people stood around, so serious and pretentious, looking with their magnifying glasses, comparing, whispering—'*Ja, Herr Direktor,*' '*Ja, Herr Professor,*' '*Natürlich, Herr Direktor*'—and looking at this, looking at that, and finally they said to me: 'Yes, sure, it's okay, it's genuine—how much you want?' I sometimes wanted to laugh in such people's faces. And that's what happened everywhere. It's amusing, yes. But it's also sad. What is the result of it? What is the moral of it?''

Fernand Legros, by the time he found Meadows in 1964, had definite ideas as to what Elmyr should and shouldn't paint. The Fauve period—particularly Matisse, Derain, Vlaminck, Braque and van Dongen in the years 1904 to 1908—was a sure "best-seller," very much in demand. Elmyr at one time decided he would enjoy doing some Puy and Valtat—two of the lesser French Fauve painters, but fine colorists whose best figural work was certainly on a par with early Vlaminck and Derain.

"I timidly suggested this once or twice, but Fernand yelled no. It wasn't worth it to him financially. It was the same amount of selling effort and he pointed out that you got nothing—well, relatively nothing—in return. I was also tempted by the German Expressionists—Nolde, Pechstein, Schmidt-Rottluf—because there again I felt I had an affinity for the whole school, and it had a great deal to do with my early training in Munich. But every time I mentioned it I was discouraged in no uncertain terms by Fernand and Réal. Don't be an idiot, they said. No market for it." Drawings, for the same reason, were generally in disfavor.

A good Dufy painting of any period brought a high price and was an easy sale. "He's so bright and gay," Fernand said. "People love that." Still lifes were out: "Very difficult to sell in New York and Texas," and compositions crowded with figures were in: "People feel they're getting their money's worth." He also wanted lots of red in the paintings. He explained that people were psychologically attracted to the boldness of the color, and that it usually fit nicely with the decorative scheme of most American living rooms; but he had once told Elmyr that in Farouk's Egypt only the royal family had the right to use the color red—it was taboo, he claimed, to the rest of the populace. In his youth, therefore, red had symbolized wealth, prestige, and power, which were precisely the things that Fernand wanted. The walls of his apartment in Paris were solid red velvet, his apartment in Elmyr's house was decorated in red, his Cadillacs were red, his pajamas, shirts, sweaters and the silk linings of his suits were red; and, when he had his way, the backgrounds of his Matisses were red, too.

His insistence on certain subjects finally got the triumvirate into a jam which almost killed the operation and sent Elmyr scurrying halfway around the world to temporary sanctuary in Australia.

Elmyr didn't mind painting red backgrounds or crowded canvases, but some themes bored him. One such was a favorite of Raoul Dufy—*The Reception at Élysée Palace.* Dufy had painted it several times in both watercolor and oil, and there was a strong market demand for the works.

"It has no appeal to me," Elmyr complained. "A group of men in uniform and women in long dresses. Phooey. They stand around like idiots."

But Fernand wheedled, pleaded and insisted, and Elmyr finally gave in. He did half a dozen watercolors on the subject, which he himself thought were mostly mediocre. Fernand didn't care. He rushed out to sell them—successfully, of course—and one of the purchased paintings found its way for appraisal to the Schoneman

Galleries on 57th Street in New York, where Fred Schoneman, one of the most astute and forthright dealers in the art establishment, took a quick look at it, agreed with Elmyr's critical judgment that it was a mediocre work of art; but added, on that basis, that he thought it was a fake, too.

"It's an ugly thing," Schoneman said later, "when you have to tell a client he's bought a fake. Of all things in this business—it's a kid-glove business—the thing I dislike most is being called in to tell if a painting is right or wrong. I'll do it only for clients who are very close friends. You have to do it gently. If you say 'fake' you insult a man's intelligence, you wound his vanity, and you probably lose him as a customer."

Much upset, the man who had bought the Dufy, a collector named Adolph Juviler, threatened to sue Fernand Legros. Challenged, Fernand admitted nothing. Instead, as he put it, "rather than embarrass" the noted French authority who had given his expertise to the contested painting, he brazenly offered Juviler a genuine Rouault in exchange for the "wrong" Dufy. Fernand was no piker: he had rushed out in the midst of the crisis and paid $30,000 for the Rouault. The victimized New York art collector accepted the swap. Fernand was also no defeatist: two weeks later he flew from New York to Palm Beach and sold the Dufy reception painting to Algur Hurtle Meadows.

Word had leaked to Paris, however, and in the midst of the controversy there had been considerable danger that if the fake expertise came to light, the whole jig was up. The idea was to lie low until muddy waters grew clear again. Little could be proved without the authorities tracking down Fernand's source of supply and establishing a clear-cut chain of deception—which indicated that for safety's sake Elmyr should disappear for a while. Perhaps, Fernand decided, forever.

It was the winter of 1964–1965 and Elmyr was in Kitzbühel again, assiduously painting a new series of oils. Réal stayed with him a while during the period of trouble, but told Elmyr nothing of what was going on. Of course, Elmyr had clues. There were constant telephone calls from Fernand in New York, and from Fernand's interior decorator and Fernand's father in Paris.

The police, Elmyr half overheard, were about to search the apartment on the Avenue Henri-Martin. For some reason he had the uncomfortable idea that the French Deuxième Bureau was involved, which meant that it was an espionage case. He questioned Réal, who kept saying, "It's nothing serious. What a lovely Vlaminck! Don't stop work."

Before the Rouault-Dufy swap was accomplished in New York, Fernand crept out of the city, flew to Zurich, picked up Réal there, and drove with him nonstop through the night over the Alps. They argued and screamed at each other all the way, but by some miracle the Alfa Romeo kept the road and they reached the snowbound chalet above Kitzbühel at four o'clock of a black February morning. A decision had been reached. Pounding on the door, they woke Elmyr from a deep sleep and frightened him half out of his wits.

Once inside, Réal said: "You know, we were thinking. The house in Ibiza isn't ready yet—why don't you go to Australia?"

"In the middle of the night?" Elmyr asked, furious, freezing and fearing the worst. "All they've got there is kangaroos. Can I please have my breakfast first?"

He was joking, but Réal and Fernand weren't. They didn't want to tell Elmyr precisely what had happened, but they made up a half-true tale of a New York dealer who hadn't liked one of the recent paintings and had invoked the ghost of the long-dead L. E. Raynal. They alarmed Elmyr sufficiently with tales of an impending police raid on the chalet in the mountains that he agreed to go that morning. At the time they had a large stock of paintings scattered in various cities—twenty-five to thirty oils and at least as many watercolors and drawings. This realization—that for the next year, at least, he was expendable—did not increase Elmyr's sense of physical security. And it hit a new low when he heard Réal on the telephone to the travel agency in Kitzbühel, asking for a one-way boat ticket to Australia.

It sounded ominous. "Oh, no," Elmyr cried. "I won't go."

"We thought you might open an art gallery out there, in Sydney," Fernand explained.

"An art gallery?" Elmyr's large brown eyes regarded Fernand with worried suspicion. He decided he didn't feel well and took two tranquilizers. "What for? And so what? Am I going to sit in it for the rest of my life?"

"We don't know," Réal said. "The main thing is that you're out of the way for a while, that they don't find you."

"I want a return ticket," Elmyr yelled, panicky. Eventually he got it.

By now he had to face the growing realization that his partners were selling the oils, and had been selling them for years—the head of Fernand's mother notwithstanding. But there was little he could do about it. He tried to remonstrate with Fernand—"You see, I told you . . . I told you this would happen . . . you wouldn't listen to me, you never listen to me . . . you never . . ."—but they only hurried him along with his packing. They told him he couldn't even return to Ibiza; the police might be watching the villa. Réal volunteered to make the trip instead. Finding the Villa Platero unguarded, he nevertheless decided it would be too risky to leave any evidence that would even suggest Elmyr's capabilities as an artist; he kindled a fire in the fireplace and burned all of the paintings and sketches he could find—not Matisses and Dufys, but de Horys. (Elmyr only discovered this five months later, and he was nearly in tears at the loss. Réal said: "But it was to protect *you*.") The easel went up in the blaze as well, and so did Elmyr's French oil paints and watercolors. Stuffing two suitcases full of Elmyr's summer clothing, Réal flew to Madrid, where Elmyr and Fernand were waiting at the Ritz Hotel. Elmyr was given $3000 in cash and a day later, in Gibraltar, prodded aboard the *Canberra,* bound for Australia.

By the time the ship had reached Sydney the panic in New York was over, Fernand had exchanged the good Rouault for the bad Dufy, and with a few well-placed bribes had cooled the Paris scene. It was too late to call Elmyr back, however, so they shipped him old canvas, paper and French colors and suggested that he forget the idea of an art gallery in Sydney and get back to work. "I want some gouaches by Vlaminck," Fernand said, on the telephone from Chicago. "Landscapes, with lots of red in them."

15.

in which
Cleopatra and
The Peasant
declare war on
each other,
gangsters from
Marseilles are
called in; and in
which Grandma
chooses sides.

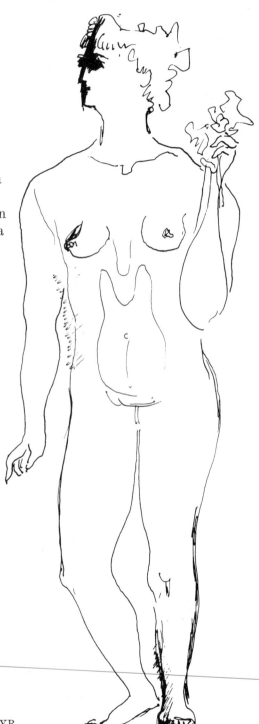

BRAQUE BY ELMYR

The Australian trip—so far as Elmyr was concerned—was a fiasco and a failure in all ways. The Mustang, which he had shipped with him on the *Canberra*, was never unloaded in Sydney for lack of a substantial cash deposit to insure that it wouldn't be sold or abandoned. No one had told him that this might happen, and to his great annoyance Elmyr was suddenly in a strange country without his luxury transport. A week after he had himself debarked and found a small seaside apartment in which to live, he began to complain to anyone who would listen that he wasn't feeling well. Since it was usually obvious even to his new acquaintances that he was an inveterate hypochondriac and pill-taker, no one paid much attention to his sighs and groans. He finally dragged himself off to a doctor, which seemed to indicate this time that his complaints were genuine; and indeed they were: he had somehow, probably in Ibiza, picked up a rare disease called Malta fever, contracted from a virus that lives in goat's milk. He was depressed and listless for the rest of his stay in Australia and spent almost all of the time in his apartment, attended for a while by a male nurse. The only positive result of the illness was that, cooped up for so many weeks, he had little else to do except read and paint. And paint he did—a huge collection of gouaches and watercolors and small oils. Fernand came out to visit in April and see what was wrong; he also brought money.

Delighted with the unexpected inventory, he crated and air-freighted all the paintings back with him to Europe and told Elmyr to keep busy, not to hurry back. "Do more," he chirped.

"I was sick, half-dead," Elmyr later recalled with bitterness, "but he couldn't have cared less. There was never enough money for his harem. They all wanted cars and credit cards. I also found out that just that winter he'd made a down payment on a house in Aspen, Colorado, where he liked to ski. And who was going to pay for it? Me."

Elmyr said: "I don't like Australia. I'm not well. I need a rest. I'm getting out of here," he swore, "as soon as I have the strength to walk out that door."

It was June 1965 when he finally flew back to Europe and moved into the new house on Ibiza, which he called La Falaise—The Cliff.

By the time he left Australia he had met most of the Sydney art dealers and had occasionally been persuaded to part with one or two small items from his "private collection." Perhaps it was coincidence, but some four months after his departure the major auction house in Sydney held what was considered the largest sale of French Impressionist and Fauve art in Australian history. Oblivious to all this, Elmyr had hardly finished unpacking in Ibiza when Fernand telephoned from Paris and announced that he intended to arrive as a houseguest for two weeks during July, with his parents, his American wife, and young Patrick.

"I couldn't easily tell him no," Elmyr said, "so when he arrived I moved out and went to the South of Spain. Already I realized that Fernand's presence was such a source of irritation to me, we couldn't stay under the same roof. I couldn't stand him any more. And I thought it was in both our interests that people shouldn't associate him too closely with me—in fact, at the beginning I'd made them promise they wouldn't come to see me except to pick up work or bring materials. I asked him please, one thing, don't make a display of your well-known colorful personality in Ibiza, because it's a simple, quiet place and the Spaniards are very dignified, and that's where I want to make my home. At the time Réal was off in Capri on vacation. Of course, Fernand couldn't stay away from making a Fourth-of-July fireworks display of his presence, which I'd begged him not to do—he gave big parties and he cruised through the town all night long with his boys, drinking and dancing."

Fernand's wife was with him, and in Ibiza she gave evidence of her total ignorance of the setup. Someone said to her, after being introduced: "Oh, yes, of course, you're staying up in Elmyr's new house."

"Who," she replied, with bland and unmistakable innocence, "is this Elmyr person everyone keeps mentioning to me?"

While he was in Ibiza, Fernand visited the local art gallery run by Ivan Spence, the giant, white-bearded sixty-year-old expatriate Englishman. Promenading as a patron of the arts, Fernand bought several paintings and entertained the local artists at La Falaise. For $1000 he bought the entire year's output, some hundred draw-

A forged
André Schoeller expertise
is shown with a
Braque oil painting
done by Elmyr
in Australia in 1965.

Le tableau reproduit ci-contre, —
peint sur toile mesurant : haut. 54 cent.,
larg. 65 cent.,— est une oeuvre authentique
de Georges Braque.

Ce tableau date de la période fauve (1905).

A Paris ,le 18 Avril 1947.

ings and gouaches, of one American painter. He and Réal later sponsored an exhibition in Paris for a young, gifted Canadian artist, Jamie Goodbrand, whom they had met on Ibiza.

"He always bought small things as a front for the big operation," was Elmyr's explanation. "It made him look a little bit more legitimate. Then he gave them away for nothing. If someone bought a Matisse he'd say, 'Here, take this lovely little gouache by so-and-so. He's a brilliant unknown painter—in twenty years it may be worth $10,000.' Oh, he knew how to sell. He was shrewd. In some ways, even, he was a kind of genius."

His genius, however, did not extend to his personal life. During this period, toward the end of 1965, the fights between Fernand and Réal grew more numerous and more grave in consequence. Elmyr, of course, found himself placed squarely—and vulnerably—in the middle of the battlefield.

For a while this worked two ways. Once the antagonism had reached such serious proportions that it seemed the business partnership might even split up, Elmyr achieved a new status as an object of desire. He was, after all, the meal ticket. Bearing in mind Réal's shrewd observation that if Elmyr had too much money he would automatically quit work, within the framework of that thesis they began to fawn over him and woo him like two gigolos after the same rich widow. They each had their nicknames to use behind the back of the currently odd-man-out. Fernand was "Cleopatra" or "Farouk." Réal was "The Peasant." Elmyr, too, supposedly unknown to him, was labeled *"la vieille"*—the old woman —or sometimes just "Grandma."

To them it was a private joke, very "camp" and very "gay." "By the way, Grandma called this morning," Réal would say to Fernand, on the telephone from Paris to New York. "She's hysterical about not being able to pay her rent. Better send her a few hundred dollars on account."

"Look," Réal said to Elmyr, visiting him on Ibiza, "I brought you this lovely Cartier wristwatch. Did Cleopatra bring you anything lately?"

"Who went out to Australia when you were sick with Malta fever?" Fernand demanded from Buenos Aires. "Did that peasant go? That thief, that blackmailer, that high school dropout? No, *I* did. Which of us is your real friend?''

Elmyr listened, frowning. A joke was a joke, but he sensed the building antagonisms. ''Cut it out,'' he said to them both. ''Don't forget, we're sitting all in one boat. Don't rock the boat—because if we sink, we'll go in the drink all together.''

Rome fell, so did Napoleon, and so does the stock market when the bulls breathe too rarefied an air; the natural direction after a spectacular and speedy rise seems to be nowhere but down, and so Fernand Legros turned a deaf ear to Elmyr's excellent advice and hastened to his fate. No one could accuse him, however, of attempting to play the role of tragic hero. He was still the protagonist of the slapstick comedy, the pursuer in the climactic chase—fierce, formidable, falling on his face. One must imagine swift cuts between shots, rapid pans of the camera and a certain herky-jerky quality in the movements of the two heroes, who are always dressed in identical dark form-fitting doublebreasted suits with red silk linings.

In the spring of 1965: in Madrid, prior to a party given by Algur Hurtle Meadows, Fernand and Réal visit Elmyr, who happens also to be in the capital staying in a suite in the highly respectable Torre de Madrid. They argue. Fernand smashes four glass table-tops and cracks a whisky bottle over Réal's forehead. Bleeding and bandaged but arm in arm, the two warriors leave for Meadows' party. ''Who's going to pay the bill for the damages?'' Elmyr demands angrily.

''We will,'' they promise.

They leave town. Elmyr pays.

The time: shortly thereafter. The place: Cannes, on the French Riviera. At two o'clock in the morning Réal pulls up in front of the elegant Carlton Hotel; he has a girl with him in the white Alfa Romeo. From out of the shadows leaps Fernand, a knife glinting in his hand. He slashes wildly at the canvas top of the convertible. After a brief struggle, the doorman subdues him. Fernand tips him. There are no repercussions.

In New York, in September 1965, no longer welcome at the Adams Hotel and somewhat wary after the recent incidents in

Cannes and Madrid, Réal books a separate room for himself—on a low floor—at Delmonico's Hotel. Furious, Fernand waits until they are alone in his suite, then picks up the nearest painting, which happens to be a Vlaminck held on consignment, of which Elmyr has also made a copy, and slams it down on his partner's head. The canvas, needless to say, splits. Réal's brown curly hair peers through. Fernand turns pale. "My God," he whispers, "that's the *real* one."

The museum's bill for having it stitched together and restored comes to more than $2000.

Throughout this most recent phase of *opéra bouffe* attack and counterattack, Elmyr had done his utmost to act as peacemaker, but his voice of reason could be best described as "a very small candle on a very dark night."

Then came the most unkind cut of all. Réal had met a young French girl with whom he had fallen in love. In January 1966 he announced his engagement, and a week later he moved out of the apartment on the Avenue Henri-Martin. He meant it as a throwing in of the towel where his personal relationship with Fernand was concerned, but Fernand took it as a throwing down of the gauntlet. It was war.

Fernand's weapons, until nearly the end, tended toward the old-fashioned and melodramatic: the shriek, the fist, the shoe, the knife, or the nearest oil painting. He never lacked for imagination in his efforts, however thwarted, to do Réal in. In recent years, since Elmyr had begun living in Spain, the two partners had had most of their suits made by Elmyr's tailor in Madrid, to whose elegant and antique precincts Elmyr had introduced them. The shop was next to the Hilton Hotel, where Fernand usually stayed. In three years, by the tailor's reckoning, Fernand had ordered and paid for thirty-two suits and ensembles. They were not all for him; he often came down with members of the Paris harem and had them outfitted with silk shirts, Andalusian calfskin boots and doublebreasted black blazers with gold buttons.

During the height of their personal quarrels, Fernand and Réal were in Madrid together for the Meadows party, and Fernand had a bill to pay at the Spanish tailor's. Busily selecting some new cloth, he took out his First National City Bank checkbook, handed it to Réal and said in the tailor's presence, "Sign my name as you always do." Réal obliged.

A short time afterward the check was returned to the tailor, unpaid, with the New York bank's notation that the signature was not quite right. The tailor accordingly wrote to Fernand, who flew down from Paris a few weeks later. This time he paid cash. Then he asked the tailor to sign a prepared statement, in Spanish with a French translation, to the effect that he had received a check from Réal Lessard with a false signature of Fernand Legros.

"But I heard you yourself ask Señor Lessard to sign for you," the tailor replied, puzzled.

Fernand impatiently explained that if the tailor wanted his continued patronage, he would sign the statement. The tailor ultimately refused.

"You just lost a customer," Fernand said, and stormed out.

There was also a weird tale that Réal told Elmyr and some friends about being attacked in Fernand's apartment by three gangsters from Marseilles. Fernand had lured him to the Avenue Henri-Martin on one pretext or another, and when Réal rang the bell and entered the door the three hoods jumped him. Whether they were hired to kill him, or rough him up and threaten him, or just steal something from him was never made clear. In any case, searching him, they found in his wallet an IOU from Fernand Legros for the French equivalent of $20,000. Therefore, Réal later explained, they didn't kill him or beat him up—Fernand had told them that he, Réal, was the one who owed the money.

Schooled as they are in the esoteric codes of the Mafia, there is evidently a certain sense of financial ethics among Marseilles strongarm men. Annoyed at Fernand's deception, they were supposed to have talked it over and said to Réal, "All right. You collect that money from Legros and give it to us and we won't touch you."

"Here," Réal said adroitly, handing over the IOU. "*You* collect it."

He never saw them again. What happened afterwards was reported by Elmyr:

"The end of the story, I heard, had a rather strange twist. Fernand was furious but he was in a very bad spot. He hadn't enough cash to pay the gangsters so he gave them one of my recent oil paintings, a Matisse, which they sold for $20,000 to a dealer in the South of France—I think Cannes. But then the paint was too fresh, it came out that it was a fake and they were in trouble, so they were ready to kill Fernand. He had to give them the money and take back the painting. They were not people to joke with.''

Réal in this period was a far shrewder combatant. From behind the enemy lines he fought a kind of modern economic guerrilla warfare. He had a passion for signatures and documents, and he had begun collecting them as early as 1961. As Elmyr explained: ''Réal not only knew Fernand's financial situation, but *only* Réal knew. Fernand lived a completely helter-skelter life with money, wheeling and dealing and spending, and half the time not knowing how much was in the various bank accounts or where the money was going to. Réal knew much more about the business side of their arrangements than Fernand did, and Réal always took the checks. Until 1966 they went on every trip and saw every client together. Fernand did the hard bargaining and then Réal, who looked so young and innocent and who people thought was a soft touch, closed the deal. It was their system. Réal always paid the bills, too. Perhaps Fernand kept some drawings for himself and sold them secretly to pay for his little boys, but the big business manipulations and the constant transfer of cash to Swiss banks was done exclusively by Réal. He was always squeezing papers out of Fernand saying that he had this and that right to this and that painting and a percentage of such-and-such property. He got Fernand finally to make him the heir to the house in Ibiza, and before that he made a terrific fuss that he wanted half the Paris apartment in his name. 'That way,' he said, 'they can't seize it if there's trouble.' But there Fernand screamed, turned purple in the face and threatened to kill Réal if he brought up the subject one single more time.''

While Fernand bought luxury apartments, hired hoods and private detectives and paid bills for hotel damages in three continents, Réal invested his share of the take in Canadian real estate— or loaned it to the partnership at usurious rates of interest. The money always came from Canada and Réal maintained that it was borrowed from his mother and various other family in Montreal. Fernand naturally wanted to know where they had made the money in the first place, since five years ago they'd had nothing, but Réal played dumb. He thus accumulated, over the years, a sizable pile of Fernand's IOUs. These were the weapons with which he mounted the first serious offensive.

Of course, while both combatants were setting out with utmost vigor to destroy each other, they continued to do business together, they traveled together, they connived together, and they sold together. Like a husband and wife in the bitter throes of divorce who nevertheless recognize a common responsibility to their children, they jointly pressured Elmyr for work at the same time that they fought like fishwives for his loyalty. But Elmyr had made his choice. It was a simple one, since he had long ago decided that Fernand was thoroughly unreasonable, maybe even insane, and had recently realized that Réal had most of the cash.

Réal also reported to him the following story. One evening in Cannes, after an opening at a local gallery, Fernand was drinking and chain-smoking at the bar of the Carleton Hotel with a group of French art dealers and critics. A little drunk, and still sulking from a squabble over money that he had had with his young partner that afternoon, he turned to one of the critics, pointed to Réal and said: "Do you know how he can afford to wear such expensive suits? I'll take you to Ibiza. I'll introduce you to the man who makes all his Vlamincks and Derains."

"They laughed," Elmyr recounted later—unsmiling himself. "They thought he was joking. But when I heard that story, *I* knew he was mad. He was a megalomaniac, a paranoiac. Paranoia people, as far I know, are violent and vindictive—he, somehow, in his confused and sick mind, must have thought that I am his friend and that I owe him my life. Without him, he once dared to tell me, I would be in the gutter somewhere—an 'old queen without a pot to piss in.' Those were his exact words. I was furious. I think it came as a terrible shock to him that when the two finally broke up I stood on Réal's side."

16.

in which the
battle rages on
both sides of the
Atlantic: an
attaché case is
stolen, Uncle
Réal is caught
red-handed, a
Vlaminck sky
fades, and
Fernand Legros
arrives in Ibiza.

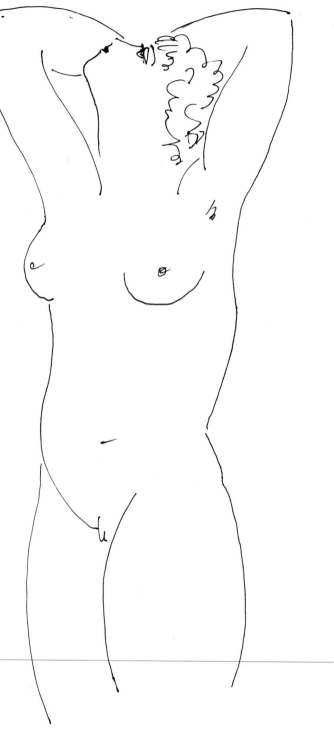

PICASSO BY ELMYR

n April 1966, shortly after he had moved from Avenue Henri-Martin to an apartment of his own in the Hôtel Montalambert, Réal secretly prepared to go into business for himself by buying the Galerie Cardo, on the Avenue Matignon just off the Faubourg St. Honoré. It was between the Knoedler and Hervé galleries, a location whose equivalent in New York would be 57th Street and Madison Avenue; in the geography of the art world, you couldn't do better. The reported price of the sale was around $200,000. The erstwhile high school dropout from Mansonville, Quebec, was not a poor man, and when the usual shouts of financial distress were heard that spring from Ibiza, it was Réal who answered them.

He had always been genuinely fond of Elmyr and, as much as was possible under the circumstances of their business relationship, felt sorry for him—that he had done so much in his life and had achieved so little. "You're not getting any younger," Réal said to him pointedly. "What you need is real security. A lot of money that you can invest in stocks and bonds, to get an income and never worry again." Elmyr agreed wholeheartedly, and Réal went into details.

The previous year, after his successful visit to Kees van Dongen in Monaco, he had hatched a plan which for audacity and shrewdness was on a par with that of the substitute tip-ins in the out-of-print portfolios. No major biography of van Dongen had been written since 1927. Réal had proposed to Mme. van Dongen, who was the family business manager, that he be the one to write it, edit it, and choose the illustrations. After all, he was a van Dongen collector of some importance, a connoisseur. He was also a charming young man with beautiful brown eyes and an air of enthusiastic sincerity. "A very expensive biography," he explained to the painter and his wife, "printed in Switzerland, with lots of beautiful color reproductions."

A contract between Mme. van Dongen and the publisher was already in the works when, in August 1966, Réal rushed down to Ibiza and begged Elmyr to get busy and turn out five or six large van Dongen oils for inclusion in the book. After publication they would surely sell for a fortune. Fernand was to know nothing.

Once again Elmyr fell into the trap of wanting to believe; Réal flattered him, begged him, promised him huge sums of money. "This is for your nest egg," he repeated, and Elmyr nodded warily but happily. Réal gave him $4000 in cash and a promissory note for $60,000 due May 30, 1967, or, in the event of Réal's prior death—he thought if Fernand found out, he might easily murder him—a 50 per cent share in ARTINVEST, the Liechtenstein puppet corporation through which he owned the Galerie Cardo.

"He pressed me hard for the van Dongen oils," Elmyr said, "because he explained if they're not ready by a certain date it's too late to include them in the book. So I painted with great haste and diligence. Naturally," he shrugged—with the stoical, slightly cynical, slightly bewildered smile of the perennial loser—"I've never seen another dime."

While Réal pressed him for work, Fernand threatened him. He wrote at the end of August: "My dear, I heard that your friend Mr. Réal Lessard is in Ibiza, that you both seem to be in a very happy relationship and you seem most delighted to have him with you in the house. I warn you, that if that man is not leaving La Falaise immediately you will have the biggest scandal in Ibiza that you can easily imagine. If I have to break everything in the house, I will. You have to know if you want him or me. Answer me immediately. I am out of my mind about that story."

He also went on in the same letter to accuse Réal of various past infidelities, both sexual and financial. He had given a Corvette to one of Fernand's lovers and then tried to talk the young man into living with him. And he had become engaged, Fernand claimed, "just to bug me." Fernand also swore that he had photostats of documents, receipts and notes which proved that Réal had pilfered huge sums of money from their joint business—"my money and *yours*," he emphasized to Elmyr—and had spent most of it on expensive gifts to the various residents of the apartment on the Avenue Henri-Martin. It takes one to know one, Elmyr thought grimly.

Constantly buffeted during this time between his two feuding partners, Elmyr began to lose a certain amount of confidence in their ability to handle their end of the bargain. He began to worry, and then he began to paint badly.

"There was so much pressure. Fernand always wanted more and more work. I did a series of Derain watercolors. I knew they weren't good but I just didn't give a damn."

He also did a watercolor by Raoul Dufy of the promenade at Deauville. It was definitely not up to scratch, and at the last minute the signature was changed to that of Jean Dufy, Raoul's lesser known and not-quite-so-gifted younger brother, who was also a painter. Fernand eventually put the watercolor up at official French government auction in the Hôtel Rameau in Versailles. In the preauction viewing, Philippe Reichenbach, a Paris dealer, noticed the obvious: the painting didn't look like Jean Dufy's work at all, it looked like a poor imitation of big brother Raoul. "I'm sure it's wrong," Reichenbach confided to the auction house authorities.

Reichenbach knew Fernand Legros from two previous occasions. The first time, in 1961, Fernand had come by Philippe's gallery on the Avenue Matignon to buy a small but important Segonzac oil painting, a still life with flowers. He had then demanded a completely documented provenance, or history, of the painting, as well as a full description of the canvas itself, all of it in duplicate and signed by the French dealer. He had been so unpleasantly insistent that, after Reichenbach complied, he said to Fernand, "Look, do me a favor. Buy your Segonzacs somewhere else next time."

The second occasion was a few years later when a private American dealer, a woman who often acted as New York liaison for Fernand, bought from Reichenbach a small and relatively unimportant van Dongen oil, period 1895, when van Dongen was just beginning his career as a painter. It depicted, mostly in gray and blue, two can-can dancers. Reichenbach had bought it for only $500 in Texas and though he was sure it was genuine he had not yet had the opportunity of having van Dongen himself look at it and say "Yes, it's mine"—so he sold it somewhat reluctantly, but cheaply, to the New York dealer for $1500. A year later he saw the painting

Kees van Dongen:
Woman with Hat.
Painted by
Elmyr in 1966.
Elmyr did a number of
van Dongens, one of which
received the artist's expertise.

again. Now it belonged to Fernand Legros and a miraculous trans-
formation had taken place. It had-lost ten years of age, become a
brilliantly colored and rare van Dongen from the 1905 Fauve period, and was priced at $20,000.

When Reichenbach learned that the Jean Dufy watercolor at
Versailles had been put up for auction by his old friend Fernand,
he understood everything. ''Now I *know* it's wrong. It was meant
to be a Raoul Dufy but it's such a bad job they signed it 'Jean.' ''
The auction house authorities had reached the same conclusion;
they took it down from the wall and handed it back to an irate Fernand Legros.

But Fernand's troubles were just beginning. Réal, accumulating
his IOUs and promissory notes like a squirrel storing nuts for
winter, had previously demanded that Fernand either come up
with the cash—the notes then totaled the sizable sum of $92,000—
or sell him the apartment on the Avenue Henri-Martin. Fernand
howled with grim laughter. ''He told me,'' Réal reported gloomily
to Elmyr, ''that he'd prefer to make an *auto-da-fé* and go up in
smoke, because that was the great dream of his life—to own an elegant apartment in Paris with golden angels on the ceiling and
walls of red velvet. He said, 'Never!' ''

Returning to Paris then at the beginning of September, Réal
presented his promissory notes to the French legal authorities. He
asked for a writ of seizure to be slapped on the apartment.

A trip to New York and Texas was impending—through thick
and thin, whatever their private battles, business was still business
—so that three nights later the two art dealers were eating
Saumon glacé au four à la Chambord by candlelight at the marble
dining-room table in the Avenue Henri-Martin when the doorbell
chimes tinkled merrily. Fernand's Spanish butler appeared, and
close behind him a grim-looking gentleman in a black raincoat. It
was the *huissier*, the French equivalent of a professional process-
server or city marshal for cases involving debt.

''Monsieur Fernand Legros,'' he said, ''in the name of Monsieur
Réal Lessard I seize your apartment and the contents thereof.''

Monsieur Réal Lessard, who hadn't realized that French justice
could be so swift, had to duck beneath the marble table and crawl

for his life toward the door, as Monsieur Fernand Legros, screaming threats of castration and murder, hurled the salmon, the cutlery
and the lighted candelabrum. A small fire broke out on the red-
velvet walls and almost destroyed a Matisse oil. The *huissier* helped
Fernand put it out.

"The seizure," Réal said later, in one of his rare understate-
ments, "came as a great shock to him."

Knowing that Fernand would fight to the death in the French
courts and that publicity would do neither of them any good, Réal
shortly thereafter proposed a deal. He and Elmyr were still good
friends, as well as partners in the new van Dongen venture. For
some time Elmyr had been fretting over the fact that Fernand
Legros was the legal owner of La Falaise. "Of course," said
Elmyr, "I have the right to live in it until I die. But considering
the circumstances, I don't sleep well when a man like that has such
a good reason for getting rid of me."

He had discussed this often with Réal, and therefore—a temporary cease-fire having been declared so that business activities
could continue—Réal proposed a *quid pro quo* to his partner: if
Fernand would give him the house on Ibiza, he would tear up the
$92,000 worth of promissory notes and relent on the seizure of the
Paris apartment. Fernand surprised him by being sensible and
agreeing to the deal. Three days later the peripatetic partners flew
off to Texas, stopped off in New York and, before a notary public
approved by the Spanish consulate, the documents for the sale of
La Falaise in Ibiza were duly executed and witnessed. For Réal,
obviously, it was a question of a bird in the hand; La Falaise, it
may be noted, was still not Elmyr's property, but Réal's.

Arriving in Dallas in November, the two went to work again on
Algur Hurtle Meadows, who was getting cagier all the time, forc-
ing them to hang around in the expensive Marriott Hotel while he
made up his mind whether he wanted the latest Chagall or Dufy.
"That way," Meadows explained afterward, "they'd have to
sweat it out and chew their fingernails while they shelled out $200 a
day for expenses, and in the end I'd usually get what I wanted at
half the asking price."

Coming back to the hotel one evening, Réal discovered that his attaché case was missing. It was a heavy, bulky case stuffed with bankbooks, expertises, photographs, personal papers, including his passport, and all the documents relating to ARTINVEST and the Galerie Cardo. Fernand, the natural suspect, had been with Réal all the time. To give further proof of his innocence, Fernand called in the Dallas police, accused one of the Negro hotel maids of the theft and then offered a reward of $1000 for the return of the attaché case. Réal was frantic. Obviously, he informed the police, someone had stolen it thinking that it contained jewelry.

At that point, getting despondent and needing advice, he placed a call to Elmyr, who was in London. For the autumn months he had taken an apartment in Kensington, and in the supposedly locked guest room was busily painting the needed van Dongens, as well as a few Marquet gouaches that Réal had requested for "a quick turnover." On the telephone Réal told the unhappy tale of the missing attaché case. Without hesitation Elmyr replied: "Don't be such a dunce. Fernand paid someone to steal it for him."

"No, no," Réal explained. "He was with me all the time. And he swore on the head of his mother that he had nothing to do with it."

"Then it's certain he took it!" Elmyr shouted (it was a poor connection)—but twenty-six-year-old Réal, who was deeply attached to his own mother and would never have put her dear gray head as forfeit for a lie, refused to believe a man could stoop so low.

A week later he flew to England to pick up some of the van Dongens and Marquets that were drying in Elmyr's rented apartment in Kensington. There were two spare bedrooms and Elmyr invited him to stay for the few days he would be in town. That first morning, at three o'clock, the telephone rang—it was Fernand, calling from New York. "Just a minute," Elmyr said sleepily, "I want to shut the window." He rushed into the spare bedroom and woke Réal. "Pick up the telephone in the living room. It's *him*."

Not realizing that Réal was in London, much less listening to the conversation on Elmyr's living-room extension, Fernand ranted to Elmyr on his now favorite subject: "That blackmailer, that thief, that peasant! He has a $200,000 corporation in Liechtenstein and a gallery in Paris and thousands of dollars invested in Canadian government bonds! I have no money at all—''

''If you have no money now,'' Elmyr said, after he had listened for nearly an hour, ''you're going to have five hundred dollars less when you get this bill from the telephone company.''

Fernand finished by pleading with Elmyr to dump The Peasant and come back to faithful old Cleopatra. To put a stop to the harangue, Elmyr promised to think about it.

''How did he know my telephone number here in London?'' he wondered aloud, after Fernand had hung up.

Réal, his face bone-white with shock, charged out of the living room.

''Because it's in the attaché case,'' he raved. ''That's how he knew the details about Liechtenstein! And the gallery, and everything else! This time,'' he cried, ''he's gone too far! This time,'' he vowed, ''I'll get him.''

Scorning sleep, he was on the early-morning Pan Am jet to New York, and that afternoon in Dallas he swore out a complaint to the Dallas police. By dinnertime Fernand Legros was in jail. By midnight, inexplicably, he had confessed. Yes, he had hired someone to steal the attaché case and mail it to an address in New York. Yes, he would return it; it was a ''ghastly affair,'' he was ''terribly sorry.'' ''I have these black fits of depression,'' he explained, ''when I don't know what I'm doing.'' An upset Algur Hurtle Meadows put up his personal bond and a weeping, apparently broken Fernand Legros was led from the Dallas jail back to the Marriott Hotel. When the attaché case was returned to him from New York—Fernand, needless to relate, had already photostated the contents—Réal dropped the charges.

''I felt so sorry for him,'' he said later to Elmyr, trying to explain this aberrant lenience. ''Meadows did, too. To see him that way, behind bars, screaming like a lunatic, crying like a baby—it was awful. The thing I most regret,'' he added, in the light of what happened afterward in Paris, ''is that the day they let him out of the Dallas jail there was no Jack Ruby waiting in the courtyard.''

A week later, growing more and more uneasy after the incident of the attaché case, which threw a certain doubt on Fernand Legros' integrity, and having recently learned that his Spanish collection was something less than authentic, Meadows sought the advice of Donald Vogel, a reputable Dallas dealer. Vogel suggested that a quintet of experts and gallery owners—Klaus Perls, his brother Frank from Beverly Hills, Mr. and Mrs. Daniel Saidenberg, and Stephen Hahn—all of whom were to be in Dallas for the Picasso show in February, be invited to the house to have a careful look at the French Post-Impressionist collection. Meadows agreed. Vogel, on a trip to New York, showed some photographs of the collection to Klaus Perls.

"I told him," Perls said later, "that judging from the photos, they were fakes. We went to Mr. Meadows' home one afternoon in February. I turned to Mr. Meadows and said, 'Before I go any further, I would like you to tell me if you are prepared to hear the truth as we see it or whether you would prefer we look around and make a report later.' He said, 'By all means, tell me what you think.' "

Daniel Saidenberg, who with his wife had taken Paul Rosenberg's place as the American representative of Picasso's dealer in Paris, recalled: "Just inside the front door of the Meadows house was their Picasso—a portrait of Jacqueline in Algerian costume. It wasn't a bad painting, but it was wrong, all wrong. I knew the year, I knew the palette Picasso had used, and I recognized all the elements in different paintings that had been put together to make this one. I said instantly, 'It's a fake.' " With refreshing modesty for an art dealer, Saidenberg added: "I could be fooled perhaps by a wrong Dufy, but not by a Picasso."

Stephen Hahn and the brothers Perls then issued the same ruthless verdict for forty-three more paintings. They were abrupt in their judgment and Meadows was most upset. "With most of them," Hahn said later, "we knew in a second. It's subjective, based on looking at hundreds of the painter's real works. You feel something is wrong. You look a bit closer, and then you know it's a fake. There was one big Vlaminck oil which would have been a major work of art—if it had been right. But it was wrong, and so was almost everything else." Klaus Perls, on the other hand, was later quoted as saying that he recognized this particular Vlaminck —*La Seine aux Environs de Chatou*—as a "brutal, awful fake." When Pierre Matisse, the son of Henri Matisse, examined a photograph of *Femme aux Fleurs,* which had been attributed to his father, he commented, "I won't say it's a fake, but I wouldn't give you fifty cents for it." Another dealer examined Elmyr's *Portrait de Jeanne Hébuterne* and said: "It's terrible, it's embarrassingly bad. Look at the dull way the lines of the upraised arm parallel the lines of the dress. How could anyone *ever* believe it was a real Modigliani?"

The point, of course, is that no one could believe it was a real Modigliani—or a real Vlaminck, or a real Matisse—once they had been told that it wasn't. If there was a bear market in the making for Elmyrs, there was already a bull market for hindsight. At the same time none of the dealers who visited the Meadows collection realized that all of the fakes had been done by one man. "I found it impossible to believe," Klaus Perls said, "because the styles and the quality varied to such an extraordinary degree."

Fernand Legros, however, was scarcely concerned with such mundane developments or academic debate. He had returned to Paris with something else on his mind: the personal humiliation he had suffered in the Dallas jail, and his consequent plans for revenge on Réal. It was typical that in such a moment of crisis his entire energies should be focused on his personal vendetta, and he made no secret of it. In December he ripped off a letter to Elmyr in Ibiza. Gone was prudence and "that ooze of charm." Here was the warrior bold, singing his exploits and ready for the fray.

You know me well enough [he wrote (one must remember that English was not Fernand's native language)] *that I don't take too easily things from people, and that I have a rather revenchefull mind, and a lifetime won't be long enough to punish him* [Réal], *his entire family, mother, father and little brothers, to punish that son of a bitch. If necessary I would mind to kill the man myself in public, in front of everyone, and afterwards I don't mind to spend the rest of my life in jail, as it is a limit of what people can take. As soon as I went out of jail in Dallas I went officially to Ottawa. At the passport bureau, with a lawyer I told his authorities the practices of the man, making his false passports and afterwards trying to blackmail people. I also went to Washington telling them as well that he is blackmailing me about taxes, when that whore never paid taxes in his life and manage to have a half million dollar corporations, all paid by him, without partners, with money stolen from me and you, and still pretend to destroy me. Before I would be destroy his entire family will suffer from it as long as they life, they all will be punish to have such a monster among themself. I am not interested in that man, all I want is to forget that such crapule can ever exist. And as I say if he doesn't stop I shall kill him myself and that will be the greatest pleasure I can ever get out of that life. A little peasant from Canada, that the F.B.I. was after eight years ago, having half million dollars corporation in Liechtenstein, paid in cash and he stupidly imagines that he will get away with it! I thought he had some brains, but I understand now that the man is insane.*

The letter concluded magnificently: *"He went now to Cortina d'Ampezzo. Anyway, I am not interested in him."*

A few weeks later, on the morning of January twenty-sixth, which was his thirty-fifth birthday, Fernand gave the lie to such lofty and admirable disinterest by calling the Paris police and suggesting that they might find it worth their time to search the apartment and luggage of one Réal Lessard, domiciled in the Hôtel Montalambert on the Left Bank. The police did so. In the *consigne* of the hotel they found a packing case addressed by Réal to himself at an address in Dallas, Texas. In the packing case were four van Dongens, a Bonnard, a Marquet, a number of corresponding expertises—and the package of forged French customs stamps that had been made to order in Tokyo.

By early evening, quite in time for Fernand's birthday celebration, Réal was in prison, calling for his lawyers and shouting that he was innocent, it was a frameup, that *sale con* Fernand Legros had planted the stamps. The birthday party continued far into the night, its "gayety" dimmed for only a moment when, upon hearing that his handsome Uncle Réal was in jail, Fernand's so-called adopted son, Patrick, burst into tears. "He was always a little weak in the head," Fernand confided later to Elmyr.

In the meantime, Réal's protests were of no avail—at least for the moment. He had been caught red-handed. He was indicted, and then a month later, when developments in Texas and resulting pressure from certain influential people in the French art world made it apparent that the case was not so simple, released on bail.

But that one month was all that Fernand needed. He moved swiftly, boldly, with characteristic disregard for obstacles, and no doubt would have succeeded in his object—which was to make a quick million and reestablish himself as king of the seller's market —if, in one of those beautifully ironic twists which usually require the services of Alec Guinness or the intervention of an entire Hollywood studio story department, his luck hadn't suddenly run out, like air from a ruptured tire, in the small French provincial town of Pontoise.

He couldn't move, of course, without Elmyr's help, and there he reckoned—under the circumstances, correctly—that his appeal had to be aimed straight for Elmyr's pocketbook. For one thing, Elmyr was as usual without funds. For another, a $5000 check given him by Réal in London as second payment on the van Dongen venture had unfortunately just bounced. Elmyr was in a panic, and he couldn't locate Réal. Then Jacques Imbert, Réal's secretary, telephoned from Paris and explained to Elmyr that not only was Réal in jail for the possession of false customs stamps, but he urgently needed $5000 cash for bail money. The police exam-ination of Réal's personal effects had also brought to light the fact that he had previously pawned one of the Matisse oils for $19,000 to the Mont de Piété, the French national hockshop. It looked like big trouble. Would Elmyr help?

Elmyr apologized—he was already holding Réal's bad check for the same amount; he was hoping that Réal would send *him* the $5000.

A few weeks later, out on bail, Réal finally wrote to him. Elmyr shook the envelope, looking for a check. Nothing fell out except a ten-page handwritten letter which began: *"Mon cher,* I fear that the times of Cartier watches and Corvettes are passed. . . ."

A little desperate, Elmyr went to a friend of his, an English mil-lionaire who lived on Ibiza, was very fond of horseracing and knew nothing of the troubles that had recently befallen Fernand and Réal, and offered to sell him "a beautiful Dufy watercolor," some horses and jockeys in a paddock, from his "private family collection." It was in Madrid, Elmyr claimed, in a safety deposit box. The price was "only $5000." The Englishman thought it over and shrewdly decided that such a price was far too low; although he had no specific suspicions, his common sense told him something was wrong, and he turned down the offer.

Elmyr started to sweat, and while he was sweating, Fernand arrived smiling and bearing a check for $2000. It was a gift. All Fernand wanted in return was that they do business again. He didn't threaten him, although he did mention, *en passant,* that it would be a bad thing for Elmyr's tranquil existence in Ibiza if the scandal brought to light the fact that he had lived twelve years in the United States without a passport. There were such things as extradition laws.

"For me," Elmyr mourned later, "it wasn't a matter of wanting or not wanting. I just had to do it. I had no money. It was the moment I finally realized how much I depended on these son of a bitches."

Fernand placed his order: some watercolors by Dufy—horses, a view from a window overlooking the Mediterranean—a Fauve Vlaminck, possibly a Derain, and a Marquet. He had arranged to put a group of six paintings up for sale at the official government auction gallery in the town of Pontoise, twenty kilometers outside of Paris. It was a pleasant suburban setting, a favorite spot for important sales in the spring and summer when buyers enjoyed an outing from the city. With scandal already brewing in America it seemed wiser at this point not to put the paintings up under his own name, and so Richard Urbach, the young American houseguest Fernand was grooming to take Réal's place, was listed at Pontoise—without his knowledge, Urbach later claimed—as the owner. The auction was scheduled for the first week of April. The six paintings should have brought a total of about $150,000.

In late February Fernand met Elmyr at Barcelona airport. All the work was ready except one Vlaminck landscape, which Elmyr promised for the end of the month. By now Elmyr was deeply troubled; he was working slowly and, by his standards, poorly. He heard from Réal, too, who still hadn't made good on the bounced check but was understandably displeased that Elmyr and Fernand were doing business again.

"You were in jail," Elmyr explained when the young Canadian telephoned from Paris. "I was in a terrible predicament. I'm still sitting here without a dime. What can I do?"

A little afraid of Fernand by this time, Elmyr brought a young and broadshouldered Englishman along with him to Barcelona, to serve as bodyguard in the event of tantrums or table-throwing. Only then, in Barcelona airport, did Fernand tell Elmyr what had lately happened with the art dealers' visit to Meadows' house, and showed him a letter and several cables from Dallas in which the Texas oilman explained that he would like to see Fernand with a view to settling the dispute. Once again on the verge of panic, Elmyr counseled Fernand to fly immediately to Texas and make some kind of financial settlement, but Fernand only laughed and ordered another whisky. He insisted that Meadows would be advised by his tax lawyers not to make trouble. Fernand then took the paintings, gave Elmyr a check on his Swiss bank for $2000, and flew back to Paris on the next plane. He hadn't even bothered to leave the airport.

In an uneasy and despondent mood, Elmyr returned to Ibiza. He was even more despondent a week later when Matutes, the local bank, told him that Fernand's $2000 check had bounced, too. Hysterical, he called Fernand in Paris.

"*Mon cher*—" Fernand began, apologetically.

"Don't *mon cher* me," Elmyr cried. "I know that behind my back you call me 'Grandma.' You people have made millions, you've milked me like an old cow—and now the udder is dry. I'm sick and tired of you both. I'm without money. All I have to say to you is *adieu*, you son of a bitch!" And he hung up.

After several more telephone conversations of a similar nature, it seemed final. But now Fernand was missing one Vlaminck landscape, and it was listed in the Pontoise auction catalog. Other stories have been told to explain the final Pontoise *débacle,* but this is Elmyr's version. Fernand could easily have substituted something else or withdrawn the Vlaminck completely; but pride, or perhaps simply greed, got the better of him. He checked the two or three Paris warehouses where Réal's paintings might be stored, and sure enough, there was a Vlaminck landscape, an oil that he thought was about a year old. It looked older, too, because Réal, that past December, a week or so before he was flung in prison, had "aged" it with a spotty brown varnish that gave it a nice appearance of neglect as well as the faint hint of *craquelure*.

Unaware of such recent improvement, Fernand decided that it suited him perfectly. Expertises were prepared and he had it entered in the Pontoise auction.

A week later, according to Elmyr, one of the government auction house employees decided that the painting was a little *too* dirty. Gently and expertly, he began rubbing away the pale brown film that flecked portions of the canvas. When he looked at his rag he saw to his amazement that it was stained with the faint blue of Vlaminck's 1906 sky. The supposedly sixty-year-old oil paint was coming off with the dirt.

The auction house telephoned immediately to the police, and the police telephoned to Urbach. He telephoned to Fernand, who dashed down to Pontoise in an effort to withdraw the paintings. But they had been confiscated by the police, after the Vlaminck had faded before everyone's marveling eyes, for further examination.

Fernand decided not to wait around for the results. Hurrying back to the Avenue Henri-Martin, he burned all his records, packed nine leather suitcases full of clothes and jewelry, stuffed them into his red Buick convertible and that night, with Richard Urbach at the wheel, headed south. A telephone call to Richard's brother in Ibiza informed him that Elmyr had left the island for a few days to attend Lord Maugham's theater opening in Madrid.

Fernand and Richard took the boat from Barcelona. They arrived in Ibiza, broke into La Falaise by climbing over the wall and smashing a pane of glass in the kitchen door, changed the locks, moved into the Red Apartment, and took over.

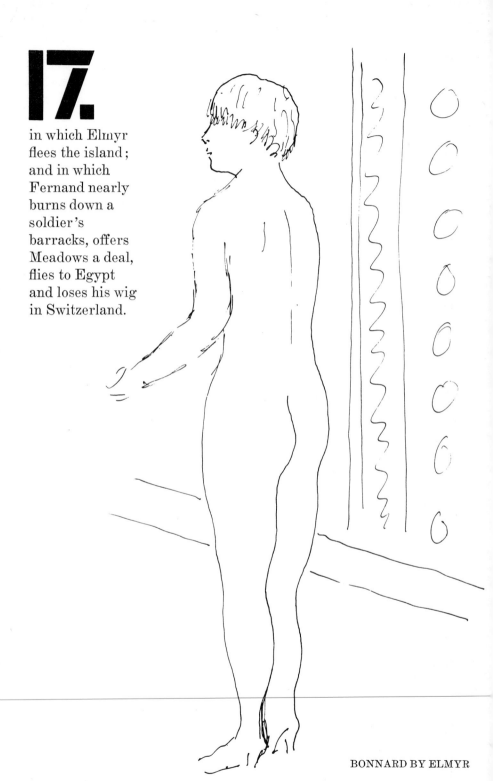

17.

in which Elmyr
flees the island;
and in which
Fernand nearly
burns down a
soldier's
barracks, offers
Meadows a deal,
flies to Egypt
and loses his wig
in Switzerland.

BONNARD BY ELMYR

t was the beginning of the end and, for the Ibiza police and the fascinated foreign colony, a long hot summer they would not soon forget. Fernand's career as an art dealer was finished. Shortly before the Pontoise scandal a Paris antique dealer and Legros customer had showed an alleged Marquet to the painter's widow for verification. Mme. Marquet, it was now revealed, had said an emphatic *"non"* and taken the painting to the police. Later in the spring a show called *Fauve et Cubiste* opened at a Left Bank gallery in Paris. A great hue and cry rose up almost immediately, and the first examination of the paintings revealed that there were thirteen probable fake Derains on exhibit. The dominoes were beginning to topple.

"I think," Elmyr said, "Fernand went down to Ibiza because he had no other place to go. The police, the collectors, the art dealers were all after him. It probably became unbearable—even for someone as slippery and callous as him. Réal also claimed that he was really broke at the time. He might conceivably have hidden out in his parents' house near Cannes, but he was afraid to stay in France. He always had it fixed in his mind that since he'd never sold anything in Spain, the Spanish authorities wouldn't extradite him."

Sometimes Fernand laughed with genuine mirth at the accusations. "It's a plot," he explained, "on the part of jealous American art dealers. They'd like to ruin me and discredit the French experts at the same time. And I've done nothing wrong. Really, if I were guilty of selling $35 million worth of fakes I should have been guillotined a long time ago."

And sometimes, like a cornered rat, he gnashed his teeth, arched his back, and bit.

"Marquet's widow? Matisse's daughter? Those half-blind old ladies?"

Or, he snapped, the whole affair was "a conspiracy on the part of those jealous art dealers in Paris." The general principle on which he operated seemed to be, as usual, one of "Vilify! Vilify! Some of it will always stick." Elmyr, he said, was a madman. "Did you know," he let slip, "that he's wanted for murder in Mexico? I swear it to you!" At night in Ibiza town he brandished a gas pistol in the form of a silver cigarette case, and the maid in La Falaise later testified that he slept with a revolver next to his bed and that his young guests carried switchblades.

Elmyr was understandably queasy about sharing the house with them. Anyway, he had papers to prove that Fernand had sold it to Réal before the Spanish consulate in New York. The case came before the local *juez de instrucción* and Fernand, after variously claiming that his signature in New York had been extorted from him under duress and then that it was a forgery, produced his trump card: a private document between himself and Elmyr in which he not only gave Elmyr the right to live in the house for life, but also abrogated his own right to sell the property. This made the sale to Réal in New York an illegal one.

"Then why did you break into the house when you got here?" Elmyr demanded.

"I didn't break in, my dear," Fernand said blandly. "I used my key."

"Not true," Elmyr cried. "I had the locks changed before I went to Madrid, and I can prove it!"

Somewhat perplexed by now, the court ruled that for the time being the house was large enough for both of them to live in. It was a dramatic moment in the little courtroom. Elmyr was pale, nearly in tears. "I am sixty years old," he cried in French (he had never before admitted to more than fifty-two)—"a refugee, a man without a country. Here, at last, I thought I had found some peace, some freedom from persecution." Glaring at Fernand, he pounded his fist on a wooden table. "This man is a maniac! He's wanted by the French police, he's living up there in my house with two boys who carry *knives*! How can you make me share the house with criminals?" The judge was sympathetic, but pointed out that in the eyes of the law it wasn't Elmyr's house to share.

Elmyr's legal and public protests had failed. Privately he pleaded with Fernand to "just, please, go away." His presence on Ibiza, much less under the same roof, would surely link the two and bring Interpol agents swarming to the island.

Fernand coolly replied: "If I go to prison, for thirty days or thirty years, it will be my greatest pleasure to take you and your criminal-minded friend with me.'' Perhaps in this moment he was finally taking his revenge for that night, nine long years ago, when Elmyr had said ''He stinks'' and asked him to leave his chic cocktail party in Murray Hill.

But it was too much for Elmyr. He was frantic and couldn't tell anyone the true reason; he was miserable in his own home, where Fernand smoked his cigars and the bodyguards played rock-and-roll music until three o'clock in the morning, threw him cold-eyed glances and swiftly depleted his supply of French champagne; and he was broke. Some well-meaning friends, under the belief that Elmyr had innocently signed some papers which linked him to Fernand's illegal operation, and would undoubtedly perish or kill himself if as a result he had to spend five years in a French jail, met with Fernand and begged him to listen to reason: to go.

But Fernand only laughed. ''I am being very kind to him,'' he said. ''I let him live in *my* house. Why does he tell such terrible lies about me?''

The friends finally counseled Elmyr to leave the island, for Fernand appeared adamant. He was living quietly at the moment, but obviously that couldn't last; he was bound to do something eventually that would bring the Spanish authorities thundering up to his door. Or the scandal would erupt, Interpol agents would arrive and he would be carted off to prison in France. In either case, it would be wiser for Elmyr to be absent.

Elmyr had lost the battle. He agreed to go. In early June he left the island—no one knew to where, and no one knew for how long. Neither did he. In time, rumors sifted back to Ibiza that he had been seen in Basel, drowned in Paris, arrested in London, and murdered in São Paulo, and then that an unknown Hungarian painter had committed suicide in Madrid. Worried friends waited and wondered. Then an unsigned but recognizable postcard arrived from Switzerland; he was deeply depressed, and he was positive that a plot had been laid to do away with him. But so far, at least, he was alive and kicking.

The summer season had arrived in Ibiza. There was sailing,

swimming, cocktail parties and new arrivals. "Have you heard anything from Elmyr?" people asked one another. The answer was usually no, and after a while people stopped asking.

Gradually Elmyr Dory-Boutin, the missing Hungarian, became only a brief tale to tell to newcomers, and an amusing if confusing memory.

Fernand, in the meantime, had announced his intention to take up permanent residence. He imported a speedboat from the South of France and made a down payment on a bar to be run by the Urbach brothers. No one could say that Fernand in the twilight of his career was bereft of humor: he called the bar The Sharks. All was relatively calm on Ibiza until, toward the end of July, Réal arrived from Paris to speak to the *juez de instrucción* about the house and hopefully negotiate a peace with his erstwhile partner. Then all hell broke loose. Within hours it was Tom and Jerry, Grand Guignol and the Keystone Cops all over again.

This time, bearing scratches, bites and cuts from the forehead to the waist, Réal limped off to the police and denounced Fernand for assault. Fernand's private defense was: "He used to *adore* it when I bit him," but publicly, to the police, he made a counterdenunciation. The fed-up Ibiza judiciary solved the problem by sentencing both claimants to fifteen days for disturbing the peace.

Ibiza jail is hardly an Alcatraz or Devil's Island. It occupies a pleasant building high in the old city next to the town hall, and the individual cells, though not quite so spacious and clean as a room in the Madrid Hilton, face a sunny, flower-bedecked patio. Prisoners are allowed to do their own cooking and import all their own amenities, including food, which is lowered in a basket into the patio from the guard's balcony above. Réal, however, wanted no part of such arrangements, however humane. He excused himself to pack his valise, skipped out the back door of his hotel and made straight for the airport, where he boarded the next plane for Barcelona and then Paris. Fernand, perhaps with no other place to go, went along to jail, taking with him from the house Elmyr's best sheets, monogrammed towels, cashmere sweaters, hi-fi set and about fifty pop records, most of which he eventually left in his cell for the comfort of future inmates.

He was a model prisoner, and he received his reward. He was released forty-eight hours before his fifteen-day sentence had run its course.

Climbing the long hill to La Falaise under a hot morning sun, he thus walked in the front door long before he was expected. The house was in complete disarray, unknown and naked girls lolled about the swimming pool and the Urbach brothers were only just waking up with powerful hangovers.

Bellowing with rage, Fernand skipped twice round the pool like a nanny goat in pursuit and then chased one French girl out the front door. Her rented car stood nearby on a slope. When the girl tried to get in and make good her escape, Fernand pushed her away, vengefully released the handbrake and sent the car spinning merrily down the narrow dirt road. It got halfway, then careened to one side and down the slope into the military barracks, where it burst into flames. Scrambling back to the house, Fernand was met by Richard Urbach, who angrily shoved him back down the steps. The fall fractured Fernand's ankle. A gaggle of sweating police, two doctors, the barracks lieutenant and a troop of smoked-out soldiers arrived at La Falaise simultaneously. The girls were dispersed, the Urbach brothers were taken into custody, and Fernand was placed under house arrest.

That evening he lay with his leg in a cast to receive Lord Kilbracken of the London *Evening Standard,* to whom—obviously with the realization that Ibiza's official hospitality had been strained that morning to its limits—he coolly offered to sell La Falaise for $200,000. Lord Kilbracken had to decline. He didn't decline, however, to act as Fernand's ambassador and special correspondent to Algur Hurtle Meadows, who happened at that time to be visiting Madrid in the hope of authenticating some of his Goyas and El Grecos.

The aristocratic English journalist subsequently reported to Meadows in his Madrid hotel room the following extraordinary offer by Fernand. For $350,000, Fernand would buy back all the alleged fake paintings sold to Meadows in Dallas, provided that payment and delivery were concluded "on neutral ground," and he proposed Switzerland. In return, Meadows was expected immediately to drop all legal proceedings. The offer had already been made through Fernand's lawyer in Paris, but Meadows hadn't heard about it yet. Kilbracken said: "He was clearly taken aback."

Lord Kilbracken also reported, in the *Evening Standard* of October 19, 1967: "It is common gossip on Ibiza, as Legros agreed (though firmly denying he was in any way involved), that a 'stable' of highly skilled forgers or copyists had been operating on the island. I had the names of several suspects."

Only two more scenes had yet to be played in the personal drama between Fernand and Réal, and the first followed hard upon Réal's clandestine return to Ibiza in early November.

Réal was still trying to make some sort of deal, but Fernand, despite the fact that the Ibiza police had seized both The Sharks bar and his $12,000 Chris-Craft and had suggested he leave the island now that his leg had healed, still wasn't playing ball. There was a brief flareup of the usual window-smashing and light fisticuffs, with the result that Réal's presence on the island was discovered and he was carted off by the weary cops to spend *his* fifteen days in jail. He wasn't too uncomfortable there. Elmyr's sheets, towels and cashmere sweaters were still scattered throughout the prison cells, left behind by Fernand in August.

A few days later, just before his departure from Spain, Fernand had one of those inexplicable seizures of soft-heartedness to which, no doubt, even the most hardened criminals are subject, when he decided to bring a hot meal to the jail to feed Réal and the other prisoners, some of whom he fondly remembered from his own incarceration. He arrived about two o'clock in the afternoon in the company of a restaurant waiter who carried in his hands a steaming skillet of chicken-and-shrimp *paella*. Fernand chatted with the prison guards, whom he knew well, then called cheerily down into the patio to Réal.

"I wanted to do you one last favor," he explained, "to show you

I have no hard feelings, so I ordered this food for you. But I just went to pick it up at the restaurant and I suddenly realized I'd changed my pants and didn't have a single peseta in my pocket. Can you lend me three hundred pesetas? I'll pay the waiter and then he'll give you the *paella*."

All the Spanish prisoners waited eagerly. The basket was lowered and came up with three crumpled notes produced from Réal's pocket. Then the basket was lowered again with the *paella*.

"Drop dead," Réal screamed.

"Hearty appetite," Fernand called down, then "*Au revoir, mon cher*," and then he left.

He flew the next day to London, where a consignment of nine paintings awaited him at a forwarding agent. They were the remainder of the stock of fakes that he had taken out last year to South Africa, and Fernand had shipped them from Johannesburg in the name of André Robert, a pseudonym he used on several false passports. The apartment on the Avenue Henri-Martin had already been mortgaged and finally sold in October by his Paris lawyer. Fernand telephoned the lawyer from London, just to find out how things were going, and learned that an international warrant for his arrest had been issued that same day, following a final charge by Algur Hurtle Meadows, who had turned down the offer delivered by Lord Kilbracken.

Fernand hung up the telephone, packed his luggage, called his forwarding agents and instructed them to have his crate of paintings placed aboard the next plane for Cairo. Then he paid his bill and took a taxi to London Airport. When the plane left for Cairo, he was on it.

For three months Fernand lived in Cairo and Ismailia, where he had been born, claiming Egyptian citizenship and thus avoiding extradition by the French authorities. He might have stayed there forever if in February of 1968 a young man giving the name and passport of André Charles Martin had not passed a reported $12,000 worth of bad checks in Switzerland. The young man was caught, and under interrogation he admitted that his real name was Réal Lessard. Where Réal had spent the last of his money, and why he should have taken such a risk under the circumstances of his new notoriety, is still unknown; after he was jailed in Geneva to await trial he refused to make a statement. But this was only prelude to an even stranger development.

With all the bitterness, denunciations and furious fights of the last few years, Fernand must still have felt something resembling tenderness for his former partner. Either that or he was afraid that under pressure Réal would talk. In early April a swaggering, suntanned blond man in his late thirties, bearing a British passport in the name of Fernand MacDonald, checked into a Geneva businessman's hotel. He wore what was later described as "hippie clothing." The maid thought it strange that he had a complete make-up kit on his bedside table. The Swiss hotelkeeper thought it strange that he spent the whole day on the telephone to Paris and New York trying to arrange the release from a Swiss prison of one Monsieur Réal Lessard.

The Swiss police were tipped, and when they got a glimpse of him in the bar, despite the dark glasses and yellow hair they thought they recognized their man. A call went out over the loudspeaker: "Paging Monsieur Legros. Telephone call for Monsieur Fernand Legros."

Fernand MacDonald hesitated a minute, got up from his chair, took two steps, saw the law bearing down on him, turned pale and tried to run for it. In the scuffle he lost his dark glasses and blond wig. That evening, as the *Frankfurter Allgemeine* reported under its column "Cultural News," "one of the most successful fakers of the past years [had] been arrested and jailed in Geneva by the Swiss police."

It was the end of the line for Cleopatra and The Peasant.

18.

in which
Elmyr
comes home
at last, is
accused of
a crime
he didn't
commit, and
takes his deck
chair to prison.

MODIGLIANI BY ELMYR

During all this time the hapless, harried Hungarian was fleeing through the capitals, fleshpots and culture centers of Europe, from Madrid to Lausanne to Berlin and back again, a human yo-yo with neither a resting place nor a clue. A weary and unhappy refugee once again, Elmyr longed for the peace and anonymity he had known, if briefly, on his once-tranquil island home.

The first place he had gone after leaving Ibiza was Paris, to see a lawyer recommended to him by a close friend on the island. By complete coincidence, the man turned out to be the lawyer of Mme. Duthuit as well. Elmyr found himself in an office surrounded by Matisse drawings and lithographs. After his first natural expressions of admiration he hardly dared look at them a second time, for fear that his knowledgeable interest might reveal his identity. A casual glance, in any case, convinced him that none of them was his.

The lawyer, on Elmyr's behalf, tried to contact Fernand on Ibiza in an attempt to convince him to evacuate La Falaise, but Fernand refused to answer cables and letters and finally hung up in the middle of a telephone conversation. Elmyr then decided he didn't dare go back to the island until Fernand left. When that would be, he had no idea.

He was miserable. He had no money. He borrowed from his friends until in late July when he heard from Réal, who had just finished his brief jail sentence in Ibiza and had returned to Paris. Looking as always for some fast profit, Réal bought a Giacometti bronze—cheap, for $8000—and he gave it now to Elmyr to sell in Switzerland. No sooner did Elmyr get his hands on it than word of a minor scandal flashed through the art world: the Giacometti, a female nude, was one of six unauthorized casts made from the original bronze, and therefore considered a forgery. Réal was shocked, enraged—how could they do such a thing to *him?*—and he threatened to sue. But somehow, in Geneva, Elmyr finally managed to sell the bronze for $3300. The money paid what he considered his most urgent bills, including one for garaging and repair of the Corvette in Barcelona. Somewhat shaken, Elmyr holed up for a while in Sitges, on the Costa Brava.

By October he was broke again. He went to Berlin, where he had been invited by friends. Every day, or so it seemed to his anxious eyes, the Paris newspapers carried articles about *Fernand Legros et les faux tableaux*. In every art gallery he visited the talk was about Meadows, the scandal at Pontoise, the faked expertises. In his dreams, waking or sleeping, Elmyr saw the blade of the guillotine poised above his neck. He didn't dare to sell. He called for help to Réal in Paris.

"That Legros," he said bitterly, "has ruined the art market."

Then, finally, in late November a telegram from a friend in Ibiza informed him that Fernand was gone, fled to sanctuary in mother Egypt. Elmyr drove to Barcelona and garaged the Corvette, which, under a Spanish law that says no foreign car may be operated in the country for more than six months, he no longer had the legal right to drive in Spain. A day later, wearing dark glasses and his blue blazer, he alighted jauntily from a DC-3 in Ibiza airport.

La Falaise looked as if a California motorcycle club had spent a long weekend there. Windows were shattered, chairs overturned, his phonograph and records were missing, dedications had been torn from the flyleafs of books, ashtrays were full, clothes were strewn about and ripped, cigarette holes had been burned in the leather upholstery of his favorite easy chair. But it was still home. With the aid of his Spanish maid, he set about cleaning up. Then he went off into town to the Café Alhambra to announce his arrival.

"El-*myr*!"

Within a few weeks the easel was set up in the studio off the bedroom and Elmyr was at work, soft brown eyes aglow, painting brightly colored landscapes and portraits of his friends. Finishing each one, he signed it, as if in final compromise with the many pseudonyms of his life—*Elmyr*.

Most other painters who saw the new oils, however, were disappointed. They seemed strangely sentimental, out of tune with any of the vital contemporary art movements. It was as if Elmyr were still living in the days of the Académie la Grande-Chaumière, and even of the Akademie Heimann in Munich. The color was vivid and the compositions were sound, but somehow the guiding hand behind the brush seemed unsure of itself. A passion and a direction were lacking.

Although he had never seen the work, Jack O'Hana of London's O'Hana Gallery had foreseen at least the initial results. "De Hory," he said, after the scandal broke, "is a genius at faking, or copying—but not a creative genius. For him to have been able to fake so *many* artists successfully is astounding. But for that very reason I'd be extremely surprised if he could paint well now, I mean his own work. You get too much into the habit of borrowing from other men. You forget who you are."

"But," said Elmyr, who was basically disinterested in such criticism, "the faking is finished. I came out of it without a dime. It's the dealers and the art galleries who made a fortune, buying as cheap as they could from me and selling as dear as they could to the collectors. I've suffered enough. I just want to paint my own paintings and hope that people will buy them because it's good art, not because the signature is famous. And I want to keep on living here. I like the sun and the sea. I like Spain. I love Ibiza."

He made the point often that he had never abused the hospitality of his Spanish hosts; in the rare moments when he admitted anything he still emphatically denied having painted any of the fakes in Ibiza or any other part of Spain. "This is my home," he said, "and in it, something which Fernand Legros did never understand, I try to live with dignity."

This try for the dignified life was, unfortunately, fated to be shortlived. In February he briefly met with Réal in Barcelona, and so he knew the worst. Later he read in the French newspaper, *Le Monde,* first about Réal's imprisonment in Geneva and then the tale of Fernand's capture. About Fernand's fate he couldn't have cared less, except insofar as his own liberty was endangered. Despite his being convinced that Réal had tried to poison him during their final farewell in Barcelona airport—"We had a coffee together," he related somewhat ingenuously to a friend, "then Réal got up suddenly and said he had to go, and an hour later in my hotel I did have these terrible stomach cramps"—he had to admit that he felt sorry for the younger of his two former partners.

"He's only twenty-eight years old," he said, "and look—his

life is already ruined. He was corrupted at too early an age. If there was *any* way I could help him, I would do it. But my hands are tied. I may be next,'' he added uneasily.

Elmyr had known all along that there would be some sort of reckoning to be faced. Coming back to Ibiza was the act of a man who was tired of living on the run, tired of using false names, tired of a secret and underground existence and tired of practicing a tainted profession—in short, tired. Staying there now was the gamble of a man who had no other place to go. Somehow he believed that even if his name were linked conclusively with the scandal, even if Fernand Legros or Réal Lessard confessed and implicated him—which was unlikely, since only *his* confession before the law could conclusively convict *them*—the Spanish authorities would show leniency and let him live out his days quietly in La Falaise. He dreaded the final reckoning to the point where he thought he would commit suicide rather than face even a five-year prison term, but at the same time he could only face day-to-day living by deluding himself that somehow, some way, nothing would happen to him. He would be spared.

It was wishful more than intelligent thinking. Still, in one way he was right. He had been advised by a Spanish lawyer that if he hadn't personally sold any of the false paintings in Spain, hadn't painted them in Spain, and hadn't faked any Spanish masters, then he had committed no crime under Spanish law and Madrid would neither imprison him nor permit his extradition to France or the United States. So far, so good. Jean-Louis, his old friend from Paris, provided him with some money and he had borrowed a further $700 from Réal the week before that unfortunate young man was nailed by the Swiss police for passing bad checks. He collected a few old debts while explaining to patient friends on Ibiza that he couldn't pay his own, he made a tentative arrangement to dictate his memoirs for sale to *Look* magazine, and he continued living and painting in La Falaise. Nothing happened. Everyone gossiped, but no one accused him. Most people still didn't believe he had either the genius, discipline or discretion to have done what a few gullible others said he had done. If anyone asked him point-blank, he simply smiled and said, ''What do *you* think?'' No Guardia Civil or Interpol agent knocked on his door. He invited local Ibizenco dignitaries to his house and they accepted the invitations; they returned his greetings in front of the Café Alhambra where he sat each morning sipping coffee with his friends. Gradually he felt more and more secure. He was a bird of bright plumage and it was not his style to walk round in sackcloth and ashes with bowed head. Once again he began to give lunches and parties. He brought his fire-engine-red Corvette Sting Ray convertible over from Barcelona, applying for a temporary customs permit on the grounds that he wanted to sell it, and tooled round the streets of Ibiza with the top down like a free man.

Perhaps this last act, among others, was his undoing—a pardonable and human indiscretion, but unwise. By now the Spanish authorities in both Ibiza and Madrid knew very well his connection with the imprisoned Legros and Lessard, and an article in the French newspaper *L'Aurore* named him specifically as the painter. Perhaps the Spaniards resented the fact that this man, Elmyr Dory-Boutin—if not actually a criminal, then certainly the accomplice of accused criminals—flaunted so flagrantly the fact that he was at liberty under the warm Spanish sun. But when this was suggested to Elmyr by a friend, a high-ranking Spanish diplomat from Madrid whom Elmyr had openly embraced at a party attended by many Ibizenco officials, Elmyr was visibly shocked.

"What do they expect me to do?" he asked, deeply offended. *"Hide?"*

At heart he still believed—or wanted to believe—that he had done nothing wrong. And if he had, then surely he had paid the penalty in the seven months when he was on the run throughout Europe. Was he to be hounded for the rest of his life? The thought was intolerable.

In any case, and for whatever reason, Madrid in late June began a routine investigation of the man known to them then as Joseph Elmyr Dory-Boutin. Since he had apparently broken no law, the inquiry was conducted by the Madrid court for *Vagos y Malientes* —a colloquial translation of which would be "vagrants and socially undesirables." The ultimate threat was permanent exile from Spain. Elmyr flew back and forth from Ibiza to Madrid three times in the months of June and July, conferring with his lawyer and rounding up hopefully influential people in the capital who might provide affidavits and exert some pressure in his defense. A petition also was circulated in Ibiza, signed by a number of French, Danish, English and American actors, writers and singers, all friends of Elmyr, stating in effect that he was a gentleman and a scholar and didn't deserve at his advanced age to be once more made homeless and booted out into an unfriendly world. The lawyer tried unsuccessfully for a postponement of the case until October. But on the eve of final judgment, to be rendered in *camera oscura,* Elmyr was oddly confident. Somehow, some way, something would work out. He was a refugee, there were conventions of international rights to protect him—they *couldn't* throw him out. Where could he go? More to the point, who would have him?

But the Madrid court proved more prone to considerations of Spanish law and morality than the well-meant opinions of Elmyr's actor and writer friends. A decision was reached the first week of August. The indictment contained a potpourri of charges ranging from homosexuality and consorting with known criminals to "no visible means of support," but considering that he was a refugee the penalty of permanent exile was not imposed. Instead, a sentence was given of two months in prison—and possibly more, depending on further evidence. The police arrived at La Falaise that same evening to escort Elmyr to Ibiza jail.

At first Elmyr was depressed beyond belief. He was allowed visitors, and the spectacle he presented to them was that of a broken man. His shoulders were bowed, his cheeks looked waxy and sunken, and he had neglected to touch up his hair so that now for the first time it was gray. He spoke so softly that people had difficulty in hearing him.

"My dear," he confided to a friend, "I'm going to kill myself."

"Don't," she said. "I'm sure they won't keep you here for more than the two months, and we all still love you. Is there anything you need?"

The Ibiza jail, as has been mentioned before, was not run along the lines of Alcatraz. He gave a list, which included food parcels, his bed from La Falaise, a deck chair, books, phonograph, toilet articles, sleeping pills, tranquilizers, some clothing, and money. All duly arrived. Other of his personal possessions were already in the jail, left there by Fernand Legros and in use by other prisoners.

The bed was set up in his cell, the deck chair just outside in the prison patio.

If anything, Elmyr was a survivor. The other prisoners were for the most part young foreigners, hippies without money who had been apprehended naked on the beach or sleeping in parked cars, a few boys charged with possession of marijuana and petty theft. The English Vice-Consul came to visit them regularly, cheer them up, and try to get their sentences commuted. Within a week Elmyr had hired one of them as his personal servant; he cleaned Elmyr's cell, washed Elmyr's plates and cooking utensils, and set up Elmyr's deck chair in the shady or sunny part of the courtyard as desired. It was even rumored that Elmyr kept his drinks next door, in the *ayuntamiento,* or town hall, in the mayor's refrigerator. His requests to his friends on the outside began to include extra bars of soap, a pair of sandals for a barefoot cellmate, and a number of combs. He had never liked to be surrounded by anything unclean or distasteful to his sensibilities.

Most of his friends came regularly to see him. To one of them, one Monday morning, he said ebulliently: "My dear, yesterday, on Sunday, I had not twelve—not thirteen—but *fourteen* visitors. What you think of *that?*"

Obviously it was not all so gratifying; no jail is a paradise, though the lack of external pressures may suggest it to the uninitiated. In one letter to the outside he wrote despondently: "I get heavy sleeping pills every night, and most of the night I am awake, looking at the locked door, the dirty walls, the dirty floor. . . ."

But the following day an English visitor came to see him, and while he was waiting for the guard to go downstairs and notify Elmyr, he peered down through the one narrow window into the prison courtyard. Most of the prisoners, pale and bearded young men, in faded jeans and worn T-shirts, sat or lay about in the shade, heads folded on their arms or staring listlessly at the hot blue sky overhead.

In the center of the courtyard in the sunshine was Elmyr. Wearing dark glasses, an orange sport shirt and white Bermuda shorts, he lay on the deck chair which had previously graced the side of his swimming pool, reading yesterday's edition of *Le Monde.* It was an image difficult to forget.

19.

in which, after numerous other authorities render their verdicts, Elmyr has the last word.

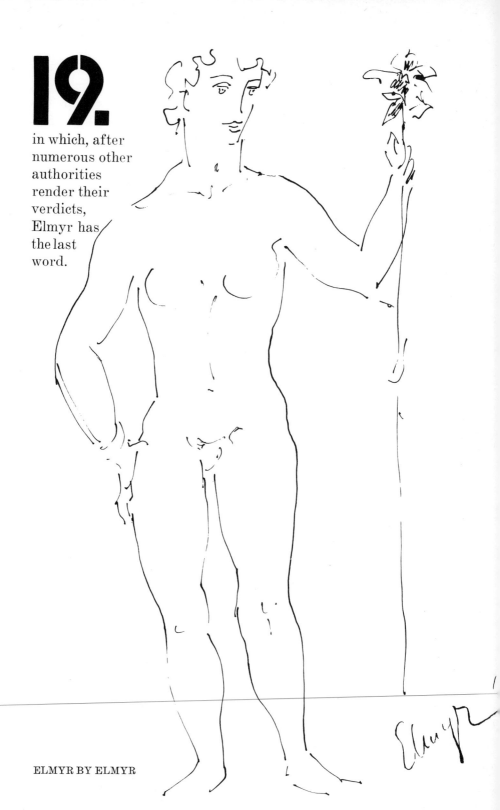

ELMYR BY ELMYR

n early May 1968 Fernand received a three-month suspended
sentence for entering Switzerland on a forged British passport,
but was kept under arrest pending a decision on whether to
hand him over to France to face charges of fraud. He also owed
the American Express Company more than $25,000 for credit-card
expenditure in half a dozen countries. In October he attempted to
commit suicide by taking an overdose of barbiturates, but failed.
French efforts to extradite him have so far been equally without
success. "The Swiss," explained Maître Roger Hauert, who once
played the rôle of Fernand's lawyer in Paris and owns the magnificent Dufy that was featured on the catalog of the *Hommage à
Dufy* show, "are protectors of humanity."

A good many rumors have wafted through Paris art circles to
explain this curious situation. The most flamboyant—and the one
most often repeated by responsible dealers on Madison Avenue
and the Avenue Matignon—is that Fernand Legros was on intimate terms with not one, but two ministers in the French cabinet,
one of whom reportedly dined in the apartment on the Avenue
Henri-Martin several times. Both are thought to be homosexual,
and the story goes that Fernand bribed them—that is, sought their
good will and protection in the event of future trouble—by procur-
ing and offering young men, both in and out of his harem. Privately, Réal Lessard laughed at this accusation, then added: "If
there was any bribing, it was done with paintings." Certainly it
seems odd that for so many years Fernand operated as openly as
he did, as a suspect art dealer, without once being tagged out by
the authorities. Undoubtedly the French police, with their unex-
celled network of paid informers, previously knew the whole lurid
circumstances of his private life. For years he had used three passports, French, British and Canadian, under the assumed name of
André Robert. He was never arrested, never interrogated. He was
only finally indicted, after the scandal had already reached gigantic proportions, when a foreigner, an American, Algur Hurtle
Meadows, pressed charges. What pressures were applied from
above we may never know until Fernand Legros writes his
memoirs—and even then perhaps not.

"I have no idea if we'll ever get him," said Gérard Lorin, Commissaire de Police of the Paris Brigade Criminelle. "As for the man who calls himself Elmyr Dory-Boutin, it's impossible. We'd have to have witnesses who saw him paint the paintings, sign them with false signatures and turn them over to Legros and Lessard. We'd have to prove he knew they were going to be sold as Vlamincks and Derains and Dufys, and not simply hung on the walls of Legros' apartment. I frankly don't think it can be done." In New York, however, Joseph Stone, the Assistant District Attorney who successfully prosecuted David Stein, has been painstakingly amassing evidence in an effort to bring forth an indictment of the swindlers. In June 1968, the closets and walls of the somber Leonard Street offices of the District Attorney of New York County contained enough fake oils, watercolors, drawings and gouaches to start a small museum. There were more under lock and key at a downtown storage house.

Fernand and Réal, of course, won't reveal the list of those to whom they've sold, and the records had been destroyed in 1967. Elmyr doesn't know, and the buyers themselves can scarcely be expected to come flying forth from anonymity and say "I'm the idiot who . . ." and "Yes, I took a tax writeoff back in '63 on. . . ." The exceptions to this are Meadows, who pressed charges in Paris, and two New York collectors who are suing the Parke-Bernet Galleries and their former appraiser, Carroll Hogan, on the grounds that the Dufys they bought at auction in 1962 were not Dufys at all (both were watercolors by Elmyr, consigned to Parke-Bernet by Fernand) and that Parke-Bernet had "impliedly [sic] warranted that the painting was an authentic painting by Raoul Dufy, had been signed by Raoul Dufy and would pass as such without objection in the trade."

Parke-Bernet denies every allegation and points to the much-debated disclaimer in its auction catalogs, which then explained that "all property is sold 'as is' and neither the Galleries nor its consignor warrants or represents, and they shall in no event be responsible for, the correctness of description, genuineness, authorship, provenience or condition of the property."

Since being taken over by Sotheby's of London, the New York auction house has adopted the somewhat more liberal disclaimer of its English big brother, which says in effect that if within twenty-one days of the sale a purchaser informs Parke-Bernet that he thinks he has a forgery and can prove it "beyond reasonable doubt" within two weeks after that, the man's money will be cheerfully refunded. Alvin Lane, legal counsel for the two art collectors who have filed suit, scoffed at the new provisions. "What meaning is the twenty-one-day clause," he asked, "if the auction house won't tell you the name of the previous owner? They never do. How can any buyer conduct an intelligent investigation?"

"We act merely as agent," explained Peregrine Pollen, the young Englishman who is president of Parke-Bernet under the new Sotheby's management. Regarding the art auction bill then before the New York state legislature which would limit the authority of general disclaimers in auction house art catalogs, he said: "The Attorney General's motive in protecting the consumer is admirable but his experience of the fine-art market is limited and there is no need for such legislation. It is an attempt to change the centuries-old practice of auction sales. If the Governor signs this bill in the form in which it was drafted, it will drive business out of New York, particularly estate sales, and will severely undermine and possibly destroy this city's pre-eminent position in the world's art market." Regarding Fernand Legros himself: "Obviously the previous Parke-Bernet shareholders failed to take sufficient precautions. We can't be held responsible for their mistakes."

But the bill, sparked by Attorney General Louis J. Lefkowitz, who spoke of a climate in the New York art market "where chicanery and fakery thrive," was approved by Governor Rockefeller and became law on September 1, 1968.

The international art market, of course, is in difficulties—and they may only have just begun. Dealers are searching everywhere for reasons and excuses. One who doesn't is Fred Schoneman. "Anyone who buys a painting for the value of ten cents on the dollar," he said succinctly, "must be an idiot or a crook."

But the others disagree.

"We're only human," said Herbert Kende, formerly a partner in the defunct New York auction house and now owner of Selected Artists Galleries. "There is no dealer, from the biggest to the

[NUMBER 64]

RAOUL DUFY

FRENCH: 1880-1953

64. *LA MOISSON*. View looking across an open wheat field with harvesters resting at left, another figure at right; the outlines of a village in the distance. Signed at lower left RAOUL DUFY.

21½x 25¾ inches (54.5 x 65.5 *cm.*)

Note: A certificate from M. André Pacitti, dated December 2, 1963, accompanies this work.

From the Galerie Blanche Denis, Paris

Exposition, Hommage à Raoul Dufy, Honfleur, 1958

[See illustration]

34

A page from a catalog
of the Parke-Bernet Galleries
in New York.
~~The painting shown,~~
La Moisson,
is supposedly by Dufy.
It was painted by
Elmyr in 1964.

smallest, who has never been stuck with a wrong painting once or twice."

"I'm not infallible," Jack O'Hana confessed in London. "I bought two Picassos some years ago from a young French forger named Schoecrunn. He was caught. But I guarantee every painting I sell, and so the loss was mine."

From another London gallery owner: "I can't understand why the New York dealers made such a fuss over the Legros affair. It's hurt our business badly over here, especially with American customers. Perls and Hahn and their clique wanted to call attention to themselves. The ADAA—the Art Dealers Association of America —is trying to set itself up as a kind of art Mafia."

"But it's not just Legros," said the wife of the owner of a large Paris gallery. "It's all the in-between people who have ruined the market. Running about like rabbits, buying and selling from dealer to dealer, trying to make what the Americans call 'a quick buck.' My husband's family has been in the art business for three generations. These new people have neither the taste, the experience, nor the capital to back them if they make a mistake."

"All this trouble," lamented Mme. Margouliès of the Niveau Gallery, who tore up the fake Chagalls she had bought in order to keep them off the market forever, "started with the expertises and certificates of authenticity. Before that you never dreamed of giving one. My husband, if you'd asked him for one, would have shown you the door. A dealer's good judgment and personal guarantee were sufficient. And now," she added, pinpointing the post-Elmyr problem that has begun to arise in the art world, "I wouldn't buy a Dufy or a Fauve Derain from *anybody*—not under *any* circumstances."

But the meaning of her words, and the full effect of the scandal, seems still unfelt. In April 1968 Sotheby's in a three-day sale knocked down 388 modern paintings, drawings and sculptures for a total gross of $5 million—including a Picasso that went for $300,000 and a Braque that brought $276,000. Then, in October, Parke-Bernet auctioned off ten Impressionist and modern paintings for over $3 million, including a Renoir landscape which established the world auction record for an Impressionist painting:

$1,550,000. The following evening seventy paintings from the collection of Dr. Roudinesco went on the block—including a Fauve-period Dufy, a Vlaminck landscape and a van Dongen—bringing a total of $2,785,250.

On December 10 *Look* magazine published an article which definitely named Elmyr as the forger who had provided Fernand Legros with his inventory. In the following issue *Look* published a letter from Ralph F. Colin, Administrative Vice-President of the Art Dealers Association of America. After making the amazing statement that it was "largely the result of the Association's activities that Messrs. Legros, Lessard and de Hory were all put in jail"—which is about as far from the truth as it was possible to get—Mr. Colin went on to write: "We feel that the public should be warned against assuming that the entire art market is fraudulent because the press from time to time reports sensational art frauds. Hundreds of millions of dollars of authentic works of art are sold annually by honest art dealers. The situation in the art market is akin to that in the airplane-transportation industry. Airlines fly their planes millions of miles without press comment. Only the rare airplane accident is reported." What Mr. Colin failed to mention was that the safety of the airline passenger and the price he pays for his air ticket are respectively supervised and regulated by an agency of the United States government, and a comparable supervision and regulation in the art world would put virtually every art dealer and gallery owner out of business overnight. He might also have pointed out that an airplane crash or a violation of safety regulations instantly becomes public knowledge, whereas a fake painting can be sold—and has been, thousands of times— without the buyer, much less the public, being any the wiser. Obviously, most dealers, auction houses, museums and galleries are looking the other way and pretending that Elmyr de Hory and Fernand Legros never happened; while those that admit it shrug their shoulders and say "It's of no importance." But the art establishment, had it known back in March 1968 that Fernand was definitely shuttling back and forth between Cairo and Ismailia, might well have paid him a handsome income just to stay there, or perhaps even taken the more secure step of contacting Israeli intelligence to see if something could be worked out.

Elmyr himself, in one of his final statements before he went to jail, may have had the last word on the subject of the art market.

"It's absolutely out of proportion," he said—"the money that's been paid in relation to the value of the paintings. Certain old or disfigured postage stamps have an immense value, not for their beauty or the art work in them, but for their rarity. But modern paintings—by that I mean twentieth-century so-called French masterpieces, Matisse, Dufy and so forth, and the Fauves—are not really rare at all. Those men were prolific painters. Their works are in every big gallery and museum in the world. And they haven't necessarily got this great value because they're *masterpieces*—not at all. If you think of long-dead, fabulous and fantastic artists like Franz Hals or Rembrandt, and the other great pre-Renaissance painters, and then you realize that some of their paintings fetch comparably smaller prices today than a Miró or a Renoir or a Picasso—then your hair stands up like you touched an electric wire! Really, it's just incredible that someone like a Picasso, a living artist—between two cigarettes he makes a little drawing and that is transferred immediately into gold. John Paul Getty is supposed to be the richest man in the world, but in a given year, if he wanted to, Picasso could make more money than Getty. He can make a line and sign his name to it and get cash for it in five seconds by just picking up the telephone. Fantastic! It's a situation unparalleled in the history of art or commerce. I heard a story from Fernand Legros that he sent one of my Picassos to Picasso for an authentication, and Picasso, who wasn't quite sure, asked the man who brought it, 'How much did the dealer pay for it?' The man mentioned a huge amount, maybe $100,000, and Picasso said, 'Well, if he paid that much, it must be real.'

"The whole situation today," Elmyr continued, "was built up artificially over the years by a group of art dealers around the world. The public has been completely duped. And now the dealers are forced to keep up the market because there's so much money involved. That's one of the reasons that Fernand Legros will never be transferred to a French or American court and have to defend himself—because it would do terrible damage to a big, big business. Not only the interests of the great galleries, which are worth billions, but also the interests of museums, public institutions who have paid fabulous prices over the last twenty years, and often with public money. Also the great fortunes, like Ford and Rockefeller and Du Pont in America, have spent immense sums on paintings, on the recommendations of experts and museums, as an investment. They all want to keep their investment secure in the same way the stock exchange wants to keep blue-chip stocks secure —they don't want that they should stumble down like in Wall Street in 1929. And in the kind of scandal that could be created in front of a court by a Fernand Legros—who will accuse, who will not *hesitate* to accuse, two dozen big dealers who helped him sell paintings, two dozen experts and four dozen big museums—these things *will* come stumbling down. It would be a 1929 crash for the art world.''

Whatever the crash, Elmyr's own position—such as it is—seems secure as *le maître* of fraudulent art. Since the beginning of his career in 1946—first in Europe, then during twelve fugitive years in the United States, and finally in Europe again with one trip to South America—he had drawn or painted an estimated one thousand works of art which were then attributed to French masters from Modigliani to Picasso, sold by major art galleries and hung in modern art museums and premier private collections from New York to Tokyo and Capetown to Stockholm. The range is so wide that in some cases, confronted with reproductions of what was indisputably his own handicraft, he was unable to recognize it. ''I never understood,'' he said recently, ''the scale of the thing I was doing.''

In fact, had it not been for the bizarre personal problems and slapstick shenanigans of his two far-ranging salesmen, Fernand Legros and Réal Lessard, the truth about Elmyr might never have been discovered—that his product had bolstered the international art market and yet gone virtually undetected, as had his true identity, for more than twenty years; that his enormous output, his scope, his vision and artistic skill, are unmatched in the history of his strange underground profession. He was and is the most prolific and successful art forger the world has ever known.

The value in the art market of his life's work is difficult to calculate, but *Le Figaro* estimated that what was sold worldwide by Legros and Lessard alone, in the years 1961–1967, if undetected as forgeries, would bring at today's bullish prices about $60 million. This is probably an exaggeration; Elmyr himself laughed at the figure. Still, it represents less than a third of what he himself peddled during his previous twelve years as a fugitive journeying back and forth across the United States.

"Undoubtedly," said F. R. Fehse, owner of the Galerie Münsterberg in Basel, "he is some kind of genius. But which kind, I don't know. All I know is that no one quite like him has ever existed before. And," he added solemnly, "we all pray that no one like him will ever exist again."

Not every authority, however, agrees with Fehse, or with the New York gallery owner who recently said (but refused for obvious reasons to have his name linked with the statement) : "When it came to doing Matisse, de Hory was better than Matisse."

"There is no such thing as a good fake," said Philippe Huisman amid the eighteenth-century decor of the Wildenstein Foundation in Paris, which was given the task of making the final judgment on the ill-fated Meadows collection. "No faker," Huisman explained, "has the talent and the passion of the master. The work is weak or stiff. The line lacks the essential vitality. You might say that de Hory's *faux tableaux* are on a par with the worst work of the great French geniuses he copied."

Fiery little Philippe Reichenbach, on the other hand, who moved his gallery seven years ago from Houston, Texas, to the Avenue Matignon, laughs with Elmyr at the experts and at the more pompous of his fellow art dealers.

"I was there," he related, "when the President of the Academy called in four experts to look at a little Derain that he thought was 'wrong.' It was on the floor, propped carelessly against the wall, unframed, and the four experts came into the room—looked at it each one for, I assure you, not more than a second—and then laughed. They smirked, they sneered: 'How ghastly! What a joke! How could anyone believe for a second that it's a Derain? It's so *obviously* a fake!' *Voilà.* Then the President asked the four experts to look at a Derain that belonged to *him,* and tell him what they thought of it. They looked, they rubbed their hands, they rolled their eyes with admiration. They cooed: 'How beautiful, how masterly, how typical a Derain,' and so forth until you wanted to throw up.

"Well," Reichenbach confided, "I can assure you, the Derain that belonged to the President was *awful.* A real Derain it might have been, but even Derain, you know, had his bad days when his wife burned the toast and his cigarette ashes fell on the palette. And the little fake on the floor was really, in some parts, quite lovely. But the experts had made up their minds before they entered the room.

"I will tell you, the only sound test for a painting would be to put a fake Derain in a room with nine real Derains and then have four experts pick out the wrong one. Let's make the test," Reichenbach chortled, his eyes aglow with anticipation. "I'd love to be there!"

"It is difficult to explain how you recognize a fake," Klaus Perls once stated. "The first look at a work of art has to give you the emotional response of truth or fake. You can write whole books on what this first look implies. It is the summing up of all the knowledge you've acquired, all the things you've seen of the artist, all you've read. . . . I've handled the works of Vlaminck for over thirty years and I know what his works look like. One of the fakes we saw [in the Meadows collection] was supposed to have been painted in 1905. Paintings of this period have mellowed in sixty years. The particular picture I saw is totally unmellowed. It's brand-new. What happens to colors is that they age and blend chemically. Colors on a brand-new painting change as they blend together in the process of drying. This process takes several years. That is why it is comparatively easy to spot a fake five years or more after it is done. It will have aged differently from the way the original works of the artist aged. . . .

"No one who produces a fake can avoid putting his own personality into it somehow, and that personality just isn't the personality of the artist you know so well who is being forged. The better you know this personality, the easier it is to detect the forgery. A work of art is a direct extension of the personality of the artist. This is something the forger cannot do.''

Elmyr might legitimately have disagreed. Out of a confused cynicism, relating the tale of a museum director who had given his expertise to some Matisse ''lithographs,'' Elmyr had once asked: ''What is the sense of it? What is the moral of it?''

Contemporary art dealer Ivan Spence's answer is right to the point. ''Anyone who paid fifty or sixty thousand dollars for one of these paintings,'' he said, ''deserves to be taken for a ride. I think it's all highly amusing. Is a Matisse so beautiful or so rare that it's worth that kind of money? Nonsense! Let's end this veneration of what's old and outdated. Let's end this bloody business of an art 'market.' What one can hope for is that the whole scandal will teach people to buy the work of young, living painters.''

The other side of the coin was expressed by a Boston art collector who, ten years ago, bought two Renoir watercolors from one of the top New York galleries and now realizes that he owns a pair of Renoirs-by-Elmyr. ''I would be a complete hypocrite,'' he admitted, ''if I bore the artist a lasting grudge. I don't buy paintings the way I buy stock in A.T. & T. and Xerox. I've had ten years of pleasure from my Renoirs—or Renoirs-by-Elmyr, call them what you will—and I'll have twenty more years if I'm lucky. Then I'll leave them to my two sons and tell them, 'These are things of beauty. Enjoy them for what they are, not for the signature they bear or what someone else tells you they are or aren't.' ''

A similar story is told by Joseph Faulkner of the Main Street Art Galleries in Chicago. In 1956, after he had learned that the drawings and paintings he had bought from the man he knew as Raynal were fake, Faulkner informed his clients of the fact and offered to give them back their money. One collector in Minneapolis, who had bought a Modigliani drawing, said: ''I think I'll keep it awhile, if you don't mind.'' Shortly afterward the collector traveled to Europe and showed photographs of the drawing to various experts and gallery owners in Paris, who examined them and assured him that the original was "undoubtedly genuine." Recently, after the scandal broke and L. E. Raynal was revealed to be Elmyr de Hory, Faulkner spoke to his client again and said, "Can I have it back now?"

"Are you serious?" the collector said. "Never! I wouldn't give it up for anything. I want you to come up here to Minneapolis and write on the back of the drawing—'I, Joseph Faulkner, certify that this is an original and genuine Modigliani fake by Elmyr de Hory.'"

Despite the apparent lack of expert knowledge on the part of the art establishment, when one asks why Elmyr was so consistently successful as a forger one must take a more positive approach toward *le maître*'s personal skill and vision. He knew what he was doing. He chose his subjects exclusively from the period he understood best—he was a product of the same epoch, the same European background, the same schools of artistic thinking—and he was never tempted to stray. He had been friendly or acquainted with Léger, Vlaminck, van Dongen, Picasso and Derain; and, until the end, when he was influenced and then pressured by Fernand Legros, he only painted subjects for which he had, as he put it, "an affinity," such as his Modigliani heads and his Matisse nudes.

This personal preference for portraits and figural work, coupled with his ability to implement it, was one of the major factors in Elmyr's success. There is no quicker way to spot a fake or a copy of a masterpiece than by studying the rendering of an ear or a hand, or the expression on a face. All the greatest painters (until the abstract-anything goes-pop-op era) had that knowledge in the hand which with a simple line would capture a mood, make a personal statement and leave no feeling of accident in what had been drawn or painted. Beyond doubt, Elmyr had it, too. A lesser artist would have been forced to avoid nudes and portraits like the plague, or be quickly challenged by the *Herr Direktors*. The dealers were right when they looked at Elmyr's Matisse and Picasso figural drawings and thought: "Yes. It's the work of a craftsman and a master."

Beyond that, he took the infinite pains which are often associated with genius. If he was going to paint a Dufy interior from 1928, he brought out the books and studied the specific objects—the kind of chairs, the shape of the musical instruments, the type of windows—that usually appeared in Dufy backgrounds, and then used them for his *pastiche*. For his fine Modigliani portrait in oil of Jeanne Hébuterne he simply combined the features of Mlle. Hébuterne and the pose adopted by Mme. Lunia Czechoswska—a raised, slender hand supporting her chin—in another Modigliani portrait. Confronted with a reproduction of the Modigliani-by-Elmyr Hébuterne, which was bought by Meadows in Dallas, an art dealer's first reaction is to think: "Yes, of course, I know that painting well." No expert or dealer had ever doubted its authenticity prior to 1967; told the truth now, with few exceptions they evince nothing but admiration for the artist.

"I read somewhere," Elmyr said, "that David Stein, the Englishman who did a few Chagalls and Picassos and right away got caught, claimed that he put himself into the mind and soul of the artist. If he was painting Chagall, he *became* Chagall. If he was painting Matisse, he *became* Matisse. I personally think that's all the worst sort of nonsense. Could you write a story like Hemingway by trying to put yourself into Hemingway's mind and soul? Could you *become* Hemingway? No, it's a terribly vulgar and romantic explanation . . . though I'm sure the public eats it up. What *I* did was study—very, very carefully—the man's work. That's all there is to it.

"With Matisse, for example, I had to be particularly careful. At the beginning—say, around 1948—I used a very easy, flowing line for a Matisse drawing. Because he had, I thought, a very simple line. And then suddenly later on I realized that his hand was not as secure as mine. Obviously, when he stopped work to glance up at his model, his line stopped, too, with just that tiny little bit of uncertainty. Where I went very securely on, Matisse was hesitant, insecure. I had to correct that; I had to learn to hesitate also. Of course I never have had much respect for Matisse anyway. I thought he was a very mediocre painter, greatly overrated. He juggled with colors and lines very cleverly, but to be clever is one thing and to be a great artist is something else. He was far and away the easiest artist to fake. (I don't like that word 'fake,' but I'll use it. I made paintings in the *style* of a certain artist. I never copied. The only fake thing in my paintings was the signature.) I could do a Matisse drawing in about five minutes, so I assume it took him even less time, like with Picasso, between two puffs on a cigarette.

"Picasso was terribly easy for me, too, especially the classical period—but dangerous, because everything was registered and photographed by Sabartés, his secretary, and then put in a huge catalog of seventeen volumes by Christian Zervos. You can still get away with a small drawing from the blue or pink period, before everything was photographed, but not a big one. Anyway, I don't think Picasso's produced anything important in the last twenty years—he's just, literally, banking on his reputation. He's a great artist, but I think his last masterpiece was the *Guernica*. He's done many beautiful things since, but he didn't produce anything any more that was great.

"Modigliani, also, was someone I did with great success—not because he's easy, but because there was such an affinity between us. I don't think there's anyone in the whole art world who knows more about Modigliani than I do. I know him *à fond,* and I think I got the most satisfaction and pleasure out of doing Modigliani.

"The most difficult to do were Cézanne and Braque. Cézanne is a very great artist; his technique is so cerebral, his knowledge so complex. Braque and Monet are very great painters, difficult to copy. Monet was a genius.

"Dufy, on the other hand, is amusing. I knew that world intimately: Cannes, Deauville and Longchamps. I did a lot of Léger gouaches and oils, but I never really found any affinity. Maybe it was because he had been my teacher—I felt peculiar about it. Fernand and Réal bugged me for a long time for more Léger, there was a good market for it, but I finally did give it up. I also felt he lacked spontaneity. I did a little bit of van Gogh and Toulouse-Lautrec from time to time, but not much. It was another era, not my scene. I never went further back in art time because of my moving around so much. To sit down and paint something from the nineteenth or eighteenth centuries, or before that, you have to live in a house and prepare everything very carefully, then dry it for years. I had neither the time, energy, money, or patience to do that. I did a few Chagalls, but he was alive, too, and it was risky. He's quite intolerant about fakes. There are some painters and painters' families who don't seem to care—for example, the family of Paul Klee refuse to give any expertise, they say it's none of their business. I did no Klee. I don't think he's a great painter, and anyway I was never tempted to do the more contemporary abstract painters.

"Utrillo and Corot had been copied so much I never even bothered.

"I never did Miró, either—it seemed to me so terribly easy that I never did dare to try it. Even the real Mirós look like fakes."

These words were spoken a few days before Elmyr was taken to Ibiza jail. He was at work on a portrait of a friend, a young American from Indiana. He put away his oversized French palette and began to clean up. Some friends, writers and painters, were expected for lunch and would probably stay for a swim in the pool; in the evening a visiting Spanish architect from Madrid and the young Prince Adam Czartorisky of Poland were invited for dinner. Ivan Spence had indicated he might drop in, too; he had hopes of giving Elmyr a show at his gallery high in the Old Town of Ibiza.

"I've always been an optimist," Elmyr added. "I look to the future. Not that I have any special regrets about what I've done in the past. It proved to me that in spite of having absolutely no personal recognition for myself, I obviously was an artist of consequence. I would have preferred in my life to become a recognized good painter in my own way, but that may come yet, too, because for the first time in my life I feel I have a choice. After the war, in a great sense, I didn't. I had no trade, no instinct for business, none of the shrewdness and toughness you need to shove the other fellow aside and get ahead. I might have wound up as one of those old artists *manqués,* who wander around cafés and restaurants trying to make a dollar by selling little pastel landscapes to tourists. You see them everywhere. I saw one in Paris last summer, outside Notre Dame. He was an old white-haired Czech refugee, and he came up to our table and offered to do our portraits for a few francs. My friends politely said 'No,' and turned their backs. I gave him ten francs for a little watercolor sketch of Montmartre.

"I watched him walk away. He was a derelict. I realized all too well that if I hadn't done what I'd done in my life, it might have been me."

At the end of his two months' sentence, in October 1968, Elmyr was released from Ibiza jail. He looked well: silver-haired but deeply tanned. He was given two weeks' grace to close up the house and wind up his affairs, and then required to leave the island for a period of one year.

Within a few days of his release he gave a small luncheon party for his friends at La Falaise. Unfortunately, although it was a warm and brilliant afternoon, the party had to be held indoors; in his two-month absence the filter system for the pool had broken down, and the surface of the water was covered with a green, foul-smelling slime. But the atmosphere round the table, where chicken *paprikas* and vintage Marques de Riscal wine were abundantly served, was jovial and fresh. Although he painstakingly avoided any discussion of his most recent experience, at one point when it was carelessly mentioned by an old friend, he said, rather forcefully: "You know, my dear, you are mistaken. I was not actually imprisoned. I was *interned.*"

"Interned?" she burst out, her eyes widening in mock horror. "Good God! Is Hungary at war with Spain?"

But Elmyr didn't reply to this unkind and insensitive quip. As always, he held his head high.

It was quietly noted that day—and might be of interest to those who are bound to ask "What now?"—that during the period of his "internment," the two things Elmyr had never requested from his friends were art books and painting materials. "I need a holiday," he said when the lunch was over—with which the visitors who had glimpsed him reclining peacefully on his deck chair in the sun of the prison courtyard might perhaps have disagreed—and left the island the following week for the South of Portugal.

His easel and his library on twentieth-century French art stayed behind in La Falaise. He boarded the boat to Valencia alone. To all appearances, Elmyr had finally quit.

Unless, of course . . .

INDEX